Cheshire Within Living Memory

Compiled by the
Cheshire Federation of Women's Institutes
from notes sent by Institutes in the County

Published jointly by
Countryside Books, Newbury
and the CFWI, Chester

COUNTRYSIDE BOOKS
3 Catherine Road
Newbury, Berkshire

ISBN 1 85306 279 0

The cover photograph shows the Stretton and Whitley motor bus

Designed by Mon Mohan
Produced through MRM Associates Ltd, Reading
Typeset by Paragon Typesetters, Clwyd
Printed by Woolnough, Northamptonshire

Contents

CHESHIRE

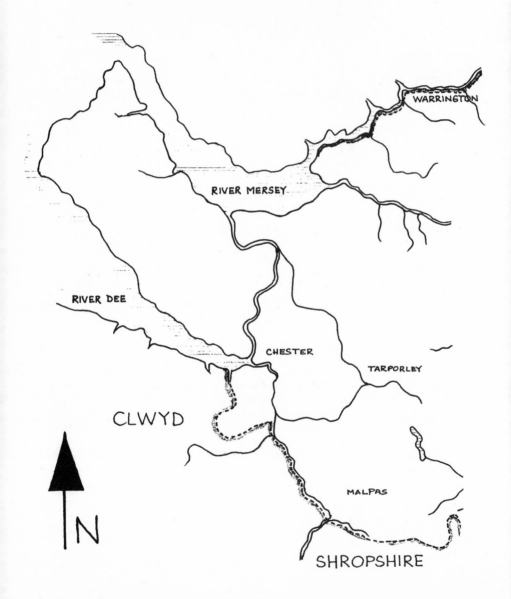

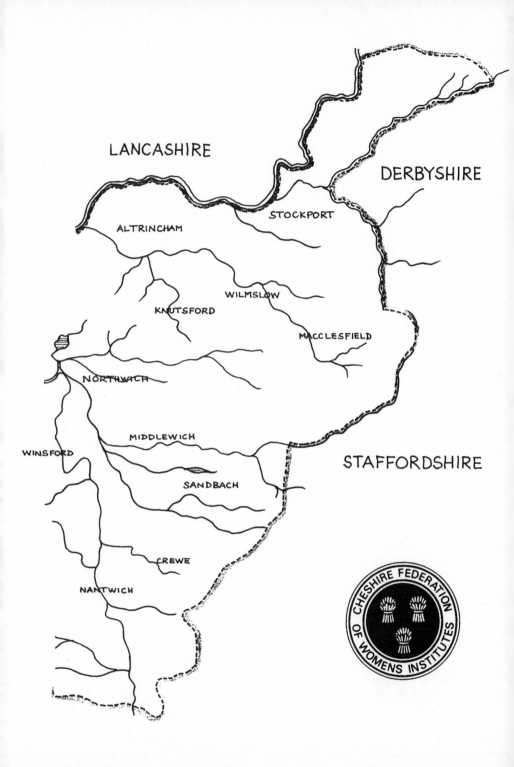

List of Contributing Institutes

Contributions have been received from the following Cheshire Women's Institutes:

Acton Bridge, Acton & Reaseheath, Adlington, Antrobus, Astbury, Audlem, Barnston, Barrow, Barthomley, Blacon-cum-Crabwall, Blakenhall, Boothsmere, Bostock & District, Boughton Heath, Brereton, Bridgemere & District, Brimstage, Broxton & Bickerton, Buerton, Bunbury, Burton & Puddington, Burtonwood, Byley, Capesthorne & Siddington, Cheadle & Gatley, Chelford, Childer Thornton, Churton, Comberbach, Cranford, Cross Town, Crowton, Cuddington & Sandiway, Culcheth, Darnhall & Wettenhall, Davenham, Dean Row, Dodleston, Duddon, Clotton & District, Glazebrook, Grappenhall, Great Sutton, Grindley Brook & Tushingham, Hadlow Green, Hale, Halton Village, Handbridge, Hartford, Hatherton & Broad Lane, Helsby Hillside, Henbury & District, Heswall, Higher Bebington, Higher Hurdsfield, Huxley & Hargrave, Ince, Irby & Thurstaston, Iscoyd, Kelsall, Kettleshulme, Little Budworth, Little Stanney, Lower Peover, Lymm, Lymm Jubilee, Malpas, Marton, Mere & Over Tabley, Mickle Trafford, Middlewood & Higher Poynton, Minshull Vernon, Morley Green, Mottram St Andrew, Moulton, Mow Cop & District, Ness & Little Neston, Newton & District, Norley, North Rode, Odd Rode, Ollerton & Marthall, Over Alderley & Birtles, Over Peover, Park, Peckforton & Beeston, Pickmere, Plas Newton, Plumley, Prestbury, Preston Brook, Pulford, Rainow, Ringway & Hale Barns, Row of Trees, Saighton, Saughall, Shavington, Stretton, Tarvin, Thelwall, Thornton Hough, Tytherington, Vicars Cross, Wallasey, Weaverham, West Kirby, Whitley, Willaston (Wirral), Withington, Woodchurch, Woodford, Worleston, Wrenbury & District, Wybunbury.

Foreword

'What is all knowledge, too, but recorded experience and a product of history . . .'

Thomas Carlyle.

A varied landscape extending from the Dee estuary, across the Cheshire plain to the Pennine hills, divided by a busy motorway network and bounded by the conurbations of Manchester and Liverpool – this is Cheshire.

A county of sand, salt, chemicals and rich pastureland, it has a vibrant and diverse heritage which can often be forgotten in the frenetic activity of modern times.

So often past customs and traditions go unrecorded but this book, compiled in its 75th year by members of the Cheshire Federation of Women's Institutes and their friends, gives us an opportunity to look back and treasure the earlier values and way of life of our parents and grandparents – and to leave their memories for our children and their children to read.

On behalf of the Federation, I would like to thank all WI members who supplied material for this project through their local Institutes, and everyone who has in any way contributed. A great deal of time and effort has gone into researching the facts and we are most grateful.

Unfortunately we were not able to include extracts from every submission; to do so would have meant some duplication of content, and of course we had to take into account the total amount of space available in the book. However, all the contributions, without exception, were of value in deciding the shape and content of the book and we are grateful for them all.

Particular thanks go to Jackie Woolsey and Pat Holbrook for co-ordinating, collecting, collating and chasing up the contributions and to the entire Cheshire News team for a great deal of very rapid copy-typing. Thanks too to Janet Seddon for supplying some of the delightful line drawings.

Helen Carey
County Chairman

TOWN & COUNTRY LIFE

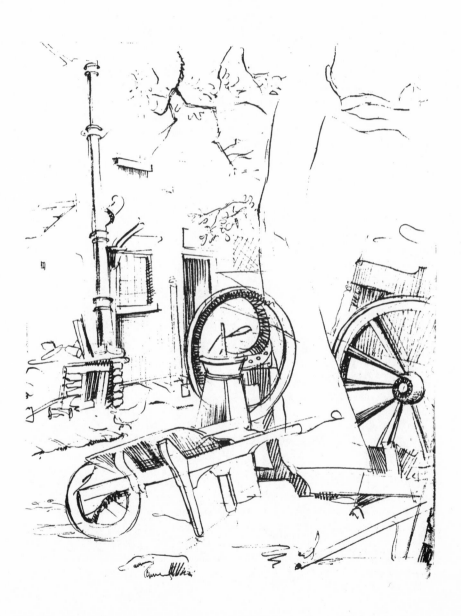

SOME TOWNS AND VILLAGES REMEMBERED

Close knit communities that bore the sorrows and the joys of life together, small shops and businesses run by local families, open countryside where now lie factories and housing – we all have memories of Cheshire as it used to be. Here are just a few of those towns and villages, and the characters who made them unique, as they were within living memory.

KNUTSFORD

'Knutsford was a sleepy market town before the 1960s. The population was about 5,000 and you knew all the roads in the town and nearly all the residents who lived in them. There were and still are, two main shopping streets, Princess Street and King Street, known locally as top and bottom streets respectively and there were numerous quaint alleyways between the two, where you would stumble across a cottage or two, often with lovely little gardens. Sadly most of these alleyways have now gone.

At one time there were six grocers in King Street, two being old established firms, Watsons and Allsops, and four multiple stores; Burtons, Melias, Meadow Dairy and Seymour Meads. The bus station was in Canute Square, where shops were only on one side, the other side being houses belonging to the Tatton estate. When Lord Egerton died in 1958 the house, gardens and park went to the National Trust to be financed and administered by the Cheshire County Council, and was opened to the public in 1961. The remainder of the Tatton estate, mainly farms and buildings in Knutsford, was bought by a firm for a businessman who came to the area.

Before 1961 you could not go into Tatton Park in your car, or take your horse or boat into the park, but you could walk in on certain days between certain hours and to do so you had to first obtain permits issued annually from the estate office near the farm. It was peaceful in those days with no cars in the park. Just sheep grazing and Highland cattle nearer the hall.

You were able to walk down to the lake, but could not go past a flagpole erected there. At the end of the golf course on the left-hand

10

side, where Beech Drive is, was another flagpole and you had to imagine a line between the two which you could not pass; but you were able to catch a glimpse of the hall and gardens from the lake.

Three times a year on Wednesdays in June you could visit the gardens, which were open supporting the National Garden Scheme in aid of nursing charities and if you were lucky you might get invited inside the hall to have tea with Lord Egerton, who kindly invited around 30 ladies each time.

He didn't invite people himself, although he walked round the gardens and spoke to people, but most people wouldn't know who he was, because he was dressed in tweed clothes, shabby and worn in parts, often wearing a cap and not really as one would expect a Lord to be attired. His friend on the other hand was smartly dressed and carried a shooting stick. It was he who invited the people in for Lord Egerton, especially if he saw you admiring the furniture in the state rooms, or the music room with its lovely red silk wallpaper.

The writer of this article was once one of the lucky ones to get invited in, during either 1946 or 1947 when Sir Winston Churchill's government had been defeated and we had a Labour government. Why do I tell you that? Because at the tea table in the spacious entrance hall Lord Egerton said that, "We must get these socialists out," much to the delight of a party of Conservative ladies who monopolised him all of the time afterwards.

Food was still rationed then, but we enjoyed sandwiches, scones and cakes and lovely cups of tea from his plantation in Kenya. After the meal Lord Egerton showed us some of the downstairs rooms, telling us who the portraits were, which decorated the walls. It was a lovely experience, never to be forgotten.

Before the war, Knutsford was an even quieter, sleepier market town, for there were very few aircraft flying over it then and Tatton Park was even more peaceful, with the pheasants and the herons rising up in front of you as you walked.

Knutsford got its first evacuees soon after the war started, when schoolchildren came from Stretford. After Dunkirk, we got train-loads of the BEF straight from the beaches. Local halls were taken over as canteens to feed these hungry and weary, gallant soldiers.

The then prime minister Winston Churchill decided that Britain must start to train parachutists, but where was it to be? Flying from Ringway his aides discovered Tatton Park, the ideal spot, and it wasn't long before Knutsford received more soldiers. These were billeted in local houses and became our first paratroopers. Living near the park, we would see them descending from Whitley bombers like giant mushrooms above the trees in the park. Some of these men married local girls and settled in Knutsford. Others, sadly, were killed at Arnhem in Holland.

Then the government decided to store armoured cars, army vehicles and tanks in the park down Beech Drive under the trees, which was a natural camouflage.

The local workhouse was turned into a military hospital, housing both our soldiers and prisoners from Germany and Italy. Some of the latter died and were buried in our cemetery before being moved after the war, to a war cemetery elsewhere in England.

Then the Americans came. Nearly everywhere there was a camp on the heath, with black soldiers except for the officers, who were white. Out at Over Peover with his 3rd Army, General Patton had his headquarters in the hall and he was to be seen in Knutsford, with his white dog sat in his jeep outside local shops.

Other Americans were stationed in Tatton Park near the Mere village end of the park and they bought bicycles and could be seen going down Manchester Road back to their camps every night.

The American Red Cross took over our town hall with its lovely ballroom, where dances were held for the troops with Glenn Miller-type bands. In the basement which was originally a market place, there was a canteen selling coffee and doughnuts to the Americans and their partners who were British girls and women who were asked to be hostesses by the American Red Cross. My sister and I were two of them.

Then came Knutsford's second batch of evacuees, this time from London, to avoid the doodlebugs and rockets. These children must have had a bad time. One little boy aged ten would wake up around 12.30 every night and scream for his family to "take cover under the table".

Well, the Americans left us one night and no one knew, for they went down south in preparation for the D-Day landings, and for the end of the war.'

'My father owned the corn mill by Birkin brook, where the Birkin centre now stands. A horse belonging to the goods station, when delivering to Mobberley, used to turn in automatically to the corn mill and refuse to go any further until he had been given some oats. I can recall the driver's name was Fagin, but I cannot remember the name of the horse!

In Canute Square, where the newsagent's is now, stood a row of cottages, and when they caught fire each and every member of the public passing by had to take a turn at pumping the old hand-pump fire engine. Once Knutsford fire brigade drove their fire engine into the loading bay at Mobberley Road paper mill to fight a fire there, when the roof collapsed and the fire engine itself was engulfed in flames, much to the embarrassment of the firemen. No lives were lost.

When the traffic lights were installed at the top of Adam's Hill, my father was not too good at double-declutching to change gear in his car, so if the lights were on red he used to roll backwards down the hill in the hope that when he returned to the top, the lights would then be on green. Just try that these days!

A kindly nursing sister who did private nursing used to walk up Brook Street (on a hill) on her way to night duty. She was a strong, well built lady and she often saw a frail elderly man pushing a wheelbarrow up the hill, and she offered to help him with it. Of course, there were no street lamps at this time. This happened on many occasions. It was eventually discovered that the elderly man was stealing coal from the station coal-yard and taking it home in the wheelbarrow for his own use. You can imagine the embarrassment of the dignified sister when she realised she had been "aiding and abetting"!'

HENBURY

'Visualise if you can, in place of motorists racing through Henbury along the A537, a more leisurely ride with a pony and trap, past the Cock Inn, past Pleasant View, turning into Church Lane, past the church and the vicarage, then down Dark Lane past Yew Tree Farm, Rough Heys Farm and some cottages and left on to the main road, by Park House Farm, then on to Chelford, Knutsford and Northwich – this was part of the old salt road of Roman times.

Later the straighter, wider piece of road replaced this narrow lane although at first it was not tarmacked, this came later still. It ran past The Blacksmith's Arms and Spink's Farm (a pig farm and a tiny shop) and two cottages, with a petrol pump and a repair shop as cars started to become a more common sight.

Turn your eyes south from the A537 and there before you lies Henbury estate, the home of the Brocklehursts covering an area of about 1,000 acres. Around the turn of the century and up to the 1950s, this included seven tenanted farms, namely the Home Farm, Bearhurst, Sandbach, Ruewood, Park House, Broomfield and Pexhill Farm, along with a tenanted smallholding on Henbury Moss. Whilst some tractors started to appear in the area as the century progressed, most of the farmers still used horses for ploughing as they thought they made a better job.

Potatoes, carrots, swedes etc. were all hand-picked and Barlow's threshing machine was a familiar sight. The farmers paid their rents to the agent at the Tenant's Hall, then later at the Cock Inn.

As well as the hall itself there were the stables, where Argyle Brocklehurst Esquire kept his prize-winning horse Usury, and the head gardener's cottage and the walled garden where fruits and

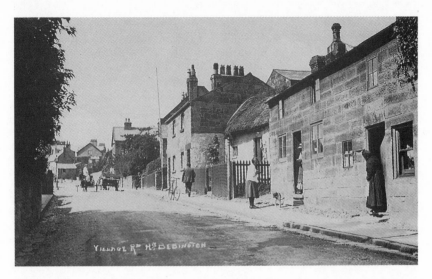

Stopping for a chat with neighbours was part of village life, when everyone knew everyone else in the street. This is Higher Bebington in the 1920s.

vegetables were grown for the hall. To the west of the hall was the gamekeeper's cottage, called the Cave, and at the entrance to each drive a lodge, one in the School Lane and the other on the main road.

Down through the Bluebell Valley was the smithy, a busy place in the first part of the century, and at the top of the School Lane was of course the school itself, with the caretaker's cottage next to it. Across the road were two cottages, in one of which lived a feared gentleman with a bowler hat who chased up children who were absent from school. Woe betide the hapless youngster who failed to produce a good reason for his absence!

One mustn't forget the little shop and post office right up on the top of Henbury where Bearhurst Lane and Pexhill Road meet. Many a youngster walked or cycled up there to buy a few sweets.

The biggest changes came on the death of Mr Edward Brockle-hurst, in the late 1950s when the contents of the hall were auctioned and the estate sold. The end of an era indeed.'

A WARRINGTON FAMILY

'My parents were born in Warrington in 1909. Warrington is now Cheshire but then it was Lancashire. My grandfather was a sergeant in the army during the First World War, serving in Salonica, Mesopotamia and other places. Serbia was an ally of Britain then, and my grandmother often told the tale of how he rescued the

14

Crown Prince of Serbia, driving him to safety across the war zone for which he was awarded a Serbian Gold Medal. While he was away my grandmother opened a small general shop on the Manchester Road. With her business flair and efforts it began to do quite well. When Grandfather returned and tried to get back his old job as manager of the local Co-op store they said his wife had to close her shop as it was conflicting with his interests. She refused, he left the Co-op and they opened up a fish and chip shop next door.

Grandma used to stuff all her money in a big leather bag; she also took bets and was keen on racing. My mother helped in the shop, rising early to serve the mill girls as they clattered down the street in their clogs on their way to the cotton mills. They bought Woodbines – they nearly all smoked.

When the shops were established in the 1920s my grandfather got a job as a traveller and came home with a parrot one day and on another occasion a marmoset monkey, bought at the Liverpool docks from sailors. Mother used to say that her cousin teased the monkey with grapes until one day it retaliated by pulling all the flowers off her hat. She complained about it and the monkey was sent away to Chester Zoo.

From 1909 to about 1935 the family lived in a tiny room at the back of the shop and washed in cold water from a tap in the yard. Nevertheless, they cooked hams and sides of beef for the shop and no one seemed any the worse for it. In the 1970s the shops and houses were condemned and demolished.

While all mother's family were in trade, my dad was studying as a highway engineer and his father was a teacher. There was a tremendous amount of snobbery about new money, and although she had done well with her shops my Grandma apparently encouraged my mother to stick with Dad as he was in "a profession" and not "in trade". A favourite saying of my mother's when referring to someone with obvious wealth and pretensions above their station was, "She is no one, you know!" Mum was in no hurry to get married, she was a qualified librarian and a keen tennis player.

Other members of father's family were in show business. His aunt, my Great Aunt Eulalie was a showgirl appearing with Wild Bill Hickok in the 1920s. She had hair down to her waist, rode a horse bareback and played a guitar!

One of the major events in Warrington was the annual Walking Day which survived, I think, until the 1960s. All the chapel, church and Sunday school children dressed in white and paraded through the streets. Old cine films from the 1920s still exist showing what a massive affair it was.

The arrival of the Americans at the huge Burtonwood base had quite an effect on Warrington. A style of team dancing to pop music with girls in short skirts waving fluffy mops emanated from this period. They call it Fluffy Morris, but traditional morris dancers view it with disdain!'

GROWING UP IN BIRKENHEAD

'I was born in Birkenhead and my early memories are of a terraced house lit by gas, with one cold water tap. We were lucky, we had a flush toilet at the end of the yard. Later the landlord put a lighting circuit in the block of houses but it would not take electric fires without fusing the system.

I grew up through the depression of the early 1930s and, of course, the war years. In spite of the collapse of the firm my father worked for, costing him his job, we were always happy, well-fed and clothed. Holidays were unknown but afternoons and days out were not. We enjoyed going down to Woodside Ferry on the tram, to walk down the floating roadway, to wonder at the great gush of water from the Shore Road pumping station and then to spend an afternoon on the landing stage watching the luggage ferry disgorge its load of horses and carts, lorries, vans, cars and even the occasional bicycle. There was always much to see on the busy river with the nippy tugs leading and pushing cargo vessels, liners and sometimes a vessel just launched from Cammell Lairds.

We loved going to Liverpool by ferry – a penny each way for children. The ticket was a really solid cardboard one obtained from a lovely red machine with a brass handle. I miss the sounds of the river, especially on New Year's Eve when all the ships sounded their sirens at midnight. A great treat was to be taken to Birkenhead market on a Saturday night in winter. The noise and bustle, the bright, cheery faces lit up by the naphtha flares and the sight of the china merchants throwing up the whole dinner sets and catching them again without breakage have all remained in my memory – I can almost smell that wonderful mixture of odours. Our markets today may be more hygienic but they are not half so much fun!

I was fortunate enough to live near the Birkenhead Central Library when it was being built and watched the arrival of George V and Queen Mary to lay the foundation stone. They had just opened the Mersey Tunnel, Queensway. We had been allowed to walk through the tunnel which had special black glass so far up the walls, called "unbreakable", and to prove it men jumped on pieces laid across two piles of bricks!'

CREWE BEFORE THE FIRST WORLD WAR

'When I was born in 1900, Queen Victoria was still on the throne and the Boer War was raging in South Africa. As a tiny girl, I used to sing *Goodbye Dollie Gray*, one of the Boer War "pop" songs.

There have been many changes in the world during my lifetime, probably more than in any similar span known to man. One that stands out in my memory was the arrival of the motor car in our town in, or around, 1906. At first they were so rare that children would rush out to watch a car go by.

I was born over the bakery and general store owned and run by my family. It was built by my grandfather when he retired from service as butler at Wistaston Hall, three miles away. The shop was just outside Crewe town boundary, and people thought he was mad, building a shop in an open field, albeit it was five minutes' walk from the Crewe railway works gate. As he had predicted, the shop was soon surrounded by houses and the business flourished, but not without hours of hard work.

When I was small, my grandfather had died but my grandmother lived with us. She used to say she remembered the "hungry forties", the rinderpest (a terrible cattle plague), Queen Victoria's wedding and once, while visiting relatives in Gloucestershire, she passed Florence Nightingale walking in the street. My grandmother worked in the shop and bakery, where she cured hams, cooked jam and meat pies, and we employed a maid in the house and a washer-woman. When my grandmother served tea she would wear a lace cap and preside over the tea pot like the lady at the manor where she had worked as housekeeper. When I was small the business was run by my father and his brother, as Grandmother was a very old lady.

When my mother died, I was three and a half. To help my father, the headmistress of the local school admitted me to the "babies class"; I felt rather demoted. We sat in a gallery, the back row on a level with the high windows. There were real slates to write on, with slate pens. I think they were made of graphite, and they made a horrid scratching sound. Crewe Works was seeing hard times and many men were out of work. There was no dole then and for those badly hit and for children of widows, free breakfasts were given. I hopefully joined the queue for breakfasts, because I reasoned that my father was out of work – he didn't go through the works gate, he only worked in our shop! Needless to say, my application was turned down.

Behind our shop ran the river Waldren, known locally as the Valley Brook. In fact the area was known as "The Valley". The name of the river is said to have come from the wolves that roamed the area when Cheshire was covered by Delamere Forest. I was always a little scared in case a wolf or two might still be lurking around. During school holidays, my uncle would make a jar of kali, made from icing sugar and something added to make it fizzy. The Valley children bought halfpenny-bags full and we all sat on the sandy shore of the Valley Brook, dipping our fingers into our kali until it was gone. We girls would make daisy chains whilst the younger boys bathed in the brook in their birthday suits. In those days children played in the streets and in spring, out would come whips and tops, skipping ropes, hoops, jacks and chalk to draw out a hopscotch pitch.

The highlight of our summer was the Sunday school treat. Wooden benches were strapped firmly onto coal lorries, pulled by two strong horses. A kind farmer would let us use his field for tea and games. We each had an enamel mug hung round our necks with tape, so we couldn't lose it, this was for drinking our tea. I had three whole pennies to spend at the sweet stall. I asked for them all in halfpennies, and I felt really opulent. An ice cream cornet cost a penny and Spanish laces (liquorice), bullseyes (which changed colour as you ate them) and other delights could be bought for a halfpenny.

On the Thursday before Good Friday my father and uncle never went to bed. After the day's work, they stoked up the bakehouse oven and made hot cross buns. At 7.30 in the morning the buns were being sold outside the entrance to the yard on trestle tables, since the shop itself was closed on Good Friday.

At Christmas time some people would bring turkeys or game to be cooked in the oven after the last batch of bread came out. The oven was still hot enough to cook them, as well as large hams which were boiled to be sold on the bacon counter. There were no bacon slicing machines then, my uncle had a steel strapped on a belt for sharpening his knives. The shop had a mahogany counter. Woe betide any mother who sat her baby on that counter!

There was always a lovely aroma of coffee coming from the hand-operated coffee mill. The beans were freshly ground and weighed in a bag made from a square of strong paper shaped into a cone. Tea was sold from a big, foil-lined chest and also weighed and put into a similar cone. Each piece of paper had a picture of our shop printed on it, with my father and uncle standing in the shop doorway. At harvest time, my father made two eight pound cottage loaves which were placed on the chancel steps at church harvest festival services. Afterwards they were cut up and given to needy families.

In 1911, King George and Queen Mary visited Crewe and toured the railway works. A huge grandstand was erected for all the schoolchildren to sit on. We each had a Union Jack to wave. After we had seen the king and queen we returned to our schools and had a celebration tea and buns. We were each give a celebration mug with a picture of the king and queen on it.

The family business was largely concerned with the outlying farms. My father took bread, groceries, cattle and poultry food to the farms. In return he brought home cheese, home-cured bacon, butter and eggs. He would contract for a field full of potatoes with the crop still in the ground. Often no money passed, it was a kind of barter. As required, the farmer would deliver a cart load of potatoes in sacks to refill our warehouse as the potatoes were sold.

My people had two delivery vans, a large one and a small one, drawn by a pony and driven by a teenage boy waiting to be taken on as an apprentice by the Railway. Jessie pulled the large van. My father drove her for 18 years and neither ever had a day off because of illness. Jessie was a bay mare with three white "socks". My father was very fond of her and she of him. I often watched him lovingly washing Jessie's white socks with a bucket of soapy water. Then he would paint her hooves with black Stockholm tar to protect them from weather and to look smart. When he wanted to call her from the field he would rattle his keys and make a whinnying sound. Jessie would come running to him, whinnying in response.'

THE VILLAGE BOBBY

'I was born in Prestbury in 1899 and have lived here all my life. The cottage where I was born is in the village street. When I was a child the village was very quiet and peaceful, and we played on the road outside our house without any fear of traffic.

The village bobby lived just across from us, and every morning he came out and stood in the road, hands on hips, and looked all round the village, just to let everyone know he was there. He wasn't just watching for people doing wrong, he was there to help you if you needed him. He was a nice man with a pretty wife and a very pretty little girl. Sometimes if the village boys misbehaved, he would put them in his cellar for an hour or so until they decided to be good.'

BYGONE PEOVER

'I was born in 1901, almost a stone's throw from Lower Peover church, The Warren De Tabley Arms (now The Bells of Peover) and Smithy Green. My entire childhood, apart from a few rare visits to my granny, who lived a few miles away, was spent around these places. I spent many happy hours rambling around the fields looking for wild flowers. I knew every inch of the fields and every curve in the winding brook which ran through the village.

My father was born at Charity Farm, Allostock, in 1867. He had to walk over two miles across the fields to Lower Peover church and school. His parents paid twopence each week for his education. The vicar at that time was the Rev John Holmes, who was also the schoolmaster. According to the stories my father told us about him, he was a remarkable man. He once caught a man stealing his coal, so he put a full bag of coal on the man's back and made him carry it all the way to the foxcovert without stopping for a rest. He thought that was the best punishment to fit the crime. He was also confined to bed for several weeks with pneumonia (there were no antibiotics in those days) and in the meantime his garden had got very over-grown with weeds, so he got one of the locals to help him to tidy it up. When they had finished they stood together looking at their handiwork, and the vicar said, "Now you see, my good man, what can be done by the grace of God." The local was not very pleased with this remark and replied, "Oh, be damned to the grace of God, He let it get into a reet yold mess when He had it all to Himself." The vicar told them these stories in school.

There were many skilled craftsmen in Peover when I was a child. Mr Sam Harrop was the local shoemaker and cobbler. I think he did actually make shoes. My mother would send us along with our old shoes to be mended and when we collected them, they looked like new. He would say, tell your mother you won't get your feet wet in these. He would mend all our shoes for a few shillings and always gave us a sweet.

Mr Walter Buckley was the village tailor. He and his wife, who was the daughter of the original village tailor, lived in a lovely old-world cottage near the Crown Inn. Their garden was full of sweet scented roses. Mr Buckley's workshop was full of coats, all with miles and miles of tacking in them, waiting for his customers to be fitted on.

James Gough & Sons were builders and timber merchants. Their yard was a hub of industry and always had a lovely smell of wood shavings.

Mr Johnnie Jackson was the blacksmith. We children must have been an awful nuisance to him, we were always hanging around, but he never got cross with us and he would call us into the smithy to warm our hands at his roaring fire. We loved to watch him shoeing big horses and beating pieces of red hot iron into all kinds of shapes. We also watched him putting the iron rims on wooden wheels, which were made at the Gough's yard – we were kept well out of the way as they rushed about with red hot iron, which had to be put on the wooden wheels very quickly. They would then throw buckets of cold water onto the wheels.

Across from the smithy was Mr Lea, with several threshing machines. These were always along the lanes going to the farms. The men on them would slow down and wave to us.

At the end cottage on Smithy Green the old lady Mrs Newton sold sweets. She had a shelf with glass jars with humbugs, pear drops, aniseed balls and sticks of liquorice. I always spent my penny (when I was lucky enough to get one) with her. She would let you have a halfpenny worth.

Mr and Mrs Wakefield kept the post office. Mrs Wakefield was "Peover". She knew everybody and everything that was going on in the parish. My mother often said she had a heart of gold, she was very kind to everybody. There were no telephones in Peover and telegrams would come to the post office. Mr Wakefield would take them out on his bicycle. If he was not available Evelyn and I would take them. My mother would often take us along with her to the post office and she and Mrs Wakefield would discuss all the local news – usually someone in the village had pneumonia, and everyone in the village was waiting anxiously for the "crisis" which meant they would live or die. There were many families whose parents had died leaving eight or nine children and there were no pensions or benefits in those days.

Mrs Cragg kept the shop by the church. She sold everything from shoelaces to paraffin. She would have a pig killed almost every week. (I always went sick and faint when I heard it screaming.) She would make brawn and Mrs Rimmer who lived in a cottage in the fields made black puddings, which were well-known everywhere. Mrs Cragg made lovely humbugs which were always called "Peover Humbugs" – these were quite a part of Peover.

The Bells from the Warren De Tabley were the centre of the village, though they were a very tragic family. About this time cars were in the news and the Warren was the rendezvous for all the new car owners. We were handed down the Bells' cradle which had served all of their family. It was very elaborate, solid oak with carved cherubs on the hood. I often had to rock my brothers in it and when my mother was out of the room I would rock it violently from side to side – it is a wonder my brothers did not grow up cross-eyed.

I was brought up, from a child, that we had a wonderful heritage with our beautiful old church. Our Sundays started on Saturday night, when we were all rubbed and scrubbed in a tin bath in front of a huge fire, with lots of carbolic soap. I can still see the proud look on my mother's face as she turned us out the next morning to go to Sunday school. After Sunday school we went into church. We children always sat in the Shakerley Chapel. We called it the calves cote. We had to sit all through the service, sermon and all. After- wards we had our dinner, which was the best part of the day for me, a joint, roasted potatoes and lots of fresh vegetables which my father grew in the garden. We had to go again to Sunday school in the

21

afternoon and often when my mother went to the evening service I was always the one to be dragged off again. My mother would wear the same coat year in and year out but she had a feather boa, which when she put it on made her look rather elegant.

The church was lit with paraffin lamps and the corners were very dark. They once had a cross made of honesty, high up on the oak beam over the choir stalls. I whispered to my mother how did it get there, she nudged me to be quiet – one was not even allowed to whisper in church. I never took my eyes off it and came to the conclusion it was one of those miracles they had told me about in Sunday school.

The footpath from the Smithy to Barrows Brow was called the "Ostritch". It was almost as wide as a bridlepath. All the children going to school used it – the Wakefields, Goughs, Jacksons, Ashleys, Bartons and all the children on Middlewich Road. From our back bedroom we could see the people a'coming and a'going across the Ostritch.

The Old Oak Tree – we called it the old oak tree over 80 years ago – was very much part of my childhood. It was only yards away from our cottage. When I had been naughty and my mother was cross with me, I always went and sat underneath it – there was a niche in the roots which I seemed to fit into. One day I was sent home from school very sick and feverish. They found me later fast asleep underneath the old oak tree. I awoke feeling as fresh as a daisy. I have heard people say that if you put your arms around an oak tree it will give you strength.'

MACCLESFIELD

'I was born at my parents' shop in Church Wallgate, Macclesfield, and my earliest memory is the tinkle of the shop door bell and Mum deserting me to attend to a customer. I could just reach the bottom of the net curtain on the glass half of the door to peep into the shop. My brother Bob, eleven months older than me, would be sitting on the floor happily taking an old clock to pieces, his favourite hobby until Meccano made its appearance. Then Kathleen came to help in the shop and Mum had more time to take us out.

In the 1920s we could do all our shopping in the Wallgate. Starting from the top of the steep cobbled hill there was a shop which sold bicycle spares and batteries, and I think the first wireless sets; then there was a millinery and baby-linen shop, a hairdresser, a butcher, a furniture shop, a fishmonger, a piano tuner and sheet music shop, a pot shop, a printer's and the Castle Inn. Then came an iron-monger, two sweet shops, a boys' and gents' outfitters (our shop), a secondhand shop, small electric goods, another household goods, mainly clocks, a barber and a cobbler who sold lots of clogs in those days. From the top of the street on the other side was a chemist, with a row of large coloured glass bottles on the top shelf of the window, a bespoke tailor, an auctioneer and a shoe shop. Then, after a long stretch of high stone wall, which happily still exists, came a confectioner and teashop, a greengrocer, a fish and chip shop, a grocer, tobacconist and a newsagent. I can remember all the shop-keepers, some of them by name; I visited one or another of them every day until I was 13 and we moved away. One by one they have all closed and now the only useful thing you could buy would be a house or a lampshade.

Most shopkeepers lived on their premises and all had cellars with removable gratings. I remember the loud rumbling as the coal was tipped down into the cellar, and the big horses straining up the hill with their loads.

Saturday night markets were exciting occasions with the stalls lit up by flaring acetylene lamps until nine o'clock closing time when a man walked round with a loud handbell. Crowds of people would walk up and down Church Wallgate from the top market to the bottom market on Waters Green. All the shops would be open until nine o'clock and the Salvation Army band played on a corner under a handy gas lamp, sending their collection ladies into the shops and the Castle Inn, their busiest night of the week. It was also their noisiest night at closing time! Bob and I, supposed to be in bed, watched everything from the front window above the shop. A special Saturday treat for both of us was a reading book and comic from Howarth's stall and for me a whipped cream walnut from Barnshaw's sweet shop next door. Barnshaw's had tables and chairs in the shop where customers could sit and enjoy Granelli's ice cream served in glass dishes. If you had a penny or twopenny cornet or wafer you were supposed to eat it outside the shop. On market days farmers' wives treated themselves to a welcome break from shopping.

Our milk was delivered by a farmer's wife. She would walk through into the living room and fill our big jug from a can and I can remember the rich creamy smell as it was poured out. In the hot weather it had to be scalded, and then I would have the cream off the top with brown sugar on my porridge next morning. My father was always up first in the morning, lighting the fire in the winter, and making the porridge for breakfast. Baths were taken in front of a big fire with towels warming on a clothes maiden. I don't remember all the filling of bath water, and the emptying, but I remember my mother's bliss when we acquired a bathroom.

In those days Macclesfield seemed full of mill chimneys which deposited black smuts on the washing, so my mother told me. Also you never overslept on a weekday morning because the mill hooters started at 7.30 am, the last one sounding off at eight o'clock, time to get up and ready for school. I suppose I was lucky because I always had plenty to eat and warm clothes. I used to take an apple to eat in the playground and one day a very small, thin girl asked me to save the core for her. In the backstreets of Macclesfield you often saw children barefooted.'

RUNCORN

'My earliest years were spent in the small north Cheshire town of Runcorn. Sitting on the banks of the Mersey it was at that time about as far north as one could go and still claim to be in Cheshire, for the other bank was situated in Lancashire. Runcorn's character, that of a small, compact, industrialised town, seemed far more representative of Lancashire than Cheshire for it had little of the mellow prettiness one usually associates with this county. It had not always been so and there still remained evidence of a more gracious past and indeed of the period when it enjoyed a reputation as a small town. Unfortunately it would appear that its proximity to the river was the very feature which at the turn of the century attracted the attention of first the canal builders and then the industrialists which transformed it into the no frills, plain Jane of a town in which I grew up.

In the 1940s and 1950s it was still very much a town of chemical works, tanneries, pharmaceuticals and a thriving dock and canal trade. It had many of the amenities one would associate with a Borough Council, including its own grammar school, a hospital, gas and electricity works and a main line railway station. There appeared to be an inordinate number of Co-operative Society shops and more public houses than one could have believed possible in a town of its size for it was still relatively small, and whilst it had a very respectable library, presided over by a five foot, seven stone dragon lady, it had no art gallery or museum – those I feel would have been considered pretentious.

But what there was, which seemed to enforce the work ethos, was a plethora of churches, chapels and missions. It was a town where most people knew most people, if not directly then by reputation. Where, in the town centre, industry, commerce, professional services, housing, entertainment and chapel still existed cheek by jowl. In all a comparatively self sufficient town, perhaps with an air of self satisfaction. A town in control of itself. An impression heightened by its then relatively isolated situation. For before the building of the Runcorn–Widnes road bridge, the only way across the river was via a transporter bridge which carried approximately six vehicles together with a cabin full of passengers, and which didn't run at all in bad weather. Then the foot passengers could cross via a high-level footbridge adjacent to the railway and the vehicles had to go via Warrington.

Its essential parochialism was reflected every year in one event, the Whit Monday Walk. At that time almost every family in the town had an affiliation to one or another religious establishment and on Whit Monday each year members, particularly the Sunday schools, would don their Sunday best and walk behind their respective banners. Many of these banners were quite magnificent, very large and richly embroidered, and were carried on two enormous, often ornate poles. Carrying them was considered an honour, much sought after for it gave the young men chosen an excellent opportunity to show off in front of the young women, particularly if there was a high wind when crossing Delph Bridge. Many a heroic struggle took place there. The young ladies were equally anxious to be chosen to hold the guide ropes, since that presented an excellent opportunity for a little mild flirting.

It always appeared that the whole town turned out for the occasion with those not walking lining the roads cheering us on and then as the procession passed, tagging on so that eventually everyone, brass bands and all, arrived at the Big Park where after a short service of thanksgiving we would all sit in family groups until called to reassemble and return to our respective schoolrooms for tea.'

LITTLE SUTTON

'Taking a walk up Ledsham Road on a sunny day, as always I enjoyed the view of the Welsh Hills which I have loved since I was a boy, trying not to look at the nuclear fuels plant. As so often before, I remembered how I played in the fields and sometimes shuddered a little at the thought of the ancient cemetery under, or near the farmhouse, where "lay the bones of (mighty) men", to quote from Tennyson's Morte D'Arthur. Actually these were thought to be the bones of the Benedictine monks of St Werburgh. It was quite a discovery. The old hall (manor house) was taken down about 1747 but when the foundations of the present farmhouse were being dug (about 1817) the workmen found the ancient cemetery full of bones and skulls; 24 compartments with stone pillars which had supported a floor over, stone steps and a stone door frame with an inscription. When the historian Ormerod arrived to investigate he found that "the whole was barbarously destroyed and the stones new cut and worked into the foundations of the farmhouse." Perhaps that vital bit of information, a stone with the inscription "11 237" cut into it, will be revealed again some day. Who knows?

I continued my walk to the spot where once was Ledsham station, now disappeared under a new road bridge over the railway as part of a road improvement project. Before there was a railway link through Little Sutton this was Little Sutton station. The story was told of an elderly, rather stout gentleman who was driven to the station each day by horse and trap – both rather decrepit. The driver was also old and very deaf. The gentleman climbed aboard, the trap moved forward. At that moment the floor of the trap gave way and the passenger, his feet now on the road beneath but still in the trap, was running like mad to keep up with the horse. The more he shouted to the driver to stop the more the driver urged the horse on. He thought his employer was shouting that he was going to miss his train. You would love to know what the outcome of it all was. So would I.

In the last 60 or 70 years the village has changed considerably. The decision to widen the Chester Road through the village rather than bypass it like adjoining villages on the Chester–Birkenhead route meant the demolition of many buildings and cottages, some of 17th century origins. Amongst the remembered buildings was the Presbyterian hall where I went as a young boy to the Band of Hope meetings and joined in the singing, with *Dare to be a Daniel* and *My drink is water pure*. The hall was built in 1857 and was initially used as a school, the first in the village.

That the water was not always considered so pure comes to light in a report in the *Birkenhead News* in July 1897. The new Wirral Water Company's pumps had broken down. Having previously persuaded the villagers of the dangers of using the village pump and private wells they were now told to use them till the water service was restored. "Strong utterances" were expressed by the angry villagers, who described the supply by the water company as a miserable one. "If it had not been for the village pump we should have had a water famine."

Where the telephone exchange now stands there was once a large house called Briarfield. It was the home of the Read family, its last occupants being three spinsters, the Misses Read. The house was a wedding present for their grandmother and was the first in the village with a bathroom and running water laid on. I knew the ladies well as they attended our Little Sutton Methodist church regularly. They were much respected because it was their family whose financial assistance and encouragement made the building of the church possible in 1877. They always arrived during the singing of the first hymn and made what almost amounted to a stately entrance. They arrived as usual one Sunday morning, sat for a brief prayer and must have been quite put out when the hymn ended and the minister pronounced the Benediction to end the service. British

26

Little Sutton in the early 1900s, a village that has changed considerably since this peaceful scene.

summer time had begun and they had forgotten to put the clock forward.

We have a shopping precinct in Little Sutton – just a small one. To make way for it the old Presbyterian hall had to go and a row of adjoining cottages. In one of them Tommy Spruce had his hairdresser's shop – sixpence for men, fourpence for boys. He always asked politely how you liked it, but you still got short back and sides. He never closed for lunch but his father would arrive with his flask and sandwiches. As there was no other room to which he could retire he would say, "Excuse me gentlemen while I have my lunch," and the waiting customers just had to go on waiting till he decided he had had enough.

Then there was "Daddy" Arthur. A tough nut if ever there was one. He always wore what had once been a shiner – a top hat – but was green with age. When he broke his arm the doctor set it and put it in plaster. "Daddy" then picked up a bucket of water with the broken arm and went off to see to his horse. Of course the arm became permanently deformed. He would lead the horse with a rope round its neck and he walking in front as though he was towing it. This led to his death. Taking the animal through a narrow passageway it is thought he must have stumbled with the horse treading on him.

A shop in the village was occupied by two spinsters, the Misses Price. You jingled a bell which stood on the counter and after a suitable period of time one of them would emerge from a dark passageway at the back of the shop to enquire what you wanted. One of them when out wore a hat with a long feather and was never

27

seen wearing any other. It was seen lying in the rubble when the building was demolished. Underneath the brickwork was the wooden framework of a much older building and experts concluded that this was probably the remains of an old tithe barn.'

DUDDON AND CLOTTON CHARACTERS

'Life in these villages in the early 1930s and 1940s was never easy – much harder than it is today, but there was a spirit of kindliness, eagerness and cheerfulness.

The small cottages were always spick and span although they housed very large families. There were as many as ten, eleven or twelve children in each home.

In Duddon there were the White family, the Rowlands and the Vernons. In Clotton the Evanses and Lewises. The men of the house worked on the local farms, they had to if they lived in tied cottages. The wives very often had to go milking the cows night and morning. There was always an older child to look after the little children. Most of the boys would help out on the farms to get a few pence – in the potato field, the hay and cornfields. It was hard work but cheap labour for the farmers.

Every summer all the children looked forward to a big party at Duddon Lodge, the home of Mr Dick Linnell and his sister Miss Bertha. On the big lawn children enjoyed games and a lovely tea of ham sandwiches, cakes, jelly and pop. There was a repetition again for Hallowe'en – children had to dress up and black their faces and sing in the hall at the Lodge. They were rewarded with pennies and fruit from the orchard.

Every fortnight Jessie Franks used to come from Chester selling her home-made ice cream. Her painted cart the shape of a tub was drawn by a little pony. Oh, how the children used to be first with a bucket of water to water the pony. Yes, you've guessed it, a free cornet – but even though families were poor nearly everyone had a halfpenny cornet.

Another well known character came from Chester, Joe Deponio (Hurdy Gurdy Joe) with his barrel-organ. Sometimes a big child would turn the handle, while Joe went round the cottages collecting his dues. Joe was always too tired to go back to Chester the same day so Mrs Fred Crimes of Fir Tree Cottage made him a bed in the shippon, gave him a supper and an egg and bacon breakfast to help him on his way.

There were two shops in Duddon – Price's and Capper's, and a shop in Clotton – Miss Holmes'. Price's Stores and Capper's kept open very late on one night of the year, that was Christmas Eve, so that mums could go shopping when all the children were in bed to

28

pick up a few things that had been put away for the children's Christmas stockings. Most children thought the mums had gone to meet Father Christmas.

A large wooden shed stood by Capper's shop. One half was the post office run by Nancy Dutton and the other was the shoe shop. Mr Alf Jackson made clogs and Mr Fred Vernon ("Cobbler Fred") repaired shoes. This was the meeting place for the local youths – topic of the day, football!

The Cheshire Hunt met at Burton Wood twice a year. There was a character, "Tommy the Runner", who used to dress in huntsman regalia but followed the hounds on foot (hence the phrase) with a little Jack Russell dog. Later as he got older he followed on a bike with the dog in a basket.

There were three people who received long service awards from Lord Leverhulme for working on one farm – Mrs Margaret Vernon and Mr Tom Walker worked for the Sherwin family for 47 years, whilst Mr Jim Grundy worked for 51 years at Clotton Hall for the Nicholas family. Mrs Vernon was highly respected in village life and was always called on at births, marriages and the last offices. She was called for by Nurse Wright the midwife, and Dr Campbell the local respected GP, for many years.

Two more characters that frequented the village were Polly and Biddy Larkin (mother and daughter). They had a rag and bone cart and came from Tarporley. Polly, the mother, always wore a man's cap and coat and big boots, although she was very tiny. She led the horse and Biddy sat amongst the junk but she never spoke a word to anyone.

Then there was Mr Cowan the chimney sweep who lived in a lovely white caravan by The Headless Woman pub. His daily task took him round all the local villages. He reckoned to cover about 15 miles a day on his bicycle in all kinds of weather. He lived alone but was very popular with the village children.'

PLUMLEY

'My native village, Plumley, was a scattered hamlet of less than 100 houses, many of which were tied cottages (mostly thatched, with the "small room" – sometimes a two-seater! – down the garden), farmhouses, and a few larger houses built for businessmen from Manchester at the time of the cotton trade boom. The lanes were narrow, and some of the thatched homes were painted black and white, constructed of timber and wattle and daub. Lucky folk had a well in the backyard, otherwise one went to the community well or just ladled water from the brook! Easy of access, the village had Holford Street (the A556) on one side, and the Cheshire Lines railway passing through the centre. A meandering stream, the Peover Eye, divided Brunner Mond's (now ICI) estate from that owned by Tabley House, and most people were tenants. Holford Mill on the stream ground the local farmers' corn. A former miller, Mr Dodson, started Methodism in Plumley and this resulted in the chapel being built.

The farms were mixed Cheshire businesses. Cattle were hand-milked, calves reared, manure spread back on the land which had crops in rotation. Mostly early potatoes were grown and sent to Manchester in hampers. One never knew until the cheque came from the merchants how much would be paid. As soon as potatoes were lifted, white turnip and kale seed were sown to feed the animals. Hay and oats, and some wheat (called catch-crops) were again grown to feed back to cattle. Horses were used to do all the work so each farm had a waggoner, a cowman, and many other helpers. The village had a rate collector, a thatcher, a slater, a game-keeper, a blacksmith, a wheelwright, a saddler, a pig-killer, and a man who seated rush-bottom chairs. It also had two inns, but no day school.

In the First World War, "Plumley Works" was a munition works where TNT was manufactured. Neighbouring farms sent men and horses to do paid work at the works in the daytime, and farm cultivations were squeezed into the evening hours – hard work for everyone as milking and feeding needed doing. Eventually, war over, the chimneys were blown up, and now we have the Plumley nature reserve with rare flowers growing on the old lime hills.

When, in 1913, Brunner Mond & Co erected their first bore-hole for brine, the coal had to be carted to it with a horse and cart. When a man's leg was broken while working there, he had to be taken five miles in a horse and shandry to the Infirmary at Northwich and then had to wait outside until a magistrate's signature was obtained. Another man working there fell backwards into five feet of water and came to our farm to borrow? – a pair of socks!

There was no shop in the village but the butcher delivered, with horse and van, once a week, the baker twice a week, and the grocer once a fortnight. The nearest shop was five miles away so Mother considered it was a poor housekeeper who ran short!

The old (pre 1899) Brook House Farm was thatched. There was also a thatched cattle building which was burnt down – a cinder from a railway engine setting it alight. Often cinders from engines fell on growing corn and caused fires. Talking of fires, Brookside Cottage was thatched, wattle and daub. Part of it fell down one day but was repaired with bricks. The same thatched house was formerly occupied by Pickerings, who had a large family. The children helped the parents to grow pansies, daisies, and other bedding plants which were taken by horse and cart to the local markets to sell. This cottage caught fire when a spark from the chimney set the thatch alight. Neighbours quickly rescued an invalid son and an old lady in her nineties. Everyone came armed with buckets, and a chain of them was passed, person to person, from the brook. After that the fire brigade arrived, put a hose to the brook but found the pipe full of holes, so back to the former bucket chain! All the roof was burnt off so neighbours housed the family pro tem. After months, the owner, failing to get the landlord to repair, adopted a DIY method and put on sheets of corrugated iron. It was their home for many years after this.'

HANDBRIDGE, CHESTER

'I was brought up in Greenway Street, or Sty Lane, as it was named in the old days. But generally it was always referred to as "The Lane". The two up and two down cottages were quite small. It seemed as if some of them would burst at the seams with the large families that lived in them. All of the cottages had small backyards and outside toilets, but those owned by the Duke of Westminster also boasted large gardens as well as yards.

Our cottage compared with those of our neighbours, it held the usual clutter of old-fashioned furniture and china ornaments. There was always a home-made rag rug in front of the huge black-leaded open fireplace, but at Christmas times it was replaced with a brand new shop-bought coconut rush mat. I was always glad when the mat wore out and the rag rug was put back in place. It was so much more comfortable and gave the tiny room a much cosier appearance.

The rest of the house was like an ice-box in winter, with ice forming on the inside of the windows as well as on the outside. Our hot water bottles were the oven shelves wrapped in old newspapers and placed between the cold sheets about 15 minutes before we climbed into bed.

My Dad grew many varieties of flowers and vegetables in our garden, and at the far end of it was a rambling gooseberry bush. Close to the house stood a lovely old spreading apple tree. The apples were monster Bramleys, and when they were in season, some of the women would often come to ask my mother, in the local dialect, "Betsy, can y'ough spare a couple of them big apples to make a pie with?" They always offered her a few coppers, but she never took their money.

At one time Dad kept hens and a rooster. He built a large shed in the garden to keep them housed. The rooster was a vicious brute. One day it attacked me in the pen while I was feeding the hens, and I screamed blue murder until my Dad came and chased it away. I

31

never ventured into that pen again, that is, until Dad screwed the rooster's neck for our Christmas dinner.

The toilet was situated halfway along the garden. Dad always joked that we needed bicycles to get to it. It really was purgatory using that toilet in the winter time, especially having to negotiate the flight of steps that led up to the garden, when they were covered in ice. Then, to have to balance on the hard wooden seat with feet tucked in around the toilet bowl, to avoid the icy wind that blasted through the four inch gap below the door.

On Monday washdays the house was like a steam bath. The fire under the brick boiler in the back kitchen was lit very early in the morning to heat up the water. Then Mum would stop her labours over the dolly tub just long enough to nip into town to collect the weekly grocery rations from Lipton's shop near to the Cross. I would run all the way home from school, anticipating the egg and chip lunch waiting for me. There would be real butter on the bread instead of eating it dry, sugar instead of saccharin, and tea would replace the Camp coffee, substitutes that we had to use when rations ran out before the weekend. Then, if we were really lucky, Mum brought back a bag of broken biscuits and my sister and I argued over who was to have the chocolate bits.

Greenway Street was a community of mostly salmon fishermen and their families. When my Dad was out fishing the river in bad weather, Mum could never settle to do any task properly for worrying about his safety. She went constantly to the front door which opened directly onto the street and looked down towards the river, anxiously waiting for sight of our family boat. When Dad finally rowed the *Betsy* into view, Mum would heave a sigh of relief, utter a loud "Thank God", then set about preparing him a hot meal. As soon as he came indoors he changed into dry clothes that she had ready for him, and his wet clothes were hung over the oven door to dry.

Every salmon fishing season brought the familiar sights and sounds of the fishermen laughing and joking together, as they mended and tarred their nets in the "Stakes" (an area with rows of poles set six feet apart used for hanging the nets) along the marsh by the river. Tarring the nets was a filthy job, and the men got covered in the black gooey substance. It was very hard to clean off and tiny flakes of it clung to their hair and skin for many days afterwards.

We practically lived on that succulent Dee salmon and other varieties of fish, like flukes and slimy eels which we called snigs. Some of the fishermen cured the skins of eels and used them for remedial purposes. Our elderly neighbours wore them under scarves around their necks, as poultices for sore throats, and they swore that they worked a treat.

After the long winters, the people in the Lane were happy to gather by the park wall, or crowd on to the two huge concrete manholes on the river bank to get a closer view of the men salmon fishing. The boats lined up, two men to each boat, and there would be much light-hearted rivalry between them as they waited in turn to cast out a draft. When a heavy net was slowly drawn in, excitement grew, and you could almost hear a pin drop as the tell-tale ripples began to appear on the surface of the water within the half circle of net. This was a sure sign of salmon lurking below the surface.

As the last few feet of net was inched to the river bank, the ripples turned to violent splashes and the flash of silver fins could be seen threshing wildly against the huge cobweb of net. Then the catch was swiftly hurled on to the bank and a heavy wooden peg was thrown to the men for the kill to begin. Many a time a fisherman has had to make a quick dive in the mud to catch a salmon between his knees, as it made one last desperate attempt to reach the water. When a salmon did manage to escape, you could hear the men curse out loudly at this lost revenue.

Every Sunday morning the Salvation Army came to play in the Lane. They took up their usual position on the brow of the hill outside Mrs Leonard's shop. Her grandson Tom Gilbride always led the band. Some of the people came out to stand on the cobbled street to join in the singing, others preferred to listen from inside their homes with the doors ajar. Everyone always enjoyed that rousing half hour of music and hymns, accompanied by the ear-shattering beat of the big drum.

Long summers were spent playing with my friends in Handbridge Park. We built grass houses when the grass was newly mown, and we made jam butties. We also made pop when we could afford the coppers to buy the kali powder to add to our bottles of water. We only ventured out of our grass houses to have a go on the swings, or when the boys crept up on us to destroy our little houses. Then we all waded in together for a good grass fight.

Concerts were held in the bandstand on the Park rock, or in the arches under Grosvenor Bridge. When the tide was in, it was a miracle that none of us fell into the rising waters, as we inched our way along the narrow ledges that led into the arches, but we never did.

Tracking in the Dingle was another favourite pastime. We rode on the cross-bars of the boys' bicycles, skirting the ditches as close as we dare. One day my friend Dorothy and her partner misjudged the distance, and landed in the putrid water of the ditch.

We spent many weeks before Bonfire Night collecting wood for our bonfire. Every year it was constructed in the middle of the river-

33

bank at the bottom of the Lane. Before it was lit, the fishermen moved their boats further down river, to avoid any stray sparks that might ignite the boats and the nets. The whole street came out to watch the firework displays and the lighting of the bonfire. It was a happy time, and long after the bonfire had turned to ashes the grown-ups sat on their doorsteps and gossiped into the small hours. We children sat around the dying embers roasting potatoes and frightening each other with ghost stories, until some of us were too afraid to look into the gathering shadows around us. It was then that we ran for the safety of the street.

Above the Craft (field) on top of the Rock nestled Bakers Farm from where the villagers purchased all their dairy products. To reach the farm you had to cross the Craft, and climb the steep steps that were cut into the rock face. The farmer's cattle grazed in the field below, but when the bull was in the field, it was a hazardous business collecting the milk. Getting to the farm was easy enough, but returning was sheer hell. It always seemed as if that cunning old bull knew just when to begin his charge. It was always when you had reached the middle of the field. Then, down went his head and the race was on. But somehow we managed to reach the stile with only seconds to spare, leaving the old warrior to paw the ground in temper.

I was eight years of age when the Second World War began. In school time when the sirens blared, we children were ushered down to the underground air raid shelters which were situated close to the playground. There, we were encouraged to sing, whilst a teacher handed out Horlicks tablets from a large tin box. But we only sang half-heartedly, because we were much too scared of the tremendous noise that was going on in the sky above us. I was always relieved when it was home-time to see my mother waiting at the school gates to take me home.

At home during the air raids, Dad cleared a space in the coal-hole under the stairs, and there we children were settled down with pillows and blankets until the all clear sounded. There wasn't enough room in there for Mum and Dad so they sat close to the fire. However, when we heard the noise of bombs dropping, they came and squeezed into the small recess with us. Mum would never let us go to the communal shelters in Edgar Park. She said, "If we are going to be blown up, then we will all go together in our own home."

When the bombs dropped on Liverpool it seemed as if they were going to fall on us. I was absolutely terrified of the doodlebug bombs as they screamed down to earth, and of that awful split-second of silence before they exploded. I remember that one night a bomb exploded very close to the gasworks, and the next morning all the

34

Haymaking in 1932.

children went out into the Lane to gather up the shrapnel.
Many young men of the Lane were killed in both World Wars.
How those cobblestones must have rung with all that cacophony of
sorrow. But it was a close-knit community that always drew comfort
from itself. Its ancestry went back 200 years or more and most
everyone there was related to everyone else, because inter-marriages
were rife in the old days. The old street has gone now, but I am very
proud to have once been a part of it.'

A VERY RURAL EXISTENCE

'In about the year 1887 my grandparents on my mother's side
bought a house called "Glenbollin" at Warburton Green. There were
several acres of land and like most people living in country areas
they had a pony and trap. Over the 31 years that they lived there
they had countless ponies but one in particular was a great character.
One of his habits when passing the Romper pub (The Lion Rampant)
was to come to a standstill, refusing to move until he was led away.
My mother was born at "Glenbollin" and subsequently married
at Ringway church. Among her many friends was a family called
Ridgeway living at Etrop Green. They were farmers and there were
seven children. When we were children I got to know the Ridgeway
family – none of whom married and all lived their whole life at the

35

small early 18th century farmhouse on the edge of what is now the airport. Each member of the family had a specific job on the farm. The eldest daughter kept the poultry, the next the pigs, the third kept rabbits and made fur gloves, the fourth helped in the fields and the fifth did the housekeeping. The two brothers worked separately in the fields. They occupied bedrooms at opposite ends of the house, never met for meals and led entirely separate existences.

It was a very rural existence but sometime in the early 1930s, the Ridgeway family was shocked and disgusted to learn that their area was to become part of Manchester – thus taking away their age-old Cheshire identity. Not only this, but shortly after, several hangars appeared in the fields in front of the Ridgeways' cottage and the area became what I believe was a private aerodrome.

What wonderful Boxing Days we spent at Etrop Green, the table groaning with Christmas fare: a roast goose, mince pies, trifle with two-inch thick cream, Christmas cake, whole hams and lots besides. Now, of course, it is the site of the largest airport in the North of England.'

CHURCH AND CHAPEL

At the heart of the community was the church and the chapel, in the days when most families attended at least one service on a Sunday, children were expected to go to Sunday school, and the rector was one of the most important figures in the village. The annual Sunday school treats and outings were eagerly anticipated and fondly remembered.

VERY MUCH THE SQUIRE

'Barthomley school was a Church of England school, and the rector, the Rev Edward Armistead, very much a country squire, took a great interest in it. He visited the school quite often and when he came into class we all stood up and said, "Good morning (or good afternoon) sir." We all respected him greatly.

He signed correspondence connected with the school, and sometimes it was my duty to take this to the rectory. I went through the back door in the basement, and was greeted by the housemaid who rang for the butler. He came down the stairs with his silver tray for me to place the letters on, and then went back upstairs to the rector, the correspondence was signed and brought back to me to return to school. The rector and his wife had quite a number of staff – butler, chauffeur, cook, parlour and house maids, gardeners etc. They built three houses on the left-hand side of the Audley Road going out of the village for some of their staff. Others would live in, or if local would live at home. On Sunday mornings their friends came along to church, and were invited to the rectory for lunch after the service. We enjoyed seeing them all, it was like a mini-Ascot seeing the beautiful hats and outfits.'

A REMOTE FIGURE

'I went to the church school at Wilmslow, thoroughly enjoyed it and didn't want to leave. Next to the school was a house where the rector's coachman lived, and woe betide any boy who trespassed on the garden. Our rector in those days seemed a very remote figure, especially as he was driven round in his horse and trap. In summer the Sunday school held a summer fete on the rectory grounds (note, not the garden) and I vividly remember the rector handing out prizes (I won a ball) across a little bridge. It was decidedly "them and us".

The so-called gentry went to church Sunday morning and their maids, having to get Sunday lunch, were more or less made to go to evensong.'

THEIR OWN PEW

'The family living at the local manor house in Ince came to church with their coach and horses and they entered the church through a special door. They also had their own pew, which is still there today. The service did not commence until the lady of the manor was seated in her pew.'

STABLES FOR THE PONIES

'As a girl in the early 1930s I went to school, four miles away, by pony and trap. When I went to Sunday school it was in a trap with a pony called Parson (he only worked on Sundays!). The chapel we attended had stables attached for the ponies while the congregation was at worship.'

THE SOCIAL CENTRE

'In 1987 the Wesleyan chapel in the heart of Plumley village celebrated its centenary. In my younger days, the pipe organ was hand-blown, and many a time the organ blower (behind a curtain and almost out of hearing) was fast asleep when the last hymn was announced! The chapel schoolroom was then the social centre of Plumley – the scene of all activities. The stage curtain often stuck, but nobody minded. Oil lamps lit the schoolroom, and once I remember the lamps, getting old and smoky, had to be turned down. Then the parson announced the next hymn – *Lead kindly light amid the encircling gloom*. We sang on, accompanied by the wheezy old harmonium.'

THERE WERE TWO CHAPELS

'There was an old lady living near the chapel at Buerton who used to invite the visiting preachers back to have dinner with her and the story goes that, when she thought the sermon was too long, she would tap noisily with her stick on the floor; she probably thought the roast was getting overdone.

There were two chapels in our village earlier, the Methodist and Free Gospel. The Free Gospel broke away over a disagreement with the Methodists and built their own chapel and are still carrying on there.

One memory I have of the Little Chapel on Anniversary Sunday: they all came singing round the houses in the morning and a very good, strong lot of singers they all were, from the oldest to the youngest. We could hear them a long way away until at last we knew, "The singers are here." The hymns I most remember were *Shall we gather at the river*, and *There'll be no parting*.

The Methodist chapel was very active too in those days – they had their anniversaries and Sunday school treats, which then took place in a field near the chapel with the usual sports and back to the Sunday school for a bumper tea. Mrs Jones' currant bread was a must at these occasions. If later the children went to a farm, they were transported on a farm waggon. Mrs Jones lived at the village shop across from the chapel. There are no shops in Buerton now.'

CHURTON METHODISTS

'For many years, Churton Methodist chapel played a large part in the life of the village. A large number of village people were members of the chapel.

Before the days of the motor car or buses, the preachers used to cycle from Chester and the surrounding area, to conduct the services. These bicycles had small paraffin lamps on them; many times in the dark winter evenings, the paraffin would not last and their lamps would go out and they would walk home. One preacher, Mr Martin from Rossett, used to come across the river Dee in a boat and walk up the River Lane, conduct the service and return home the same way. Mr Charles Ball of Aldford used to ride here every Sunday evening on a three-wheeled cycle. While Mr Ball was in chapel, some of the local boys used to take his tricycle and ride it around the village, always leaving one boy outside the chapel to watch for him so that the tricycle would always be back in place when he came out. Another local preacher was Mr Randal Barlow, the village cobbler, although he was completely blind. He walked miles to take services carrying his large Braille copy of the Bible.

On the first Sunday in August, the camp meeting was held in the afternoon. Everyone met at Churton crossroads and always sang the hymn *We are marching to Zion* followed by prayer and another hymn. Then everyone went marching round the village singing hymns and then on to the field opposite the chapel, behind The White Horse public house. There were forms around the field for people to sit on and wooden beer barrels for the preacher to stand on. At one of these services, the preacher was standing on one of these barrels, stamped his foot and, the wood being rather rotten, it gave way and through he fell into the barrel.

Another very popular event was the chapel tea party. One of these was held under Mr George Clubbes' hay bay, when the favourite food for parties at that time was white and pink blancmange, home-made currant bread, jam tarts and scones.

Another event was the chapel Harvest Thanksgiving in October, when dead cockerels and rabbits would be hung on the pegs along the chapel walls, with bunches of onions and carrots and beetroot. There were cabbages, baskets of damsons, sacks of potatoes and also gifts of home-made bread and farm-churned butter, and trays of jam tarts, which would be sold to people on the Monday evening for one halfpenny each, when the harvest produce was auctioned. In days gone by, the village people depended a great deal on the land for a living and food, and the Harvest Thanksgiving was always very important to them.

There are also memories of a Mrs Maylor, who lived in the largest house in the village, Churton Lodge, in the early years of this century. She had built two rows of tall terraced houses, which were rented to village people, and is remembered for her generosity to the villagers. There were Christmas parties held at the Lodge for the children, and they were also given gifts. Each schoolboy, as well, every winter received a red jersey and the girls a red cloak. When the First World War began she gave each young man who went to serve in the forces, a thick wool blanket to take with him. There were gifts of red flannel petticoats for the elderly ladies of the village, and soup and gruel to those who were ill, which reflects how much life has changed.'

WYBUNBURY CHAPEL

'I became acquainted with Wybunbury chapel in the early 1920s when my father, who was a local preacher and a helper in the Sunday school at Shavington, went to take a service there one Sunday afternoon. He found over 100 children in the charge of two teachers, Mr Cheshire and Mr Thomasson. As there were plenty of teachers at Shavington at the time, he decided that he would offer his services at Wybunbury. Soon afterwards I acquired a bicycle and, of course, wanted to go with him, and I have been attending there ever since.

At that time there was a Sunday school on Sunday morning at 10.30, 2.30 pm when we joined in part of the chapel service, and an adult evening service at 6.30. There were oil lamps to light the chapel (electricity had not yet come to the village), and iron railings at the front with an archway over an iron gate, in the centre of which was an oil lamp which was lit on dark evenings when there was a service or meeting, etc. There was a cross on top of the chapel which blew down one winter in a gale.

There are memories of Jimmie Salmon of The Hough who used to sing very much out of tune. His favourite hymn was *The day Thou gavest, Lord is ended* and if the preacher chose that, we knew that we were really in trouble for Jimmie would let fly! The old pulpit was a menace for preachers who walked about too much during the sermon: there was a small step each side for which they were unprepared and several of them fell down this in the course of their address.

After the Second World War, we went bilingual. A large contingent of German POWs from the camp at Walgherton joined us for worship each Sunday. We had both the Lord's Prayer and the lessons in English and German. They also formed a male voice choir and used to sing some of the German hymns and chorales on Sunday evenings. These were much enjoyed.'

SUNDAY SCHOOL TREATS

'We attended Sunday school at Byley during the 1920s, a two mile walk. We went in our Sunday best. In the summer I always had a white cotton or voile dress with lots of needlework on it and black patent shoes and white socks. My mother took a pride in washing and ironing my dresses, which must have been hard work in those days as irons were heated on the fire. We always had a text to learn each week or a passage from the Bible.

Our Sunday school teacher lived in a house with woods around and we would spend our Sunday school treat there in the summer,

The Sunday school treat was eagerly anticipated by these excited children from Byley in August 1929.

having a picnic. We would play hide and seek in the woods, have races, the winner receiving an orange or apple and, after a hectic day full of fun, we would scramble for nuts and, after giving three cheers as a thank you to Mr and Mrs Wrench, walk home. The young ones, who were too tired to walk, Mr Wrench would take home in his horse and shandry.

There was great excitement in 1929 when, for our treat, we went by charabanc to Overton Hills where we had a picnic and spent our time on the helter-skelter and swingboats and see-saws. It was quite an event in those days.'

'I was born in 1904 and lived at Norley. My father was a cobbler and we had a shoe repair shop which was kept busy with most of the villagers bringing their shoes there.

My sister and I attended the Central Methodist chapel, going to Sunday school in the morning and again in the afternoon, after which some of the other boys and I walked to Hatchmere Lake at the other end of the village. The one highlight of the Sunday school events was the annual trip to Overton Hills near Frodsham, by horse

41

and cart. We played games and had our tea, and memories all seem to be of sunny days though some of them most likely were not so good. The weeks of excitement building up to this event were tremendous and it was the only time some of us left the village.' 'When motor coaches came into being, the Sunday schools started to have a day out in Rhyl and this was a real treat. Both lunch and tea were prepared in one of the Methodist chapels in Rhyl and a visit to the funfair was great!'

'Church Sunday school Anniversary at Crowton was held in June, when all the girls had new clothes if possible and they always sang *Summer suns are glowing over land and sea*. Chapel had an anniversary too when the children stood in the balcony and sang to their parents below. Both church and chapel had their outings in the summer to Overton Hill or the seaside with tea in a tearoom for the church children and a picnic, with caramels thrown in the air at the end to scramble for, for the chapel children. Both church and chapel also had summer fetes and each denomination looked forward to the other's fete and joined in. The church fete was held on the vicarage lawns on the first Wednesday in July, the children entertained and there was always a tennis tournament and a live band playing for dancing on the lawn in the evening. The chapel fete was held in the field on the last Wednesday in July and is well remembered for the annual greasy pig competition, always entered by women. The lucky (or most agile) lady who caught the pig won it, and it was then slaughtered for the family's use.'

BROUGHT UP VERY STRICT

'We were brought up very strict; no arms on the table at meal times and only speaking when spoken to. We were brought up to go every Sunday to the chapel, it was then the Wesleyan Chapel later known as the Methodist, and as we grew into our teens, we had to go on Sunday nights with my father, so we went Sunday morning to Sunday school and in the afternoon to Sunday school followed by a service in the chapel. Sunday school Anniversary was always in June and we had lovely white dresses and always new shoes. A platform would be put up by the pulpit in the chapel and all the boys and girls used to sing special songs that we had learnt for that day. There were always a lot of Sunday school children those days and they used to go to Sunday school until they were well in their teens.

We also had Sunday school parties held at one of the farms, when the sun seemed to always be shining. At Christmas we had a party in the Sunday school and the prizes, which were books, were given out. The more attendances you put in, the better the book. We were always amongst the top marks so we got some lovely books.

In winter on a Sunday night when it was too cold and wet to walk to chapel, my mother would light a fire in the "best" room and my father would read stories to us before we went to bed. I often think of those happy days when we were all together. There is a lot to say for a big family, but it must have been hard work for my mother because she made all our dresses and knitted jumpers and socks for the boys, all done by oil lamp or candles. At Christmas, we used to hang our stockings up and we would find all sorts of goodies and little things my mother had made. The girls always got a doll made and dressed by Mother, and Father would make things for the boys like cricket bats and other wooden toys.

As we grew older my father moved to a bigger farm so we all worked on the farm as we left school, then we had two farms joining each other so we had a lot of work to do. We all had to learn to milk by hand as there were no machines then, and make the hay and cut the corn with horse-drawn machines. We would be working in the fields from dawn to dusk, but my father would never do anything but what was necessary on a Sunday. We still had to go to Sunday school and chapel, it was most important to him. Sadly, he died working in the fields when he was 54 years old and left my mother to continue to look after two farms and bring up a family; my youngest brother was four years old when my father died. My mother died when she was 91 years old.'

'Our whole family were churchgoers – very strict. It was a case of first up, best dressed.'

GETTING ABOUT

At the turn of the century we either got about by real horse-power or by Shanks's pony – we walked! Then came the bicycles and the early cars, and the first country bus services opened up new worlds to the village dweller. Steam trains were an important part of all our lives, whether we relied on them for travel or for telling the time.

CANAL, ROADS AND RAIL

'Thelwall has always been a crossing point over the Mersey, and is divided by the Bridgewater Canal. At the beginning of this century there were a number of farms, several fine houses including Thelwall Hall and its estate, All Saints church which was the centre of village life, a small school, a post office cum bakery and general store, The Pickering Arms inn, a smithy, a wheelwright, a cobbler, two tanneries, a huge wooden building where the lock gates for the Manchester Ship Canal were made and a railway station. There was no street lighting or pavements. It remained much the same until the late 1920s and 1930s when some new houses were built, the main road was widened and pavemented, and by then there were some street lamps. The population was around 200 to 300 and did not increase until the 1960s when two new housing estates built on the former Thelwall Hall estate and the Lock Gate shed site brought it up to around 3,000.

There was an excellent train service for passengers and goods, especially popular with theatre-goers on a Saturday night when the last train left Manchester at eleven o'clock, but Mr Beeching's axe fell on it and now even the lines have gone. There was a sketchy bus service started in the 1920s but a convenient bus service did not materialise until the mid 1930s. Until then people walked or cycled the two miles to Latchford and were then able to get a tramcar to Warrington. There were places where you could leave your bicycle for a small fee. Those going to Altrincham went by train to Broad-heath and either walked or got a tram into the town. The railway goods yard was a busy place with waggons being loaded with coal, hides and lime for the tanneries and other goods. Farm waggons, animals and passengers were ferried across the Ship Canal to Thelwall Eyes by a pontoon operated by pulling on ropes which lay on the bottom of the canal when not in use. The constant traffic of horses pulling the narrow boats kept the towpaths on the Bridgewater Canal wide and free of weeds and easy to walk along. Now they are overgrown, the canal being used only by anglers and pleasure craft.'

PONIES AND CYCLES

'Apart from bicycles and walking, pony and trap was the normal transport for people to go to Northwich or Knutsford. Usually the journeys were fortnightly and the laundry basket was often used as a receptacle for the bread and groceries purchased. A farm lorry took Pickmerians too and many a time it overturned, throwing the passengers off and itself into a ditch at Wincham after colliding or trying to pass a similar form of transport coming in the opposite direction, when neither driver would give way.

One lady recalls as a child out in Northwich with her parents, literally taking their lives in their hands attempting to dodge between the cycles as they filled Ship Hill, ridden by homeward-bound workers from ICI freewheeling at speed towards the Bull Ring and town bridge.

In 1958 it cost two shillings and ninepence to travel by rail between Cuddington and Stretford (on the Altrincham line) return and trains were every hour throughout the day. It was a similar amount for bus passengers to Manchester from The Red Lion at Pickmere.'

THE FIRST CAR

'My husband remembered seeing the first car in the district, driven by somebody from the "big house" where the school treats and Christmas parties were always held. When the time came for him to leave school the Great War was well on its way, and his father got him apprenticed with a local farmer. He lived with the farmer as one of the family and often went out with them to card parties some distance away. One day the farmer, who liked a drink, said it was time he learned to drive, so he did and next day was told that the farmer's wife had left her handbag at the other farm and would he take the car and fetch it – so he did. That was learning in those days. I don't suppose there was anything else on the roads.'

'During the years up to 1914 great changes came; bicycles with free wheels and gears instead of the old fixed wheel, and cars and motor waggons were seen much more often on the roads. One of the draw-backs with the cars was the clouds of dust thrown up from the stone roads. In summer wayside hedges would be white until the next rain. The problem was solved by using stone chippings with the addition of tar, thus making a smoother road. This of course did not suit the remaining horse traffic as it made the road slippery, but again this difficulty was overcome by the addition of rubber pads under the horses' hooves.'

SAVING UP

'The local garage owner from Bucklow Hill, in the 1920s the nearest garage to Plumley, had heard on the grapevine that we might wish to purchase a motor car! Father said, "Yes," he was interested but we would have to save up. Plumley with its small population already had two cars. Later it was agreed that a little black bull could be a start. We immediately gave him lots of extra food but the greedy animal fell sick and nearly died. However, with more careful feeding he sold for £20 at Chelford Auction. Mother took the cheque to the Union Bank at Northwich and started the fund. Gradually it grew and the garage man came again. Father said, "Still not enough

45

money!" However, the weather being nice to him, he agreed to a loan for the rest, especially as the garage man threw in a bargain package which included car, tax, insurance, and driving lessons. Monday morning there arrived a brand new Morris Cowley, straight from the works. Driving lessons started and continued each morning until Friday when the instructor declared one pupil safe to drive on the road, being able to steer and double de-clutch. One had to do this to change gear.

The car was a great convenience and brought much pleasure. There were no traffic lights and no queues. When one arrived home the car could go straight into the garage, but arriving home in the trap, the horse had to be taken out, the trap put away, and the animal taken to the stable, unharnessed and the various pieces hung up on hooks. Next, it had either to be fed or put into the field. So the car was well used, but we still loved horses!'

TRAMS, FERRIES AND CARS

'The trams were old friends and we loved to travel on the top deck "up front" where it was roofless. It was a sad day when the last of the trams went round the Oxton circle in 1937, but it was beautifully illuminated and looked like fairyland.

I recall being sent more than once to catch the post on the late tram, with a letter for my grandfather in Plymouth. There was a letter box at the back of the tram and the letter caught the night train to Devon and arrived next morning.

All luggage goods and vehicles had to be conveyed by ferry before the Mersey Tunnel was opened in 1934. The luggage boats *Oxton* and *Bebington* would land at the floating landing stage and if the tide was low, the floating ramp was very steep and the cart horses would struggle to pull their heavy loads up to dry land. They were lovely animals and beautifully groomed and on special occasions would be decorated with shining horse brasses and rosettes.

We used to travel to North Wales for holidays in a motorbike and sidecar. My mother with my sister and I (both under five), one on her knee and the other in the front bulge of the sidecar, where your face was pressed against the celluloid windscreen! – a far cry from today's safety standards. One older brother sat behind my father on the bike, and the other teenage brother used to cycle and meet us at the holiday cottage.

Later, in 1926, we had an Armstrong Siddeley open-top car with wide running boards which, although forbidden, we used to stand on holding tight to the car when my brothers began driving up and down the drive. Another fascination was the large rubber horn outside the driver's door.

Charabancs were a popular way to travel in the 1920s. This bus came from the garage of Sydney Jackson & Son at Butley near Prestbury, and sailed along at a stately 12 mph!

During our visits to Wales and other parts of Cheshire, we always drove through Willaston village, and nearly always met cattle being moved from fields to farm buildings to be milked. As there were several farms in the middle of the village the constant movement of different herds of cattle caused some confusion to traffic and the roads were usually somewhat mucky! Sad to realise that there isn't a single working farm in Willaston village today.'

THE FIRST BUSES

'In 1908 the first motor bus (open top) ran from Stockton Heath swingbridge, over the Ship Canal, through Stretton to Whitley and back.'

'Soon after our arrival at "Lyngarth" in Moor Lane a local, private bus service started up. It ran from Brook Lane corner to Wilmslow station and back, holding perhaps twelve people. The door was at the rear and there was a kind of retractable step which my poor grandmother, on a visit to our house, found rather difficult to negotiate and had to be given a slight lift up by the bus driver. When later she recounted what had happened on that occasion she said, "The driver came to the rear of the bus, put his arms under my rumpti-cum-fumpti-bus and lifted me in! The cheek of it!"

Soon, however, the private bus service was taken over by the North Western bus company. An alternative source of travel was provided for us by Mr Stretton and his horse and cab. Many's the time he took me to a party, sometimes as far away from my home in Wilmslow as Alderley Edge. Very few people had motor vehicles in the early 1920s and most goods were transported by horse and cart. Consequently the sound of horses' hooves and the rumble of iron-clad wheels was sometimes quite deafening, especially in towns where the streets were still paved with sets.'

THE STATION WAS A BUSY PLACE

'In days gone by, before the estates were built, the station at Plumley was a very busy place, staffed by a station master (in uniform), clerical staff, porters, and plate-layers. The station master's house is still there but the railway cottages are gone. The Railway Inn is still there, much altered and extended, and renamed The Golden Pheasant. At one end of the Railway Inn there was a cottage attached. There was also a thatched cottage opposite the Railway Inn.

By 6.30 am the station yard was full of milk floats with cans of milk (12 or 15 gallons) on their way to Manchester by the special "milk train". Later, wagons of coal, etc were unloaded and farmers had manure, grains and other goods coming in, while cattle, potatoes etc were loaded to go out. Our farm had the doubtful honour of the first brine-shaft in the district, and Father had a contract to cart coal from the station to the bore-hole. This was, of course, done by a lorry and two horses.

1914 brought the chemical works and the manufacture of TNT to Plumley. Many people worked there so a halt called Plumley West was provided on the railway. Only once did we have to evacuate when a small fire started.'

'There were eleven small farms in Acton, varying from 30 to 150 acres, all taking their milk to the station in churns by horse and cart. The station was very busy in those days, with a goods yard where cattle, potatoes and all kinds of building materials arrived. However, the main business was the coal yard; here five firms bagged the coal and delivered it to all surrounding villages.'

HELP WITH THE FIRE

'We lived in an isolated cottage in the fields outside Plumley. Not having much money, we often ran short of coal so my husband made a handsome, cheeky scarecrow and sited it near the railway line where the trains had to stop or slow down. The drivers would throw coal at the scarecrow, and later my husband would collect it up. It was a good help in keeping our fire going!'

IN THE GOODS VAN

'Dodleston, a small village, had no buses during the war and people had to walk to Balderton and then take the train. After the war, buses only went to Chester on Tuesdays, Thursdays and Saturdays so most people still used the train. It was possible to take the baby in its pram on the train to Wrexham or Chester but you had to sit with the pram in the goods van.

The Duke of Westminster had a private narrow gauge railway which ran from Balderton to Eaton. The coal for Eaton was delivered this way and also other goods. On special occasions the goods waggons were replaced with passenger coaches with red plush seats and sometimes these were used for guests staying at Eaton.'

THEY WOULD WAIT

'My husband worked in banking at Neston and would go by train from West Kirby. If he was late, not on the platform, the station-master would come up the steps and shout "Mr Williams!" and I would have to rush out and shout "Coming!" He forgot one day to tell them he was on holiday, and come next morning the train whistle blew and blew, the man shouted, and I had to get out of bed, rush downstairs and shout, "Not coming!".'

BESIDE THE LMS LINE

'In the mid 1920s when I was a small girl, the LMS (London, Midland and Scottish) railway line between Liverpool and Manchester ran alongside our garden and orchard. There was a frequent train service, the first one leaving Lymm station at 6.40 in the morning to Manchester, depositing a considerable number of workers at Broadheath station where there were several factories in the vicinity. Three more trains ran in both directions before nine o'clock, then an intermittent service until the evening rush hour when there were four trains between five and seven o'clock. The last one of the day, from Manchester arriving at Lymm station at 11.15 was popular with the theatregoers. How strange that all these trains ran so promptly one could set one's clock by them.

My father, working in Manchester, allowed himself seven minutes to walk to the station – but some mornings must have reached it in five. However, the guards, often knowing the passengers, would keep the train waiting for a few moments if they saw late-comers approaching and didn't wave the green flag until all had scrambled breathlessly into the nearest carriage. There were no corridor trains on this line but separate compartments, each one having a luggage rack above the seats and there were often pictures of seaside resorts served by the company. Occasionally there was a mirror too, into which if strangers were not present, we would pull faces.

We created many games on the railings dividing the garden from the railway line, our favourite being to see how long we could balance on the top rail without falling off. It was remarkable how often we over-balanced into the vegetable plot on the other side of them which was rented by a rather unfriendly neighbour of ours, though we did try to straighten out the cabbage leaves if they were broken.

The engine drivers always returned our waves and how we loved to see the sparks fly as the boiler fire was stoked up. One hot, dry summer they set fire to the cornfield on the other side of the line. Such a blaze and what excitement. We considered ourselves very lucky to live by the railway.'

HOUSE & HOME

THE HOUSES WE LIVED IN

Old cottages may look picturesque, but they could be cold, dark and damp in the days before electricity, mains water and mains sewerage. There were no labour saving appliances for the house-work either, which followed a regular weekly rhythm in most households. How many of us would want to go back to 'the good old days'?

ONE OF THE LUCKY ONES

'I was born during the depression. My father was one of the lucky ones he told me, he had managed to find work for 136 days one year. Mother used to clean for the more "fortunate". Life was hard for them. My father had served in the war as a machine gunner, and after he was demobbed, came to Heswall to join his elder brother. They were time-served joiners, and had left their village in Shrop-shire to find work at a local firm of builders in Heswall. My mother was a local lass.

Our house was a terraced cottage, two up, two down, and an outside loo. The front door opened into the living room, and our fireplace was a black range, which was blackleaded each week. A three piece suite, polished table, and four chairs, a high-backed mahogany sideboard with oval mirror, a big clock on the wall, a wind-up gramophone and a piano filled the room. It was only used for special occasions, Mother was very house-proud.

We lived in the back room. Its contents were a small fireplace, a stone sink, gas cooker, scrubbed top table, chairs, and a radio, which had an accumulator which had to be taken each week to be recharged. On the floor we had a coconut mat.

A cold water tap was our water supply, and on a Friday night a tin bath would be placed in front of the fire, water would be heated on the gas stove, and we would sit by the fire, getting toasted one side and frozen on the other. Otherwise it was a wash down in the kitchen sink.'

BIGGER AND BETTER

'I was born in 1908 in the area originally called Ringway, now Hale. The first house I lived in, Memory Cottage, was lit by oil lamps and candles and I remember the treat of having a bath in front of the open fire. Not a pleasure though, was to have to trail to the toilet at the end of the garden – a two-seater by the way – lighting your way with lamp or candle.

At the beginning of the First World War we moved on to bigger and better things, to a house with bay windows, decorated with leaded lights. We had the luxury of going upstairs to a bathroom, where hot and cold water were in abundance. The front room, with a magnificent suite in green plush and a piano, was lit by butterfly gas jets, soon to be followed by Bijou mantles. Down in the cellar was a wash boiler with a fire underneath, instead of the large tub we used before.'

MY GRANDPARENTS' HOUSE

'At my grandparents' house in Poynton, the room was warm and cosy with the glow of a coal fire that never went out. It just burned steadily and strongly with the lively, orange flames reaching upwards and lighting the black apertures of the chimney. As the flames licked each other, turning blue, yellow and red, they reflected on two pictures on the opposite wall, large sepia portraits, which had been coloured and framed ostentatiously in broad, gilt frames. These were the likenesses of the master and mistress of the house. He was gazing seriously down the living room, wearing his navy blue serge suit, a pink country rose in his buttonhole and his watch-albert straining across his chest. His moustache was still fair, but his hair looked darker pomaded and pressed to his head. She was dressed in her best black bombazine with a touch of lace at the neck and her hair rolled on pads, making a frame for her lovely, hand-some face. The only pieces of jewellery that she possessed, besides her wedding ring, were highlighted on the dress: one, a small gold brooch with a lock of baby hair inside it and the other a long pinchbeck chain.

Beneath these pictures a tall mahogany chest of drawers stood: the patina smooth as silk and the brass drop handles winking back a reflection from the fire. On top was a dear little mirror on a stand, with a piece of fine lace draping each side of it in true Victorian fashion. A satin apple, looking so real one could bite it, was a pin cushion and was placed next to the mirror, with two large china ornaments, into which were dropped any small items which had not got a home. By the side of the chest of drawers was a treadle sewing machine and this I liked best when it was in motion, because it made the most exciting, whirring noises and brightly coloured pieces of material went under the little, steel foot and magically emerged as a dress, an apron or a blouse.

The broad window-sill, facing south, had two scarlet geraniums on it in large china pots and from the top of the window, mirroring the whole room, hung a shiny, green witches' ball. This was supposed to be a lucky charm. A square deal table took up most of the floor space and almost always someone sat quietly rocking in the chair by the side of it.

Opposite the window was an old black settle with soft cushions on it and the grandfather clock, which dominated the room. This was a most important piece, telling the time, the season and the moon's phases. Its tick was soft like velvet. I have been nursed on someone's lap in that room sometimes and listened to the tick of the old clock, the gentle crackle of the coal as it burned and I have fallen fast asleep.

This room remained the same for many years – in fact all through my childhood. I don't think even the wallpaper was changed.

Then when I was 14 both my grandparents died and the cottage changed hands a few times. I was invited in one day recently to have a look at "the old place". How changed it was. The room is modern, sharp with tasteful furnishings, no fire now, just central heating radiators, but the atmosphere has changed too. Where is the peace of that unhurried time of my childhood? If only it could be captured again – just for a couple of hours.'

I'D NEVER GO BACK

'Clough Bank Farm is dated 1640 or thereabouts, in 1952 the house being of a hay roof, with walls far from straight and inside the floor downstairs was flagstoned, with the exception of the parlour. In the big sitting room, having the name of the house-place, the grand-father clock was let into the floor, rather than it be sawn off. Through the years the floor, as was the rest of the downstairs rooms, was asphalted.

The cooking was done on a huge blackleaded grate for the first two years of my married life. You boiled the kettle and grilled the bacon on a trivet attached to the bars of the grate. Meat, bread, etc was done in the oven at the side, and woe betide you if you did not get the heat just right, your efforts of the morning baking could end up in either a burnt offering or an under-cooked soggy mess. To wash up meant getting the bowl from under the stairs which you placed on the table. The cold water was kept in a bucket stood on the top of the scrubbed dresser top and you went outside into the wash-house for your hot water, which was obtained from the copper boiler which had to be lit every morning. This was the only source of hot water. For a bath, which you only had once a week, you carried the water into the room above the washhouse by bucket. Cold water was laid on to the bath, which stood proudly on bare boards. You *could* pull the plug out by the way!

Electric light was installed in all rooms; plugs were one on the landing and one downstairs which was in the kitchen, this was for the wireless and the iron.

The walls inside were so out of true you could lose nine inches in a pattern, so one kept clear of wallpaper which had a pattern on it. You learnt as you got older.

Clough Bank remains for me a very old house, perhaps lovely in a way. But go back to Clough Bank? Never!'

LIKE A MANSION

'Our houses were more or less all the same at the beginning of this century, two up and two down. Before the Second World War, council houses were being built which were more modern with better living conditions, we thought then, though they were nothing to what they are now. My house was newly built when my husband and I came to live in it and we thought it was like a mansion to the one we had left, because we had a bathroom with hot and cold water, electric lights and other modern conveniences.'

WE HAD ADVANTAGES

'We lived in the model village of Port Sunlight, which in itself gave us some advantages. For instance, before going on the National Grid in 1948, my father paid Lever Bros two shillings a week for all the electricity used. Later he paid twopence each for the radio, iron and cleaner. The house was three-bedroomed, with a bathroom but an outside toilet, and a fireplace in the kitchen and front room. We never locked the door. People would just open the door and call, "Anybody in?" We did not even think about being burgled.'

THE HEART OF THE HOUSE

'Families were bigger at Crowton in the past, in some cases three generations living under one roof. Cottages consisted of a parlour and a kitchen, with a solid fuel range where the cooking was done. Few people had bathrooms, and the privy was hidden behind a rhododendron bush in a quiet corner of the garden. Some privies had two seats, one child-sized. Tin containers, which had to be emptied regularly, were under the seats. At other houses the night soil man called. Bathing was in a tin bath in front of the fire. Houses were heated with open fires and if you were ill there was the luxury of a fire in the bedroom.

The kitchen was the heart of the house, remembered as having a big, solid table in the middle, heavy iron pans to go on the range fire, brass preserving pans, and a skillet for making custard. The fire was kept in all the time except when the chimney had to be swept. Cleaning was much harder work as there was no vacuum cleaner to suck up the continual dust caused by the fires. There was no carpet on the kitchen floor, which was mopped daily and scrubbed once a week. Brass door knobs were polished once a week.'

'Each cottage at Comberbach had a firegrate with an oven at the side used for baking and cooking, and the water was heated by making a nice red fire and placing an iron kettle on the embers. The grate had to be blackleaded and polished. These fireplaces were later replaced by a tiled grate, still with the oven at the side. Floors were mostly red tiled, on which you had a rag rug. Later linoleum came out and this covered the tiles and the luxury then became a wool rug, also hand-made.

Lighting was from oil lamps, the wicks having to be trimmed and the globes placed over, producing a very good light as you turned the wick up. When you went to bed you took a candle in a candlestick and if it was very cold you would have a hot shelf out of the oven wrapped in a cloth and placed in the bed at the bottom, or otherwise a stone bottle filled with hot water.'

'The blackleaded kitchen range was the focal point of the farmhouse kitchen in the 1930s, as to wander away from it in the winter was a freezing experience. The range had to be blackleaded, ie polished with a black liquid under the tradename "Zebo", almost daily as the fire cinders would constantly burn it off. Even in the hot summer months the fire never went out.

On the opposite side of the fire to the boiler was the oven, which had to have the temperature improved by shovels full of coal. The damper to draw the fire would be pulled out and the temperature of the oven would be guessed by putting your hand in – there were very few cookery failures! As the oven cooled down after the evening meal, household bricks were put in the oven to be used at bedtime to warm the beds. Each was wrapped in a cotton bag to protect the sheets. The bedrooms were very cold in winter; if you left a glass of water in the room it could be frozen by morning.'

STILL NO ELECTRICITY

'In 1958 there was still no electricity in the country areas and we, newly married, had only one Aladdin pressure lamp which we used downstairs and later took upstairs at bedtime. We had to fetch paraffin for the lamp from the local shop, and quite often the light would start to fade warning us that it was running short of paraffin. My husband would say, "Have you fetched the paraffin?" to which I replied, "No, I thought you were picking it up." Realising we had no paraffin to fill the lamp we made a mad dash to get ready for bed before the lamp eventually went out.

We then progressed to a ½ hp Lister engine which generated enough electricity to run a television and one lamp on top. We would be watching something interesting and the volts would drop, making the picture reduce in size and the light fade. My husband would rush outside to the shed which housed the engine to clear the carburettor and very often it would clear itself just before he got there and pick up again.

We had electricity in our area about 1961 and when we came home from work in the evening and we switched all the lights on, it was marvellous. Everything looked so light and bright and we were so thrilled we would not have to carry lamps from room to room or fetch paraffin ever again.'

THE DAILY ROUTINE

'Life in the farmhouse was as big an organisation as on the farm itself. Most farms had a cheesemaker, dairy maid, housemaid and someone to look after the children to help the farmer's wife.

Extra help was needed on Monday which was washday. Fires were laid the night before in readiness to heat the water for the household wash. Care had to be taken to make sure none of the farm cats were curled up in the boiler's fireplace before it was lit. A woman usually came to do the washing, which was an all day job. The ironing had to be done the same day. Usually one of the wives of the farmhands did this – she probably also did the milking.

When the washing was finished the last of the soapy water would be used to wash all the household brushes. Last bits of soap would be grated so as not to waste any.

Sunday lunch would always be a roast. The meat was put into the oven before the family went to church, with the potatoes put around the meat. There was usually Sunday school in the afternoon, and a service again in the evening.

Monday lunch was usually bubble and squeak (potatoes mashed up with the leftover vegetables from Sunday lunch and fried). This was served with cold meat from the Sunday joint. Monday supper was often toasted cheese and onions with apple sauce.

Tuesday was cleaning day. The range was not lit on a Tuesday morning. The flues were cleaned, the range blackleaded and the stainless steel trims were cleaned with silver sand. The kitchen tables were scrubbed, as were bread boards and chopping boards, and lastly the kitchen floor was scrubbed. The front steps were scrubbed, the sides whitened. The side doorstep was scrubbed and the border donkey-stoned. On Friday the range would be cleaned again, and the tables scrubbed in readiness for the weekend.

There would be lob scouse for lunch on Tuesday if the Sunday roast had been beef, or hotpot if it had been lamb. So the joint was made to last three days.

So the week progressed. There was a baking day, when pastry was made in the dairy on the cold slabs, but only when the cheese-making was completed – nothing must hinder that.'

THE SWALLOWS FLEW IN

'The only toilet we had at our farmhouse at Saughall was outdoors next to the washhouse, a quiet little place with a beam across the centre. Every summer the swallows came and built there, always one and sometimes two nests, and they got so tame they would fly in and continue building and also feeding their young while the "seat" was occupied!'

RAG RUGS AND STOCKINGS

'Winter evenings at home were spent making rag rugs. Our mother got us to cut up old coats into pieces measured with a match-box: if we hadn't the right colours we used to dye them. Red flannel was often incorporated to give brightness to the pattern. The rugs were always made on hessian and only wool cloth was used. In those days sugar was delivered to grocers in brown hessian bags and Mother bought these for the rug making. She cut a design in brown paper and put it on the rug with chalk. The strips of cloth were pushed into the hessian with a tapering wooden peg with a sharp point. They were warm and cosy rugs. My mother made a lovely rug with wool from jumpers and cardigans the girls at Wright's factory gave her. She undid them and used two or three strands. Mother also knitted our black stockings for school. She cast the stitches on, on four needles, and got them going and then we knitted them: she would do the shaping. I did not like knitting the black wool, but the stockings lasted quite a long time.'

WATER AND WASHDAY

Having to carry in every drop of water we used, from the well or the village pump, certainly made us careful. Washday is remembered as a time of drudgery, from bringing in the gallons of water needed, through to ironing with flat irons heated on the fire.

MY GRANDMOTHER'S ROUTINE

'My father died when I was two years of age, so my mother took my two sisters, aged four and ten, and myself to live with her parents, who lived "across the water" in Wallasey. My grandparents had a very large three-storey, eight-bedroomed house which always appeared to be bursting with relatives coming and going. This was in the 1920s when there were tramlines along the main roads and gaslit street lamps. We used to delight in watching the uniformed "gasman" cycling along with his long, slim pole over his shoulder, pulling the loop down at the top of the gas lamp to light it when the evenings were getting dark, and returning in the morning to lift the loop again to put the mantle out. This was a regular routine and he used to cycle for miles.

Monday was washday – what a performance. When we were on holiday from school my sisters and I used to help. At the bottom of the garden was a washhouse, complete with a large brick wash boiler. The water was poured into the lined centre and a fire was lit with wood, paper and coal underneath. With it being damp, it was always hard to light. We used to pray it would light quickly as my grandmother would become so annoyed as time was being wasted.

When it was lit, the sheets were put into the boiler with the Lux or Oxydol soap. We kept the sheets moving by using a large wooden baton. The sheets boiled for at least ten minutes. When they were gently lifted out with big wooden tongs they were put into a large galvanised container called a dolly tub. Then we used a posher – a long pole with three wide wooden prongs as feet at the bottom – to swirl them around to get all the soap out. Then we transferred the sheets to another large dolly tub with hot water in and repeated the process. This had to be done several times to make sure the sheets were properly rinsed; in the final rinse we used a blue-bag which, although blue, made the sheets sparkling white!

After emptying as much water as possible, the dolly tub was pushed in front of the mangle – this being a hefty piece of equipment,

Washday was hard work in the days of the dolly tub. At least this lady had a fine day for her washing, at Byley in the 1930s!

60

with a large iron frame with two large wooden rollers above and a big wheel at the side with a handle. My grandmother would feed the sheets through the rollers whilst I turned the handle to get all the water out of the sheets, and either my sister or mother would stand at the back and hold the sheets as they came through the rollers. (Whilst all this was being done, the second load of washing was put in the boiler.) The sheets were then neatly folded and carefully taken into the garden to hang on the many washing lines.

This, as you can imagine, was quite a performance and if the weather was wet we kept out of Grandma's way. As years went by there were laundries who collected the washing and took it away, but the sheets could never be as white as those washed at home – according to Grandma!

There were no electric irons for ironing – a heavy flat iron with an iron handle was used. It was placed on the kitchen range to get hot. Making sure to use a thick pad of material to hold the handle, the ironing was done on the kitchen table.

Tuesdays and Wednesdays were days for cleaning the bedrooms etc upstairs and on Thursdays, the dining room and living rooms.

Friday was baking day. We had a very large kitchen with a big wooden table, which had to be thoroughly scrubbed after use. My grandmother would make the pastry and make enough pies to last the week – both sweet and savoury, while Mother made the fruit cakes. We had a back kitchen where the deep porcelain sink was, with a wooden draining board (more scrubbing!). It was more like our kitchens are today, with the shelves for hanging crockery and pans, with under-cupboards containing dishes etc. Next to this was the pantry where there was a "safe" for keeping the freshly baked food. It had a fine mesh front to let the air circulate and to keep out the flies and it had shelves inside. The safe was on a concrete floor and there were marble shelves around to keep other food cold. It really was cold in there and food kept fresh for quite a while, as there were no refrigerators or deep freezes in those days. We had a large iron range in the kitchen that had to be blackleaded every day with Zebo. It was always gleaming due to the daily brushing. This kitchen range comprised a fireplace, having ovens each side of the fire, and a huge iron kettle, also gleaming, on top. In front of the fire was a brass fender and the fire irons used for poking the fire etc. Toast made with the long toasting forks held by the fire was delicious, as were muffins and crumpets.'

IT'S AMAZING

'I remember an advertisement for Rinso, an early washing powder:
    It's amazing what Rinso can do
    Just an hour and your whole wash is through
    I'm really not joking
    Twelve minutes for soaking
    And remember, for boiling – just two.'

FETCHING THE WATER

'Not many houses at Crowton had inside taps. In the centre of the village was a communal tap fed by a spring and continually running. A metal cup hanging on a chain enabled passers by to help themselves to a drink. The housewives in nearby cottages had to collect all their water in buckets.'

'There was no piped water to many cottages in Pickmere. Chapel Cottage got their water from a spring in the field opposite the chapel. When this dried up in the summer, they had to go to the well in Wellfield Close with their buckets. This was a walk of about three quarters of a mile in each direction. At Laburnum Cottage, the water was very hard so the night before washday the children had to get the barrow, put the dolly tub in it and go to the pit in the field at the back of the house to fill it with water. They had three rain tubs at the back door but if it had not rained they had to fill these up. They had a wooden yoke to put over their shoulders with a chain and bucket on each side.'

'We had to carry water from the river at North Rode to do all our washing. Our drinking water was carried from a spring, which was quite a journey across the main road, through a little hatch, up a banky field, across a plank over a brook, to a spring in a farmer's field. This water was kept in a stein and treated like gold.'

SHOPPING AND CALLERS
TO THE DOOR

Shopping was a pleasant experience and something of a treat when it involved a visit to the local market town. Much of our daily food was brought direct to the door by regular tradesmen who became almost part of the family.

CREWE SHOPPING

'Crewe market was open Fridays, Saturdays and Mondays. It was a very good market, and at the rear were dobby horses and steamboat rides that cost a penny. Another highlight for the children was Peacock's Penny Bazaar, a veritable Aladdin's cave where much enjoyment could be had deciding how much you could get for a penny.

The Co-op was quite close to the market. You could purchase anything from the Co-op – they had their own bakery, butcher, bank, joiner's shop, draper, and fish shop. Seed & Douthwaite was another big shop, known as "Joey Seeds", where you could buy anything "from a pin to an elephant". If they had not got the item you wanted, then nobody would have it. Your money went via the wires to the cashier and you then waited for the container to come back with your change. This always fascinated the children.'

SHOPPING IN NANTWICH

'Shopping was usually done on Thursday and Saturday, the shops being open in the 1930s until ten o'clock on a Saturday. Nantwich also had a market with all types of stalls – butchers, bakers, greengrocers, at least six cheese stalls, all kinds of hardware, carpets, curtains and clothes. On Thursdays the farmers brought their produce, butter, eggs etc. Nantwich was well known for its large Cheese Fair.

Bread could be bought from at least a dozen different bakers' shops. There were also numerous greengrocers, confectioners, ironmongers and butchers, and at least two large stores, namely Stennet & Afford and P.H. Chesters, selling virtually every household item. The Co-op was another large store which sold nearly everything, including clothes. The Maypole sold groceries such as tea and butter, which had to be weighed as you purchased it. Once my mother complained that the butter she had bought there was a bit rancid. Then she realised that the butter bought on a Saturday evening had been in the window all week.'

PAID ON A SATURDAY

'While we were living at Puddington in the 1920s, the farm workers were given their week's wages at Saturday dinnertime. After tea Mother and I would walk in to Neston to buy the weekend joint and the groceries. It was a good three miles. The shops stayed open late so that families could do their shopping after being paid.'

A PLEASANT PLACE TO SHOP

'In the 1920s and 1930s Wilmslow was a very pleasant place to shop. There were, of course, many more food shops and in sunny weather vegetable shops and fish shops displayed their goods in windows which held large blocks of ice – and in some cases, running water – all shaded by blinds. I think McLaren's, the cheese shop, was my granny's favourite, and I can see her now sampling morsels of cheese presented to her on the end of a large knife by Mr McLaren.

Later we did most of our shopping in Chapel Lane. There was a very good grocer's shop run by two delightful sisters called the Misses Warhurst. There were also two other grocer's shops, confectioners, a greengrocer, an off licence, a sweet shop and a pub. But the most amusing shop was a very small draper's owned by a Miss Birch. Every bit of her wares was stored in brown paper parcels secured by thick cord and stacked up the walls of three sides of the shop, making it a veritable padded cell. Searching for the required item was a long-winded business.'

WE WORE OUR BEST CLOTHES

'Visits to Liverpool and Chester were really big occasions and we always wore our best clothes complete with hats, gloves etc like we did for church.'

CALLERS TO THE DOOR

'Until the 1940s, there was very little transport to take one shopping, our nearest shops being in Middlewich, about three miles away.

Travelling shops were popular then. There was Kinseys who had a bakehouse in Middlewich and delivered their freshly baked bread

The Beehive Village Stores and post office at Stretton in 1931, with the owners Percy and Annie Mounfield at the door. Shops like this were the backbone of village life.

in a horse-drawn van. There was Pegrams and Meadow Dairy and later the Co-op who delivered groceries, and the travelling butcher's shop owned by Fittons.

Coal was delivered on a horse-drawn lorry, one cwt cost around one shilling and sevenpence or, if you collected your own from the station yard, it would cost about £1 3s 6d per ton. There was a milkman who came round in a horse-drawn vehicle. The milk was carried in a large tankard and was measured out with either a pint or quart measure and put into a covered jug which you would leave on the doorstep. The rag and bone man would also pay a visit from time to time; he would collect old rags or bits of scrap and in return give you a donkey stone which was used to clean doorsteps.'

'The shrimp lady called every other Tuesday at Lymm, with a basket brimming with shrimps which she measured out in an enamel pot.

Pat Parry, from the shop in the village called Parry's Pot Shop, came on a three-wheeler bicycle with a large wooden box fitted on the back. He brought a variety of cups, saucers and plates to the back door in a washing basket. He was known to us as "Hi-small" as he always announced his arrival by calling, "Hi, small-pots!"

Milk was delivered by Philip Moston. It was in a churn which was brought by horse and cart. Later on it was brought in cans by the farmer's daughter, riding a bicycle. Vegetables were delivered weekly by horse and cart, as were groceries and coal.

A gentleman would call at each house in Lymm selling end rolls of material which he bought at reduced prices from the mills. We would buy these to make tea towels and pillowcases. If you were lucky enough to buy two pieces alike you were sometimes able to make a skirt! The man was known as "Cheap Jack".'

'Tradesmen called regularly to the door in Grappenhall. There was a fish man named Copper. He would call with his two daughters each Thursday, just as dinner was put on the table. In a very loud voice he would call, "Fresh 'errings, Finny 'addy an' cod." There was also a time when the muffin man called with crumpets, Eccles cakes, potato cakes and, of course, muffins. Mouthwatering memories.'

'When I was a girl before the First World War, a man came to our house in Norley with samples of material for curtains, covers and clothes. We could decide what we needed and then if it was clothing we had to walk to Weaverham to Burgess's to be measured.

The postman was Sam Partington and if he had a letter for you he would stop outside and whistle. This postman used to sell one penny stamps which you could collect and then take to the post office, a way of saving money.'

'My grandparents lived in Alderley Edge, a very small village in those days. My grandmother remembers the first Belisha Beacon crossing in the village and being told by the local policeman that she *must* use the crossing even if it was not near the shop she wanted and there was no traffic!

The milk was delivered in churns on a donkey cart and we brought our own jugs to be filled. The baker came two or three times a week with a basket of beautiful freshly baked bread for us to choose. He was completely bald but insisted that we call him "Curly".'

'During the 1930s I delivered milk in Crewe twice a day, mornings and evenings, with a pony and float. My father and brother milked the cows by hand while I brought the pony in from the field and fed, groomed and harnessed her.

The milk was cooled and put into tankards, each holding ten gallons, then delivered to the door in carrying cans and measured into customers' jugs with pint and half pint measures. The price was twopence halfpenny during the summer and threepence in the winter. During the summer if there was a surplus of milk it was made into butter and sold on the round. The buttermilk was very much sought after.'

STREET TRADERS

'I can remember over 50 years ago at Harthill, the gypsies coming to collect wood from the willow trees in the wood to make clothes pegs and baskets. The women would come and sit on the doorstep and wouldn't move until you bought from them and gave them food and clothing for the children.'

'The streets of Adlington always seemed very clean. Every housewife would brush the footpath in front of her house and then swill it. Many even decorated the edges of the pavement, doors and windows with a white or yellow donkey stone. Many traders would visit the street to sell their wares or services.

Every day the milkman would call with his horse and cart. You would go out with some bread for the horse and jugs to put the milk in. This came straight from one of the two large churns and was ladled out either by the pint or gill measure. Buttermilk was often offered for sale from the cart.

The watercress man was always welcome. He would have a large wicker basket hanging from leather straps round his neck. In the basket would be glistening, green fresh watercress. You would be sent out with sixpence and a large soup plate which the watercress man would fill for you. When Granelli's ice cream came round it was a basin you were given and several pennies and then it was ice cream for tea.

The oatcake man came practically every day, carrying his warm oatcakes in a big wicker basket over his arm. They were always covered with a big, clean white cloth and cost a penny each.

An occasional visitor was the salt man, with his donkey cart. He required just a plate to put the salt he had cut off for you from his large block. The knife grinder was always busy when he arrived and generally collected a small crowd round him.

Perhaps the most popular visitor with the children was the rag and bone man, who would turn up with his pony and cart shouting "Pots for rags" up and down the street. He didn't give pots but donkey stones to the grown ups, but to the children he gave a goldfish!'

'We had travellers of different nationalities selling lucky charms, needles, pins, lace, tape, elastic and darning wools. We also had

Frenchmen who used to ride bicycles around Bunbury selling onions, carried by long strings hanging from their bikes.'

THE CARRIER

'My father was the village carrier at Whitley. He would take all the village produce to Warrington for sale and bring back to the village such commodities as coal and other needs. He had a regular order each Saturday for Marbury Farm, of one pound of Redman's tea and one pound of Palethorpe's sausages.'

OUR DAILY FOOD

Once, nearly every cottage kept a pig and pig-killing day was a necessary preliminary to all those home-cured hams, faggots and bacon. Our diet was wholesome, if more restricted than it is today, and we grew most of what we ate ourselves. Making cream, butter and cheese was everyday work to many farmers' wives.

KILLING THE PIG

'Mother knew what to expect when lots of squealing came from the farm along the road. Soon afterwards, the farmer appeared with a big bowl of offal for Mother to make faggots. While she minced all the bits and pieces, we girls had to make the breadcrumbs. Out came the colander and a loaf cut into chunks which we had to rub through. The best bit came afterwards, when we dipped the crusts into the juice from the cooked faggots. Lovely!'

SNIGGING

'Snigging was the collecting of young eels from the ditches on the marsh at Helsby, which we took home for our mothers to boil. We dammed a ditch just before it went under a bridge, knowing the eels like to collect in dark places. As the water drained away, we could collect them easily.'

'I am 93 and have lived in Peckforton all my life. We would scoop a hole in the bottom of the stream for the eels to gather, then use a three-finger catch to grab them. We used salt to grip them to skin them. Slice and fry or casserole!'

BREAD AND BACON

'When Grandmother passed on, Grandfather Bilton lived with his daughter's family at Appleton. They were self sufficient. They kept two pigs, one of which was sold to pay the rent, the other to be killed, salted on the marble slab in the larder and hung above the range, shrouded in a curtain to keep it clean, until it could be enjoyed by the family.

Bacon was cooked in a Dutch oven, which hung over the fire, dripping fat into the tray in which eggs were cooked. The Dutch oven had a hood which could be reversed to allow even cooking.

Carter's bread van called twice a week, so bread was not usually cooked at home. However, on one occasion when stocks were running low, the fire was stoked up and a large loaf was put in the oven and left overnight. In the morning, an enormous square loaf was eased out, and pronounced the best bread ever baked! The kitchen range with its oven differed from the family's old oven in Cambridge, where the oven was a brick structure outside, in which a fire of furze was lit. When the fire burnt out, the ashes were swept out and the loaves put in, the oven door being sealed with clay until the bread was cooked.'

ALWAYS THE SAME

'The menu on our farm was always the same. We would have a huge ten shilling piece of beef cooked for lunch on Sunday after we had been to church. It was then served cold with chutneys for evening meal after church. Monday we had the dripping from around it on toast. This was after we had done a massive wash. Tuesday the meat was hashed, and this was also ironing day.

Wednesday was bedroom day and the meat was made into lobby, which is a sort of Lancashire hot pot. Thursday we had cottage pie and it was shopping day. Father and Mother took a huge basket of eggs to P.H. Chesters in Nantwich and returned with the basket full of groceries.

Friday was downstairs cleaning the brasses, the blackleaded grate and rooms. We had egg, bacon and potatoes that day. The meat had all been eaten and this was a treat. All this food was home-produced, of course.

Saturday was tidy up for Sunday and clean the vegetables for Sunday and tidy the garden and then on Sunday it all started again.'

Although a lot of food was home-produced, the village shop, like Groves's in Peover, was an essential part of village life.

CHEESES

'At Newton Bank Farm at Daresbury, cheeses were put to dry in the large bedroom, which smelled musty. The floor was packed with wheat chaff under the boards to dry and soak up the excess whey.'

'In Watergate Street, Chester, the cheesemakers used to store the cheeses on long wooden benches in the cellars. The large round cheeses were covered with muslin and they used long pipes to push in the cheese to draw a little out to test.

Sometimes the cheeses were in wooden barrels with large wooden hoops around. My mother would call around Christmas time to get two of these wooden hoops. We covered them with coloured paper and decorated them with balls and stars. They were called Christmas bushes and were great fun to make.'

MAKING BUTTER

'If the churn has not been used for some time, fill it with cold water to swell the joints. Leave for suitable length of time. Make sure the rubber seal and the pressure valve in the lid are in good condition. Scald well with really boiling water – two kettles full will suffice. Rinse with cold water. Scald *all* utensils.

Put the milk in flat shallow bowls for the cream to rise for at least 24 hours. Skim into a bowl. Stir frequently during the next 24 hours. Separated cream *may* be too thick – but the thickness can be regulated.

Put the cream into the churn. Turn, but not at a furious pace. Let out the pressure at intervals. When the observation glass in the lid is clear, your butter is almost separated from the buttermilk, and will appear as small granules. Now turn very gently for these granules to collect into a mass.

Now empty the buttermilk out through the hole in the side of the churn – or perhaps this outlet may be in the lid of the churn. Now, without taking the butter out, wash it three times with very cold water to get it clean of buttermilk, turning the churn very gently with each washing.

Put the butter into a bowl – a wooden one is best but probably unobtainable these days. Now, press all surplus water out of the butter, using the fingers. Add salt to taste, using old-fashioned block salt. Now make up into pats and decorate with patterns, using corrugated butter pats. Then – we will come to tea and sample your butter. Scald your utensils well immediately after use. Good luck.'

NOT AMUSED

'My father and mother had moved to Manchester from Birmingham, my father having been appointed to Manchester Cathedral. Mother answered a knock at the door to be smiled at by a workman holding in his hand a brewcan. "Wilt mak a brew, mum?" was his request. "Will I what?" asked my mother in her best teacher's voice! Eventually mutual accents understood each other and Mother realised she was being asked to make a can of tea. She willingly agreed and took the can inside.

She examined the can and was horrified to find it blackened and with a wad of black stuff (her words not mine) in the bottom of the can. (It was condensed milk with tea leaves; but how was she to know?) She scoured the can out and made fresh tea in it and gave it back to him with a smile.

He was not amused and did not return a second time!'

THE CLOTHES WE WORE

Liberty bodices, Spirella corsets, layers of clothes to keep out the cold, button-up boots – what memories clothes bring back, and how we suffered to be glamorous!

THROUGH THE GENERATIONS

'My grandmother died in 1925 in her seventies. Elderly ladies of her time wore mainly black, voluminous dresses with tight bodices trimmed with jet beads and high necklines stiffened with whale bones, which set off the gold chain necklaces they invariably put on. I never saw this grandmother wearing a bonnet, which she flatly refused to do. Even at my mother's wedding she wore a hat with a veil. My great-aunt was a lady's companion. At the age of 90 odd she used to wear black bonnets trimmed with jet and tied under her chin with a huge black bow. I recall her wearing short black capes also trimmed with jet, and very smart she looked too. This lady was my father's aunt. She lived with her nieces in Higher Lane. I remember being puzzled as to how to address her. I already had two grandmothers and she was clearly too old to be an aunt, so I compromised by calling her "Auntie Grandma".

The younger ladies of that period were elegant in long, flowing dresses with elaborately tucked or trimmed skirts, tight bodices, high necklines and large hats perched precariously on their heads. In a head and shoulders photograph of my mother aged 21 (1897), she is in a pretty smocked, lace-trimmed blouse with leg of mutton sleeves. Her hair is simply styled with a curly fringe and a large chignon at the nape of her neck. Later she wore her hair taken up over hair pads a la Pompadour style – no bobbed heads till the 1920s. My mother normally wore black to please my father. Only after he died did she have more colourful clothes. With her long skirts her small waist was encircled by a silver belt with a large silver buckle. I used to wonder how on earth she got it to fasten round her. Jackets and matching skirts were then called "costumes" not "suits". The close-fitting jackets had either a small velvet collar or a long collar worn with a separate squirrel fur and huge muff to match, trimmed with squirrel tails. My mother had a long, green velour coat lined with squirrel

---

Opposite: *A well dressed young lady and her bicycle in about 1910. Clothing would gradually lighten and allow new freedom over the next few decades.*

fur, specially made to wear on board ship when we went to America in 1910. It was slim-fitting for those days, but Mother kept it so long it became a family joke. I used to call it "Noah".

As a young child I used to wear white needlework frocks in summer, with about two petticoats and white frilly knickers that peeped coyly under the hem. During my school days I was firmly encased in the green gymslip of Lymm grammar school – serge in winter and cotton in summer – white blouse and green and white striped tie. Green and white dresses could also be worn in summer. I often wonder how Mother got the ink stains off my sleeves. Out of doors on weekdays I wore my green gaberdine school coat, green velour hat with the school badge on (green and white with three doves, as today), and in summer a panama hat. Woe betide any girl caught without a hat and gloves. The headmistress, Miss Hubback, was a stickler for "ladylike" behaviour. For the dancing classes, taken by Miss Field at the old Conservative Club by the canal, I had a Red Riding Hood cloak and carried a little Dorothy bag for my slippers. The girls came in white dresses and the boys in Eton suits. When asking the girls to dance the boys had to bow and say, "May I have the pleasure?", and the girls would curtsey. These clothes were worn for children's parties, but for parties and Sundays I had my hair in long curls with a bow on either side, my mother having patiently put my hair in curling rags overnight. For school I had two pigtails.

When I left school in the early 1920s, waists had descended to the hips and dresses were shapeless. Only natural materials were available – silk, wool, linen and cotton. For my 21st party I had a grey crepe-de-chine dress made, with an accordion pleated skirt and very short sleeves. The dressmaker kept telling me to bind my bust tightly to attain the boyish figure fashionable at the time, but to no avail, much to my sorrow the bust always won.

In the years before the Second World War the fashion was for the "little black dress"; a black or grey tailored costume worn with a pretty blouse; tiny hats, often with an eye veil; a fox fur slung over one shoulder; sheer silk stockings and very high-heeled patent leather court shoes. In 1939 war was declared. Uniforms were everywhere – the Forces; the Red Cross nurses; the WVS; the Land Army; the Home Guard etc. Clothing coupons were issued and people had to manage as best they could. "Make do and mend" was the slogan. After the war came a great reaction to austerity with the "New Look". Skirts were longer and there was variety in styles and materials. In fact, a general return to femininity.'

WINTERS WERE SO COLD

'Winters were very cold. We piled layers of clothes on. Remember liberty bodices, with fleecy linings and loads of buttons? Thick black stockings – in those days we all had Nora Batty legs. Navy blue knickers with a pocket on one leg for your hankies! On top of everything else when you braved the elements, a great woolly scarf wound round the back of your neck, crossing over your chest and fastened with a huge safety pin at the back.

Shirley Temple was a child film star of the 1930s and boy, did we try to copy her, especially her curly hair and her tap dancing routines. I tried for the curly hair because Mum could not afford dancing lessons. Every night I had my hair wound up in rags. These consisted of pieces of rag (strips of old cotton sheets) about ten inches by two inches. Hair would be wound up and tied with knots. How I suffered. My favourite shoes at that time were shiny black patent with an ankle strap fastened in front with a button.'

TOO MUCH CLEAVAGE!

'We lived in Liverpool but always urged our parents to move "over the water". We were often there and a favourite walk was from Seacombe to New Brighton and back. We would pass Guinea Gap seawater baths. Years ago a female attendant there would inspect the girls for cleavage before they entered the mixed bathing pool. If they were showing too much she would give them a safety pin and make sure they put a large tuck in the neck of their costumes.'

WORKING CLOTHES

'Waistcoats, trilbys or flat caps with their wide-legged, turn-up trousers were the norm in the 1940s and 1950s for the thousands of men streaming out of the shipyard gates at knocking off time. Scarcely a bare head among them.

Navy bib and brace trousers, jacket and cap, grimy with soot was the everyday wear of the train driver and his fireman, shunting coal in the sidings. Dungarees in dark navy denim, a headscarf tied turban fashion, often hiding a pin-clipped hairdo, this was the workwear of the ladies who cleaned the railway carriages. I can see them now, mop and bucket in one hand, billycan of tea in the other.

Rolled up shirt sleeves, kerchief round neck, leather apron and huge wellington boots, these last two usually shiny with water. The not very pleasant aspect of the slaughterman from the local abattoir. Still less pleasant, the old clothes and pervasive pong of the tannery workers – no wonder they always stood on the open platforms of the buses!

But the pleasantest sight of all was our mums' capacious "pinnies" covering their clothes. My own mum always burst the underarms and sleeves of her summer dresses. This was due to pushing and carrying seven babies and the shopping, cleaning and washing with dolly tub, posser and mangle, all with her own hardworking hands. Her upper-arm muscle would put a bodybuilder's to shame.

Thank heaven for cars and supermarkets, fridges, freezers and washing machines. Nowadays our muscular development is usually in the hip area!'

'BATTEN ME AP!'

'We girls wore home-made red flannel quilted "stays" – the fore-runner of the liberty bodice. They buttoned up the back, and also had buttons at back and front to which undergarments were attached. These cotton knickers were unbuttoned at the back for "use". A gentleman visitor once said, "This house is full of little girls saying 'Batten me ap' – what do they mean?" Mother's Cambridge accent made the request for rebuttoning a modest one!'

OH, THOSE CORSETS!

'I was brought up by my grandmother and had to wear a whalebone corset. You can imagine how excruciatingly uncomfortable and how embarrassing this was at the age of ten. So I cut the nails and pulled out the bones and hid them under the lino. Grandmother never did discover what happened to them. They're probably still there.'

'When I was about 14 in the olden days of the 1940s, Mother decided to do something about my figure so off we went to the "Spirella Lady". She measured me up and the following week I was har-nessed up in a pink monstrosity of a corset. I used to put a large wad of cotton wool down the front to stop it rubbing but it didn't really help. I think Mother regarded it as some sort of chastity belt.

Underneath the corset I wore cream woollen combs not unlike those sported by Captain Webb on the matchboxes. Mother was taking no chances.

Strangely enough my ever-increasing bosom was ignored. It was apparently one of the unmentionables as it was never suggested that I wore a brassiere.

A few years later, with the dreaded corset now minus a few bones, I decided it was time I did something about my hair, which although curly when I was a child had now become quite straight. I put curling tongs into the coal fire and after a while tested them on a piece of newspaper. If the paper went up in flames I had an idea the tongs were perhaps too hot. But if the paper showed scorch marks of a sort of biscuit colour I was ready to start the curling. This was the exciting part, gripping sections of hair between the tongs and crimping it into deep waves. A few years later my hair-curling became much more sophisticated and after seeing Ingrid Bergman in *For whom the bell tolls*, every night I twisted my poor tortured hair, first soaked in sugar and water, with pipe-cleaners. They were miserable to sleep in but as my Auntie Agnes used to say, "Beauty must abide", although the end result next morning was an unbecoming frizz and I didn't look at all like Ingrid. A few years later I rolled my hair around a silk stocking so that it formed a sausage around my head.

On Saturday nights I sallied forth with my parents to the local theatre and with my Evening in Paris dabbed behind my ears and my nails buffed up with pink paste I thought I was the "bees knees", chewing my violet cachous to make my breath smell sweetly and with a Dorothy bag full of bonbons to eat in the interval. I wouldn't have changed places with anyone; not even the "posh" people sitting in the boxes at the side of the stage!'

INDEPENDENCE

'When I started my first job in 1936 I earned eleven shillings a week and that was good. Bear Brand stockings were two shillings a pair. I made my own dresses then and materials from Lewis's in Manchester were from one shilling and elevenpence a yard. The first long dance dress I made cost £1, which was a lot in 1937. We had to wear what our mothers decreed when she was paying the bill but now I was earning money.

I caused uproar in the house by changing my dentist, buying bras (which, although I had needed them since I left school, my mother had said I was not old enough for), and leaving off my Chilprufe vests. Then I really shocked my poor mother by buying a pattern for camiknickers, making lots and discarding my elastic-round-the-legs ones. The next stage was a streak in my hair and *coloured* fingernails. Oh yes, we've all been there.'

INTO THE 1950s

'During the 1950s we wore stiff net petticoats and black watermark taffeta skirts. The petticoats were rinsed in sugar and water to make them stiff. Flat ballerina shoes completed the picture.'

FROM THE CRADLE TO
THE GRAVE

We were more likely to be born, to suffer our illnesses and to die in our own homes in the past. The doctor's attention cost money, so home remedies were always welcomed, odd though some of them seem today. However, childhood illnesses such as diphtheria and scarlet fever seemed to touch so many lives in the 1920s and 1930s.

GETTING WED

'I remember waiting at the gate, dressed in a white dress with a broderie anglaise pinafore, for my sister to return from church where she had just been married. It was all very exciting. There was a meal ready in the parlour – there was a cake but the meal itself was rather ordinary, what they called in those days a "knife and fork tea" – ham, pork pie, lettuce and tomato with celery in a tall glass, followed by jelly and custard. Afterwards we had a glass of port wine with the cake, and home-made potato wine for the grown ups, which looked like whisky, and home-made herb beer for the young ones. Weddings were much simpler affairs in the old days.'

'After weddings at Dodleston, a shotgun was fired to show that it was not a "shotgun wedding". The last time this was done was for Dave Darlington and Freda Williams.'

'A practice which used to take place at Great Sutton right up to the 1950s was the mock imprisonment of the bridal party inside the churchyard. The local children would tie up the lychgate and refuse to let anyone leave until they had paid their dues. The couple and their guests would throw coins to their would-be gaolers, and then be allowed to pass.'

'I met my husband in 1949 and was married in 1953 when the choice of clothes was still limited. I did eventually find a wedding dress in a little shop in Chester. Weddings weren't such grand affairs. We had caterers in for the reception, which took place in the village hall, but the meal at the reception was normally in the form of a high tea. Our honeymoon was in Cornwall and it took us two days to get there by car.

Outside The Eagle and Child at Nether Alderley, just before the wedding reception. Weddings were often simpler affairs than they are today, particularly in country districts.

Life was gradually getting back to normal, but furniture was hard to find. The only furniture in plentiful supply was the mass-produced "utility" furniture, and all you could say about that was that it was functional!'

THE VILLAGE MIDWIFE

'There was of course no Health Service in the earlier part of the century. "Old Nurse Baker" who was 16 stones if she was a pound was the vehicle for all births, deaths, illnesses, accidents etc. And talking of vehicles, she rode a bicycle with coat tails a-flapping and the bike appeared to groan and wilt under her massive frame. She always wore a stiff white collar, pale blue dress and navy coat. Every child in Marton was brought into the world by her, by candlelight, often in very cramped conditions with five or six other bairns around to get under her feet. Nevertheless she is remembered for her cheerful nature and her welcoming of any new baby into the world... they were all "beautiful". She acted on her journeys as the village crier... calling out as she left one confinement for another, "It's a beautiful boy (or girl). Mother and baby doing well."'

'Nurse Bunting was a familiar figure, cycling the streets of our neighbourhood of Wallasey on her heavy "sit up and beg" bike. In her navy uniform with her black bag tied firmly on the back she was the very model of the local midwife. The children would eye the black bag curiously as it was rumoured that she brought the babies in it!

We all knew that when she hove into view, a baby brother or sister was due soon. My poor 20 year old mother, giving birth to her first child, husband away at war, mother sick in hospital, with the next door neighbour to help with the birth, begged Nurse Bunting, "Cut me open and get it out – I can't stand the pain." A horrified Nurse Bunting replied, "Where did you get that idea from, mother? This baby will come out the same way it went in!"'

CHRISTENING AND CHURCHING

'Everyone in our young days believed in having their babies christened at around three weeks or a month old. The mothers were churched after having a baby to thank God for a safe delivery. We were brought up to do this but I never seem to hear of it these days.'

HOME CURES

'Not many people went into hospital unless it was serious, we doctored ourselves. Most mothers in those days had remedies for colds and bad chests. For the children there was goose grease, which came from the goose that the family had at Christmas. There was camphorated oil, and if we had a cold my mother used to warm it and rub it on our chests. She also had a treatment for earache – she would warm a small onion and we held it to our ear. If we had a septic finger she would make a bread poultice; this was made by pouring boiling water over a piece of bread, draining off the water and placing the bread over the sore spot. All these remedies seemed to work for us. If we had the doctor, which was very rare, he would send a bill and our mother would pay threepence or sixpence a week. We could not afford any more. We had our babies at home and neighbours would help the families. We all helped each other.'

'Kaolin poultices were used for swollen and inflamed conditions like boils, with a green "Jaconet" overdressing to keep the heat in. Warmed onion centres in flannel covered aching ears.

Vaseline was used for all sorts of things from fingertips to baby's bottom. There were no tubular bandages, just straight bandages, not easy to use over legs and knees when a plaster wasn't big enough.

Sufferers from whooping cough and other chest problems were taken for a walk around the gas works, to inhale the coal-tar type fumes, which were thought to be beneficial. Inhalers as we know them today weren't invented, so steam tents were home-made – rigged from chains, a sheet and a boiling kettle for those nursed at home with pneumonia.

Because of widespread tuberculosis spitting in the streets was made an offence, punishable by fine.'

'A dampened blue bag gives pain relief when stung by a wasp.'

'If one had a hawthorn in the finger it was always said to put it in a small basin of hot water with a teaspoonful of Epsom salts added. This was a sure thing to draw the thorn out.'

'My mother would put a large onion into a dying fire for a few moments, and then take it out and put it in an old woollen sock. We would hold it to an aching ear and the warmth would be a great comfort.'

'My mother had two mixtures for coughs and colds. One called for two pennyworth of liquid liquorice and the same amounts of chlorodyne and horehound. These were put in a medicine bottle and topped up with cold water. The second was raspberry vinegar, made with one pound of raspberries to a quart of vinegar. Mix them and stand for 48 hours. Strain and to every pint of juice add a pound of sugar. Bring to the boil for one minute, and bottle when cold.'

'Daisy sprained her ankle so Aunt Sarah, hearing about it, walked all the way from Macclesfield to help. She brought a bundle of comfrey from her garden, wrapped in newspaper. On arrival, she requested a large saucepan and boiled the comfrey. Later she bathed the injury with the liquid and wrapped the stalks around the ankle. If one had a bad back the same procedure was followed. It was supposed to be a certain cure.'

'If you had a sore throat, when you took your stocking off as you went to bed, it would be wrapped round your throat, the foot being placed on your throat; more often than not, your throat would be better the following morning. My mother always kept a bran bag – this would be heated in the oven of the old fashioned grate and used for earache. Brown paper soaked in vinegar and then sprinkled with pepper was used on your cheek to ease toothache – it stung that much you couldn't tell you had toothache. Brimstone and black treacle were mixed together and taken to cure heat spots. Herbs were used too and I remember taking horehound tea for loss of appetite and rue tea for upset stomachs.'

'To treat coughs, we went to the chemist at Lymm to get either one or two pennyworth of aniseed, paregoric, laudanum and peppermint, which was mixed together with brown treacle and hot water. My mother swore by it for my brother, who was bronchial. Goose grease was used for sore throats.'

'Healthcare was simple – a visiting doctor recommended a slice off the pig to keep all the children healthy!'

THE LOCAL DOCTOR

'When at the age of eight I had to have my tonsils removed, the operation was performed at home on a deal table, and the anaesthetic was given by placing a pad over my face and telling me to count. Our local doctor performed the operation.'

'While living on Stanlow Island my sister Rose was taken ill. The island, once a peninsula, was cut off from the mainland by the building of the Manchester Ship Canal in 1887. However, a number of families still lived and farmed there.

The isolated location made it difficult to obtain medical help quickly, but Father set out in his boat along the Ship Canal to Ellesmere Port for this purpose. Night was falling fast, and it was also getting increasingly foggy during his journey.

On arrival at the doctor's, he was distraught when the gentleman refused to accompany him owing to the severity of the weather. Rose died of whooping cough the next day.

A physician more worthy of note was Doctor Madden, a much loved medical man. He treated patients in the Great Sutton area for many years it seems.

The doctor's whereabouts could be determined by spotting his chestnut horse, which would wait patiently outside, while his master made house calls. The animal did not need tying up, so well trained was he.'

A SINGLE-HANDED PRACTICE

'In 1956 my husband returned to Audlem to take over the Audlem practice from his father who was nearing retirement, and at that time the practice only supported one doctor.

The quite large house which included the surgery was made into two houses. We occupied the half which included the surgery and our front door was shared with the patients.

Bear in mind that at this time the doctor was either consulting or out on his rounds and other than that there was only me to answer the phone and the doorbell, at the same time as coping with our young family. The telephone was in the living room; no extensions or portables in those days – and I took all the calls. If a patient needed to speak to the doctor I had to bring my husband to the phone as he preferred not to hold a telephone consultation in front of a patient to whom he was attending. With no help in the house at that time I was often feeding the baby and answering the phone at one and the same time!

Our generation fell between two stools; no regular help in the house unlike our predecessors who had live-in help and chauffeur/gardener and unlike the present day medical practices with a full complement of ancillary staff.

To take the children out for a walk was not simple. If there was no one available to come in and listen for the telephone I would have to take advantage of my husband being in the surgery for a while and as long as he knew in which direction I was going he could soon get me back if an urgent call came in.

At that time most babies were born at home or in The Cliffe, the GP maternity unit at Wybunbury. Unfortunately the timing of a baby's arrival was not often convenient and my husband would have to leave his surgery, his meal or his bed when the call came. I would have no idea when to expect him back. My job, if there was a waiting room full of patients – no appointment system then controlling the numbers – was to explain that my husband had been called out and try to encourage those that could, to go home and return at the next surgery. As I had been trained as a nurse I was able to dress wounds and give simple advice to ease the situation. Meantime my small son was often to be found sitting talking to a patient's relative who was waiting in his car outside. I never worried about the children doing this, Audlem at that time was a small community and we all knew each other – we were not afraid for the children's safety as we might be today.

Until the mid 1960s my husband was on call night and day all the year round and we were dependent on his elderly father to stand in for him so that we could have some family time together. For our two weeks' holiday we had to employ a locum doctor and arrange for a housekeeper if he came unaccompanied. For an evening out to visit friends or to attend a social function we had to employ a baby sitter who was also competent to cope with the telephone calls and re-routing messages to my husband at wherever we were. Our first thought on our arrival at our destination was to make sure there was a telephone within hearing distance. Some planned outings had to be aborted at the eleventh hour if an urgent call came in. I was always thankful that I had been a nurse and understood the necessity to put work before pleasure. We were typical of other single-handed practices at that time.'

THE LOCAL SANATORIA

'I was born and brought up on a farm at Kingswood. Near to our farm were two sanatoria, one for patients from Liverpool and one for patients from Manchester. It was the latter which was to play a big part in our lives, being the nearer of the two.

In those days the only treatment for tuberculosis was rest and fresh air. The hospital was built in the form of a large country house on the edge of Delamere Forest. In the front was a sweeping lawn which came up to the forest. Just inside the forest were rest huts for the patients, which revolved so that a maximum amount of sunshine could be enjoyed.

As children we went often to the hospital to see film shows. We played badminton and tennis, went to keep fit classes with the nurses and, in fact, were invited to all the events there. Often on a Sunday evening we went to the lovely hospital chapel for evensong. The highlight of the year was Christmas Eve when we went up to the top floor of the building and stood on a balcony at the front overlooking the forest. At an appointed time Father Christmas emerged from one of the huts. He was waving a large torch and his progress was lit by a searchlight. It was so real to us as small children. Of course we realised as we grew older that it was the doctor dressed in a lovely Father Christmas outfit. He carried a sack which contained a present for each of the patients, and one for each of us kids.

The doctor and matron were husband and wife and ruled the staff with great dignity. The staff mostly lived on the premises. There was a large nurses' home which housed, as well as the nurses, some of the maids. The doctor had a maid, dressed in gingham in the mornings and black dress with white cap and apron in the afternoons. The matron too had her own maid, dressed similarly but with brown and cream in the afternoon.

Most of the indoor activities took place in the beautiful large dining hall which was oak panelled, and had a lovely large fireplace with log fires in the winter.

We often saw the patients, those who were well enough, walking in the lanes and sometimes they came to the farm. We were not afraid of catching tuberculosis from them as they were strictly disciplined in their behaviour. No kissing allowed, and each day they were issued with pieces of muslin for handkerchiefs as there were no paper tissues then. These they called their "Mickey Rags" and woebetide any of the patients if they were caught throwing them away. They had to be collected each day and burned.

We saw some very poorly patients who were very thin and sometimes, of course, they didn't get better but the happy times we had there were certainly good to remember.'

'I spent several years nursing in a sanatorium in the early 1950s. After the Health Service got started and the new wonder drugs like streptomycin were being used there were few actual deaths from TB, but the treatment was prolonged, rarely less than a year and more than one member of a family could be affected. I can remember two pairs of married couples being patients. The hospital regime was strict, no cohabiting permitted and they would perhaps see each other no more than once a week but notes would be passed from ward to ward. A large number of the patients were young, in their teens or twenties.

Occasionally there would be entertainments for the patients from local drama and musical groups and always a film show once a week. An off-duty member of staff would be coerced into keeping the sexes apart, females sitting on one side of the hall, males on the other side. Friendships between male and female patients were positively discouraged but not totally eliminated.

Because patients were in hospital for so long one got to know them quite well. I remember one pretty woman admitted from a coastal resort in mid-Wales. Having no children, her husband, a carpenter, locked up the house and took a job with a construction firm in Chester so that he could be near to visit his wife regularly. Once she had recovered and was due to be discharged, I asked her what they would do. She replied that they would go back to Wales and as for employment for her husband, well there was plenty of repair work to be done in summer and in winter there was "always the odd coffin"!

The hospital was fairly isolated but on a day off one could book a seat in the mini bus down to Frodsham and have a free rail or bus pass to Chester or Warrington, and on the payment of one shilling and threepence you could go as far as Liverpool. My first month's salary was £6 which didn't seem much, but on a day off to Chester one could have a meal of chips, egg and peas with bread and butter and a pot of tea for two shillings and sevenpence.'

IN ISOLATION

'I remember my father being taken ill with diphtheria, which was rife in the 1930s. Soon after the doctor had been, an ambulance came and took him to the isolation hospital in Middlewich Street, Crewe. Shortly afterwards, that day, two men came along and lit some special candles in my parents' bedroom, and sealed all the windows and door with tape, and we were told to "keep out".

The very next day my sister was taken ill. She too was taken to the isolation hospital. The two men duly arrived with their candles and sealed the bedroom I shared with my sister, and the living room downstairs. Again we were told "keep out" and do not visit any friends or relatives. This left my mother in quite a predicament as we had to go through the living room to get from the front room to the kitchen, and also from the bedrooms to the rear of the house. This meant to prepare a meal, we had to go round the block from the front of the house to get to the kitchen at the back, and of course, return the same way. The house was virtually cut in half. My mother and I had to share the "spare" bedroom, which fortunately was a double room. This went on for two or three days.

We were not able to visit my father or sister during the weeks they were in hospital, but every day we went down to the municipal buildings in Earle Street, where fastened on the wrought iron gates at the front entrance there was a daily progress report on all patients who had diphtheria or scarlet fever. I can't quite remember whether the actual names of the patients were shown or whether they all had a number.

Fortunately neither my mother nor myself contracted diphtheria, but about six months later, I developed scarlet fever and was duly rushed to the isolation hospital where I stayed for 15 weeks. During all this time, I was never allowed to see any of my family, as visitors were forbidden. My parents were allowed to come to the lodge gate house and bring toys or sweets etc. After they had gone the nurse would bring round the gifts to show you what "Mummy had brought". They would then be taken away again and shared between all the other children. The only exception was at Easter. I had seven Easter eggs sent in by various members of my family, and as I had been in longer than anyone else I was allowed to choose one which I could keep for myself. I learned afterwards that after I had been in several weeks, when my parents came to bring "presents", the nurse would take me for a walk in the grounds so they could see me, but I was never told they were there.'

THE MEN IN WHITE COATS

'My very first memory is of sitting on my mother's knee at the Chester Infirmary waiting to have my tonsils out. I must have fallen asleep because the next thing I knew was waking up and a lot of white-coated men were strapping me to a table. They had bands on their heads with mirrors on, and I was terrified. I was only two years old.

My father at that time worked in the old Co-op grocery shop in Foregate Street. Father and the staff wore white coats and if Mother called to see him she couldn't get me past the door without me screaming my head off!'

THE LAST JOURNEY

'The mourners at a funeral at Great Sutton would walk solemnly from the deceased person's house to St John's church. Wreaths would be laid out in the front garden of the house. I have seen this done a number of times, both in Great Sutton and Ellesmere Port, but former residents of Birkenhead, and other parts of the Wirral, have never experienced it until moving locally.'

'My brother, who was older than me, told of a funeral he saw in the village of Buerton. The hearse was drawn by two black horses wearing waving black plumes on their heads. There were also plumes on the hearse and, if you happened to be a bearer, which my brother was sometimes, you were given black kid gloves to wear.'

'You always knew when anyone was very ill at Witton because outside the house would be spread thick bark over the cobbles to dull the noise of the horses and carts that passed by. When my little schoolfriend died the horses had white ribbons instead of black and we children walked behind carrying a bunch of what we called "posies".'

'Men attended funerals more frequently than did the women. The "wake" was at home afterwards with tea, cold ham, currant bread and a tot of whisky for the men as they left.'

CHILDHOOD &
SCHOOLDAYS

CHILDHOOD DAYS

The freedom to wander the lanes and countryside without fear and a delight in simple things mark our childhood days before the Second World War. Whether we were born into well to do or poor families, we share memories of childhood pleasures perhaps no longer to be found.

A REAL CHESHIRE CAT

'I have always considered myself to be a real "Cheshire Cat". I was born in 1922 in a black and white timbered house in Bowdon, opposite the parish church and we lived by the chiming of the church clock, which chimed on the hour and every quarter hour throughout the year. We also lived by all the activities which went on at the church.

My nursery was on the first floor of the house and faced both the church and the square in front of it, so that as a child I could watch all the events which went on at the church, such as weddings, christenings and funerals as well as the special services for Armistice Day, the Scout and Guide parades, Confirmation, etc.

When I was first born, my mother was in bed for three weeks after the birth as was the custom and she had a fully trained maternity nurse for eight weeks. The household employed a living-in cook and a house parlourmaid. The latter cleaned and dusted and polished the silver and brass in the mornings in a plain uniform and at lunchtime changed into a black dress, frilly white cap and apron and was on duty to answer the door to visitors and serve the afternoon tea.

After the maternity nurse left a nanny (known as Nanny Atkins) was employed for me and she made friends with the nanny in the house opposite and her baby charge and we all went out together for walks. This started a life-long friendship with the girl opposite, who had been born one month before me.

I had two elder sisters, but their lives were very different from mine as they were much older. They were at day school and later at boarding school. My mother and father lived on the fringe of Bowdon Society although we were of very modest means compared with people in the big houses with whom we mixed. We were, however, always invited to all the big parties (and later dances) in the neighbourhood, although we could not always afford to return all the hospitality in a like manner.

As I grew older Nanny Atkins left and I was looked after by the house parlourmaid, who was called Annie, and she took me out most afternoons for a walk before tea. I would then slip into the kitchen, where Cook had just finished baking cakes, and hope to scrape the bowls. I would watch Annie get the tea for the drawing room and Cook on some days would give me a new crust of bread spread with butter, syrup or black treacle. Then I would play until bedtime, when Annie bathed me and put me to bed. She told me marvellous stories in the bath, a lot about service to the Duke of Devonshire at Bakewell where her family lived and had worked at Chatsworth all their lives. My father would then come and tell me a story in bed, but he never finished it and as he kissed me goodnight used to say "until our next". My mother then finally tucked me up. I never fell asleep immediately but listened to the church clock and often crept out and looked over the bannisters to see and hear what the grown-ups were saying and doing. If anyone had died during the day the bell-ringers would be called in to ring the muffled bell and this was quite eerie, although I got used to it.

As I grew up I had a room to myself at the top of the house with a window facing the church clock and another facing the square. I would often get out of bed and watch all the night revels in the square. There were two public houses on the other side and a pavilion where dances were held, so there was a great deal of coming and going. There were carriages and cars constantly moving about and in the middle of the square there was a drinking fountain, where the horses could be given a drink. There was also a bus service from Lymm and Warrington to Altrincham which came up the hill and across the square from 6 am until midnight. If I crept into the spare bedroom I could look across the Cheshire plain and see the lights of the traffic twinkling on the main Chester Road (now the M56) and on a clear day I could see as far as Ellesmere Port.

My friend across the way and I did a lot of things together during the holidays and after school as we grew older. Her family had a tennis court, so we played tennis. We rode our bicycles around her large garden (mine was too small) and up the side road. We later had horse riding lessons. Her family had a small car with a dicky seat and the chauffeur was directed to take us to and from the stables. My friend had a governess for a long time before she was sent to boarding school. I went to a local nursery school before being sent to boarding school at the age of twelve.

As we grew older we were allowed to go along to the local cinema and at first saw a lot of the silent films. Harold Lloyd and Charlie Chaplin films were very popular and later the Deanna Durbin and Judy Garland ones.

My mother gave afternoon tea parties and also had bridge parties

Looking for a bargain at Ince fete in 1923, held in the Park. Note the bloomers peeking from beneath at least one dress!

and she belonged to a local croquet club, where they also played bridge.

On Sunday mornings we all went to church, while Cook prepared the Sunday lunch. My father became a sidesman at the church, so it was important that the family was always there on the particular Sunday when he took the collection. After lunch, my father would take me and my sisters (if they were at home) for a long country walk until teatime.

The road where I lived was not a "through" road and it had white gates about halfway up it, as the road led directly to the gates of Dunham Massey Hall owned by the Earl of Stamford and Warrington. On Sundays the Earl would drive in his carriage (and later in his car) to church, where he had a private chapel. Next to the white gates was a cottage owned by the Earl and the tenant had to come out before church time and open them to let the Earl through and then close them when he returned from church.

Once a year the local Agricultural Show was held on a large piece of land owned by the Earl and normally used for cricket and football. On this day I would get up at 6 am to watch all the traffic going to the show, especially the animals, most of which were walked along my road – the gates were left open all day. There were cows, bulls, shire horses, riding ponies, goats and sheep. Many of the horses were decked out with ribbons blowing from harnesses polished to perfection. In the evening the whole parade started again going the other way, going home. I was always taken to the show and we always brought a whole Cheshire cheese home, which sat in one of our pantries and lasted well into the year.

We were taken to Manchester to buy our clothes at a large store and this would take a whole day. We usually went to Manchester by tram or bus and later by car. My mother's first car was a Jowett called "Joey" and later we had an Austin called "Gussey". I remember being taken to dancing lessons in the Jowett, which had a dicky and I always sat in the dicky to spread my frilly ballet dress out so it didn't get crushed.

Every long summer holiday, we went for a month to North Wales. We stayed in a farmhouse by the sea and at first travelled by train, which had basket woven seats. The farmer met the train in his pony and trap. Later we went by car. The farm beds were awful and had straw mattresses and we got bitten by creepy-crawlies. The "loo" was down the garden and was a three-holer with a bucket under-neath. The food was very good, but we had an awful lot of rabbit.'

THE BARN

'The barn at Mere was the centre of my young world. The great brick-pillared barn with its five bays and pierced brickwork and Gothic arched gable ends stood as the main building on the Squire's estate. The courtyard stables were first on the lane after the Hall Farm. The groom's house formed one corner and the gardener's house the other and the iron-railinged kennels stood next to them. The walled kitchen garden, so secret, where the vegetables and fruit for the hall were grown lay behind Jenny the donkey's stable and the small barn. Further up the lane was the barn. We lived in the old joiner's cottage at the saw-pit. The whole was surrounded by the park – woods and coverts for shooting and hunting and large tracts of grasslands dotted with small copses. By 1939 this grass had been ploughed up for the war effort, never to be reinstated.

As we ate our breakfast with the back door wide open, the linger-ing sharp smell from the Valor oil stove, where the bacon and eggs had just been cooked, warmed the kitchen. I could see past the shade of the huge beech trees to the field. Beyond was the barn where the morning light picked out the faded yellows of the stored wheat.

Later in the day I played in the barn. It was an "adventure play-ground" and, by today's standards, a death-trap to children. But back in the 1930s children took their chances and learnt self-reliance without the meddlesome and distant grown ups interfering. From breakfast to bedtime except for sorties home for meals, I was alone and unguarded. I had climbed the prickly bales of straw banded with bale-wire and had reached the dark world of the rafters. Here I could see where the white barn owls nested. The barn owls who sat in a row with their fluffy brood on the telegraph wires and watched us at night, swivel-necked and round-eyed, as we drove up the dark lane in the Morris Cowley. Here I could see the bats hanging like shrivelled leaves amid the cobwebs. I climbed to the unbaled hay and lay and slid on the bouncy, shiny bed, and jumped and flopped and rolled. I clung to my teddy bear − "Big Teddy" as opposed to "Little Teddy" who stayed at home, in the candle-lit bedroom and was built in a cuddly shape. Big Teddy had arms and legs, and feet mended with old brown dressing-gown material. He had shanked boot-buttons to replace his glass eyes which gave him a blank and staring appearance. His fur was worn away to a fawn cloth, except under his arms and chin. He wore a short blue knitted jumper and was always a good and uncomplaining companion.

I stood up and went trampolining towards the edge of the stack. The sun was dazzling on the ground far below. The long ladder was propped against the stack. I looked at it and thought perhaps Big Teddy would be a hindrance in my descent. I would require both hands to climb down the bouncing ladder to the stackyard. I stood on the edge of the slipping hay, just under the dark roof and threw Big Teddy to the ground with such force that I too slid over the side of the stack and tumbled down, down, down and lay in silent blackness on the ground.

I am dead, I thought − would they find me? Would they eat my tea? Would they be cross? After a few moments I lifted my head. The sun blinded me. The mud stuck to my face − I was not dead, just face down in soft black mud.

Later the threshing machine would come to the barn. This indeed was an event. The steam engine, black with polished steel and brass plaques, slow and powerful as an elephant, would trundle noisily down the cobbled lane pulling the thresher. This amazing box of wood with bits and levers and pulleys all over its faded red paint was carefully positioned against the barn. Men in black trousers and leather gaiters, collarless wincyette shirts and greasy waistcoats, pottered and busied themselves around the vast mechanism. Others in khaki slops and panama hats climbed up the stack holding their pikels. The long pulleys were harnessed to the fly-wheel of the steam engine, and work began. Sheaves were thrown with pikels into the top of the pulsating, roaring, shaking thresher − dust flew every-where. At one end bags were hung on steel hooks and filled with a run of yellow grain, and at the other end bales of golden straw heaved jerkily out on to steel runners and were lifted on to the backs of men and stacked in the barn. Out of another orifice came the chaff – dusty, light, pale, into bigger sacks. This wondrous operation went on for several days. When the stack was low we went in with sticks to kill the rats, now besieged in the last of the straw. We hit them with the force and effect of batsmen hitting boundaries at the wicket, some fell down our backs into our shirts, some ran with lads in hot pursuit, and some tried to escape up the newly stacked bales.

There were tales of terrible accidents with the threshing machine – the time Jack fell into the baler and came out baled – and dead. The time Harry had his flat cap knocked from his bald head by the drive belt and was scalped so you could see the bone of his skull. And the time Ted fell from the stack with a bale crushing his leg, which became infected and had to be cut off.

My father considered there were only two skills a girl should acquire for a successful life – she should learn to shoot and ride. School was to be avoided for as long as possible. Thus I did not start my hated schooldays until I was six and had learnt to handle a gun by the time I was eight and I was learning to ride. I was now fit for life.

I lived alone with my parents, an only child, with no one to play with. When encouraged to have a school friend for tea I did my best to lose them in the woods or terrify them with stories of wolves or kidnappers. I lived alone, but utterly content and always outside in the woods and fields.

In the house we had oil lamps and a petrol lamp in the sitting room. This perched precariously on a brass folding table. How it was never knocked over thus bringing the cottage to a state of inferno amazed my town-living Granny. In winter the fire roared up the chimney and the water gurgled and boiled in the pipes, but the rest of the cottage was icy. I crawled into bed and had to breathe hot air under the bedclothes in a feeble attempt to warm the chilled sheets. On frosty mornings exquisite patterns of ice covered the bedroom windows, Jack Frost had drawn delicate ferns and stars to delight me.

In summer bedtime was still six o'clock, and I remember lying hot and wide awake under a single sheet trying to go to sleep while grown up voices, laughing and talking drifted through the open window.

I built dens, one underground in the wood. I dug a deep hole about five feet across, roofed it with logs, then twigs and finally bracken and covered the whole with soil so that only the entrance, an 18 inch hole with steps down and the chimney pot could be seen. Of course there had to be a fireplace. The smell of damp earth and eye-watering wood smoke filled the dug-out. One day whilst roasting potatoes on the grid I was enveloped in smoke – white acrid billowing clouds of it. Driven out for air I crawled up the steps to find Frank, his air-gun under his arm, laughing his socks off. He had put a slate on my chimney pot.

There were other dens. These were made of branches put against a tree trunk, tent-like, and as the dug-out, were covered with smaller branches and then bracken. There was no fire installed here! All these dens were waterproof – even the igloo I built from blocks of snow in the early 1940s. And that was the year we were snowed up for three weeks – and that is why today I always keep a store cupboard and candles, just in case.

The woods and fields and the barn were my playground and escape. I remember hiding at the top of a yew tree for hours, until my hands and feet hurt with holding on while my parents called me, because the doctor had come to give me an injection. I waited until I saw him drive away down the lane, his Homburg hat straight on his head, in his little black car. Then I climbed down.

As early as my fifth year I roamed the fields and woods alone. I was warned about the "bottomless" marl pits that horses and carts had sunk in without trace. I was instructed carefully about not eating the "wrong" berries – "Two children had died instantly after eating woody nightshade berries." I was taught by my father to walk like a Red Indian, one foot in front of the other, to make the least track-marks. I was taught how to kill a rabbit with a rabbit-punch and how to wring a bird's neck. I was taught how to stand motionless to watch the rabbits and foxes and how to keep on the lee side of animals so that they could not scent me. I learnt how to make a fire, but I never learnt to ride a bike safely – a cobbled lane and a mud backyard were difficult terrain for learning such advanced skills.'

GROWING UP ON THE FARM

'Although my twin sister and I spent most of our school holidays on a mixed, arable farm on the Cheshire/North Staffordshire border between 1934 and 1945, the years before the Second World War were the best, as after the war everything changed, even in the country-side, and not always for the better.

Poverty was the norm for most farmers during the 1930s, but the shortage of money was offset by the fellowship between a farmer and his neighbours. This was most evident at haymaking (little silage then!) and corn harvesting, when each would help the other.

Barrels of beer and ginger beer appeared in the larder, ready to quench the thirst of the harvesters (and ours!). Cakes and pies were baked for the "baggins" – carrying the "baggin" to the men in the fields twice a day became our job. At dinnertime everyone returned to the farmhouse where we sat at the long kitchen table and tucked into the food cooked and served by the women, amid much laughter and teasing!

Getting ready to join the May Day procession at Bramhall in 1943.

Then there were the animals – all magic beasts to two "townies", especially the farm horses. These huge, patient beasts allowed us to sit on their broad backs while holding on to the metal "ames" on their collars for dear life. Imagining we were knights on chargers we raced along the sandy lane to whichever field they were working. Riding homewards on top of a sweet-smelling load of hay, gazing up at a star-laden sky was utter bliss!

Calves and "cade" lambs we helped to feed – the latter became bossy and butted us as they grew bigger; hens with their chicks, ducks with ducklings, all roamed free around the farm during the day. As dusk fell we helped to round them up and put them into pens for the night.

At feed times the sight of Aunty (the farmer's wife) walking across the field followed by a flock of clucking hens eager to get their beaks into the bucket of corn she carried, never failed to amuse us. When collecting the newly-laid eggs we took great care not to crack any or disturb any sitting hen from her nest. On one occasion loud shouts and bangs were heard from one henpen, and when one of the men went to investigate he found my sister, a large stick in her hand, chasing a rat around the pen!

On rare occasions the owners of the farm would visit – usually on horseback (the lady riding sidesaddle, of course) and, much to our amazement, Aunty and Uncle would bob and bow as they greeted the Earl and Countess.

97

September 1939 saw the start of the war. Our parents decided we should stay in the countryside away from Manchester, and so the autumn term saw us attending the village school. Our bikes were brought to the farm, as they were to be our means of getting to school, three miles away. Aunty packed our lunches into the saddle-bags and off we raced downhill to the village. Uphill we pushed our bikes homeward in good or bad weather!

One night we were roused from our beds to watch the Luftwaffe bombing Coventry – a huge firework display to us, but not for the grown ups as they could visualise the devastation in the city.

After Christmas things appeared quieter and, much to our regret, we returned home to suburbia, where the only animals were dogs and cats – no substitutes for horses and cows, and we swapped the green fields and leafy lanes for well-groomed gardens and tarmacked roads.'

IN THE OLD WEAVER'S COTTAGE

'As a child I lived in an old weaver's cottage in Dean Row. The cottage was quite large inside with a living room and at the back of this, looking out on to the garden, was a good-sized room with windows on three sides. This was the weaving room. We used it as the utility room.

Next door to us lived an old lady named Miss Williamson. In her weaving room she had a spinning wheel and I used to watch her spinning the cotton. Remembering the stories my mother told me about Sleeping Beauty, I used to watch in awe, never daring to get too close in case I pricked my finger and went to sleep for 100 years.

Life was very different in those days and lots of things happened that would seem strange today. For instance, there would be a great commotion today if a man appeared in the street with a bear. But in Dean Row when I was a child a foreign-looking man used to appear every so often with a big, brown, mangy-looking bear on a chain. He played a small concertina while the bear danced around on his hind legs. The bear then held out a small mug for pennies.

All the children used to look forward to the rag and bone man coming, with his donkey and cart. My mother said she could never find any of her dusters because I had given them to the man in exchange for goldfish, balloons, paper windmills or donkey stones. In case you don't know what a donkey stone was, it was a piece of rock-like material in brown, cream, white and blue which was used on window sills and doorsteps after you had scrubbed them to make them look "posh".'

GROWING UP IN CHESTER

'My memories of Chester begin in 1935 with the Silver Jubilee of George V and Queen Mary. At that time living in Newton, we were outside Chester and known as Hoole and Newton by Chester with our own council and mayor. On this occasion all the children were being presented with a book of pictures of the royal family and each child had to go and receive it from the Mayoress. When my turn came I took the book and said (not knowing any better at my age), "Thank you Your Majesty," to great gales of laughter. I am sure I must have made the Mayoress's day, after all it's not every day she was addressed as Her Majesty.

I also remember the gas lights, especially on Hoole Bridge, where we took great delight pulling the chains and putting on the lights. I think we were a great help to the gas lighter, although I don't think he appreciated our efforts, as he often swore at us.

Another great excitement was the illuminations when Grosvenor Park, The Groves and river were all lit up. The park especially looked like fairyland to us, with all the trees lit up in different colours, also the fountains. If we had been very good what a treat to be taken out on a Sunday night when it was beginning to get dark to see the lights.

Before the war, on August Bank Holidays which were at the proper time at the beginning of August, we had the grand carnival through the streets of Chester and ending up on the Roodee. They seemed better than any Mardi Gras. They did try to resurrect them but it wasn't the same.

I remember all the exitement of the romance of Prince Edward and Mrs Simpson and all the kids sang "Who's this coming down the street, Mrs Simpson's sweaty feet, She's been married twice before, And now she's knocking on Edward's door." And who can remember another ditty at that time, "Will you come to Abyssinia will you come? Don't forget your bullets and your gun, Mussolini will be there shooting peanuts in air, Will you come to Abyssinia will you come?"

The lovely shire horses belonging to the Great Western and London Midland and Northern railways pulled the covered waggons for deliveries, and we had great fun pretending we were cowboys and indians in these waggons. We knew all the horses and visited them often in the stables off Hoole Bridge. The horse manure was there for the taking and anyone could have lovely roses, in fact we often pushed each other off the high wall into the manure, which was warm and soft to land in, although we were usually in for it when we went home smelling beautiful.

There was the lady who came round in her little pony trap with the big churn of milk and ladled it out into your jugs. The lady in the house at the back made the most gorgeous ice cream in her outhouse; no worries then about health and safety.

In those days in Chester everyone seemed to know each other. At least, everyone seemed to know my Mum and Dad so we got in loads of trouble because they always told your Mum and Dad on you every time you were doing anything you shouldn't. When it got to the courting stage the parents wanted to know all the particulars of the latest boy and they were able to give you chapter and verse on the history of that family and they even knew the grandparents, so God help you if they weren't considered suitable.'

THE SISTERS

'My acquaintance with these two sisters was very short. Though they delivered milk to my parents' home for years it was not until the summer of my eighth year that I really noticed them. For the four weeks of that summer break from school, I got up at 6.30 with Dad, and as he left for work in one direction I went in the opposite direction to make a mile long walk to the outskirts of the town. At that time in the morning everywhere was quiet and I used to feel I was having an adventure.

At the end of a lane, I would meet the sisters. They were dressed identically, in riding jodhpurs, tweed jackets and trilby hats. Both had round, fat faces and figures to match and were in a horse-drawn milk float. One sat in the driving seat holding a whip, which I never saw her use. She gave me a smile but never spoke a word. The other one stood on the back step of the float and greeted me with a cheery, "Hallo, love." She would pick me up and practically wedge me between the two milk churns they carried. When I look back it seems every morning in that summer was fine; perhaps it wasn't, but I recall the utter bliss of riding in the warm, still morning air, with the sound of milk swishing around in the churns and the slow clip-clop of the horse, as well as the movement of the well-sprung float that used to gently bounce up and down as the sister who took the milk to the doors, got on and off.

She used to measure the milk out in different sized cans; she seemed able to carry quite a lot in one hand. As I, the silent sister, horse and cart made a quiet progression down each street, she would dash from door to door emptying the milk cans. Some door-steps had a jug with a saucer or plate on top and in a second she would have the milk in the jug, cover replaced and on to the next. Some steps had an empty can which she exchanged for a full one: some had nothing on the step. At these she would thump the door with her fist, shout "Milk" and be ready with an upraised arm, so as soon as a hand came out holding a jug the milk was transferred. She took her cue on how to behave from each customer, some said "Good morning,", some just smiled, some made a laughing remark, some were silent. They all got back what they gave to her, plus their milk. When we reached the road where I lived, she would lift me off the float with one arm, the other would be laden with milk cans, and I was deposited at our doorstep, where my mother would be waiting, with the same laughing remark, "Here you are, two pints and one daughter."

If I ever knew their names or where they lived, I have long since forgotten, but I have never forgotten the pleasure of those early morning journeys I had with them.'

GROWING UP

'I look back on the past and think how innocent we all were. My mother had a baby when I was ten and I didn't know anything about it. My brother and I hadn't noticed our mother getting bigger and it wasn't talked about in front of the children.

I lived in a part of Cheshire where the straight road went over the border to Staffordshire. After church on a Sunday, the girls from the Cheshire church walked towards Staffordshire and the boys from the Staffordshire church walked towards Cheshire. We passed each other on the pavement – no speaking, just looking at each other. Our parents referred to this as the "Monkey Run".'

CHORES TO DO

'It was normal for the older children to look after the younger ones and each was allocated jobs as they grew old enough to work. My father was born in 1900 and these were his jobs. On Friday mornings he got up at five o'clock and cleaned out all the flues in the cooking range and chopped wood for lighting it for the week. Monday to Thursday he got up at six o'clock and walked down to Adlington Hall (a distance of nearly two miles), calling at the station on his way for the morning papers and on occasion for a basket of meat which was delivered from somewhere along the line. He would take that to the hall and on certain days he would come back with a basket of washing which was despatched by rail to the laundry. On Saturday mornings he had a change. He was sent to help the gardener at Wych Cottage. This was all before school when he would be about ten years old.

A family anecdote takes us even further back. It concerns the temporary disappearance of my grandfather at the age of four or five who was eventually found watching the navvies building the Macclesfield to Marple railway line, a line which opened in 1869!'

VISITS WITH GRANDPARENTS

Visiting grandparents took us back in time to touch the Victorian age, when we would stay for holidays or just 'pop in to see how the old folks are getting on.'

SEE HOW THE OLD FOLKS ARE GETTING ON

'My grandparents lived in an old stone cottage in Poynton, one in a row, and often after tea my mother, who was a widow, would say she would walk down and see how the old folks were getting on.

I loved to go with her, especially in the winter. I would put on my hat and coat and Mother would tie a scarf crossways over my front and round my waist and she would put on her coat and pull her hat well down over her bun of hair and off we would go. Not far, but as there were no street lamps and no cars, of course, I would look at the lights in the cottage windows as we passed, and I would say the name of the people who lived there. We knew everybody and I can remember them now. Edie Booth's red blind, Mary Ellen's blue blind, Mrs Daniel's yellow blind, and so on until we came to Grandma's house.

Going through the stone porch and lifting the latch there was always a welcome. "Come in and sit thee down," and the little buffet would be put right up by the side of the fire for me and Mother would sit on the old black settle against the wall, a roaring fire always (because ours was a coal-mining village), the glow of an oil lamp and that cosy smell of warmth and paraffin.

The lamp stood on one side of the table where Grandfather Wainwright would be reading or writing. He was a great one for practising his writing and wrote quite a good hand. Often he would copy out a few verses from the Bible or write out the Lord's Prayer – just for the joy of writing. He had had very little schooling having worked part-time in the pit from when he was seven years old. As a child he was taken by his father to see the last public hanging in Manchester. That was in 1867 when my grandfather was twelve years old. The two of them walked there and back from Pott Shrigley getting the odd lift on a passing cart and then walking on again. My grandfather would tell me of the crowds and the beggars, he dwelt very little on the hanging. How thankful and exhausted he was when they got back home and he saw his mother again.

My grandmother never learnt to read or write but was very skilled with her hands, being the village midwife. She was very proud of a framed card in her front cottage window certifying that she was a trained midwife. What tales she had to tell! The mother who was feckless and never did a "hand's-turn" in her house which was like a pig sty but she had all her babies without any trouble and they were all beautiful; or the time she had to walk to an outlying farm in a blizzard with the snow nearly up to her waist but knowing that some poor girl was needing her help.

My mother would be dozing after a busy day with her children and household chores. She'd heard all the stories before and she became sleepy in the cosy warmth by the fire. I was not sleepy though, I drew pictures in my mind of exciting times and people and I stored it all away. The time had come when Mother and I had to go home. We wrapped ourselves up warm and braved the winter weather and I skipped along holding Mother's hand and thinking of the big cup of hot, steaming cocoa I would have before going up to bed.'

THEY LIVED IN PORT SUNLIGHT

'Birkenhead was once in Cheshire and my grandparents lived in Port Sunlight. As a little girl during the war I used to look forward to visiting them – things were quite different there from the Staffordshire town I lived in. My grandfather had a long garden with the lawn nearest to the house bordered by espalier pear trees and a friendly looking green pottery rabbit in the very middle of the lawn. As a child it never occurred to me to question why it was green! In "digging for victory" Grandad had made use of every inch of the bottom of the garden and used to push me down to play in it with him, in his big wooden wheelbarrow. I liked to help him pull rhubarb, pick gooseberries and blackcurrants. I even liked pulling up carrots but I did *not* like watching him pick off nasty squidgy green caterpillars and despatching them quickly to their death.

As my grandparents' house was near the actual port of Port Sunlight our nostrils were frequently and horribly assaulted by the strong smell of palm oil being unloaded for use in Palmolive and Sunlight soap, manufactured by Lever Brothers nearby. My mother had worked in the Lux Washability bureau there and was responsible for giving a test certificate on all sorts of fabrics sent in to them, assessing after washing in Lux soap flakes, drying, ironing and measuring the percentage of shrinkage. Mother's sister also worked for Lever Brothers in the cosmetics laboratory. My biggest thrill was a trip to New Brighton, I think on a tram, with its tower and fairground and a nice sandy beach and there was the contrasting furrowed beach at Parkgate where I'm sure that I *did* remember the tide coming in (it doesn't any more, being all silted up). There was an open-air swimming pool there too but being frightened of the water I never asked to go inside. There was also an ice cream shop there but of course they didn't always have any because, "There was a war on you know"!

Granny was a good cook who made delicious apple pies and who extravagantly put evaporated milk in her lovely rice puddings, but she taught me even then to appreciate a good "scouse" on Monday washday.

I remember once being bundled into the car in a hurry and making a sudden dash up to Port Sunlight and being puzzled at the quietness in my mother and father. I subsequently learnt that the trip was in response to a call from my Grandad to say that my Uncle Tom was aboard the stricken *Thetis* submarine, sinking bow down in the middle of the Mersey. Uncle Tom always went on secret submarine trials, usually in Scotland which is perhaps where the *Thetis* was bound that day. Tugs had got lines around the stern and were pulling in opposite directions to keep the stern out of the water ready for an escape hatch to be cut.

Unfortunately decisions to cut open the valuable submarine were not made in time; one of the hawsers broke and the boat sank. All aboard were lost.

However, within half an hour of our arrival at my grandparents' house we had a wonderful phone call from the dockside from my Uncle Tom, who it seems had changed places with his best friend who had one more payment to make on his beloved motorbike and needed the "danger money" he would receive for the trials. The house was suddenly filled with an electric mix of feelings of utter relief at the good news and profound shock and sadness at the thought of all those poor souls lost not through war, but through a tragic accident on our very own doorstep. Uncle Tom was shocked to the core and I know that his wife died a thousand deaths in later years every time he went on submarine trials.

My grandparents are long gone, but every time I contemplate a bar of Palmolive soap I swear I can conjure up the terrible smell of palm oil and hear the ships hooting on the river Mersey.'

HOLIDAYS ON THE FARM

'Whenever I visit the lovely peaceful village of Eccleston it always brings back memories of happy holidays spent there before the war with my grandparents who lived in a house called Mill Hill just outside the village. My grandmother used to say, "Bring a friend, as two are easier than one to entertain," and it certainly made the holidays lots more fun.

If the weather was fine we were expected to play outside, so we would jump on our cycles and ride up to the village, pedalling a bit harder as we passed through a sandstone rock cutting and under a bridge known as "the tunnel", a bit frightening to us children, especially at dusk as it was very quiet with only the drip, drip of water off the rocks and the snapping of twigs in the woods above, probably just a fox on the prowl! But once in the village we would visit Mrs Gillam's small general shop stocked with everything from candles to cotton, biscuits to bootlaces and soap to sugar. However, it was the large sweet jars that held our attention and it took us ages to decide what to buy with our pennies; usually chocolate drops won the day.

We always enjoyed going down to Eccleston Ferry to be ferried across the river Dee for a penny. Horses and carts and other vehicles crossed on a flat-decked ferry operated by a chain system. Occasionally when accompanied by adults we would hire a rowing boat here and row further up the river and pull in by some woods for a picnic. Other times we just sat on the river bank waving to passing boaters or fed the swans.

Some days we spent on my grandfather's farm and while he was away at business we loved the forbidden pleasure of swinging on farm gates, sliding down haystacks, or trying to punt with a makeshift raft on a pond. Once with the help of some boys we built a "secret house" under a huge pile of wood, but when a farm worker fell through it and hurt his leg there was terrible trouble! However, all must have been forgiven for soon afterwards it was arranged for us to ride on the Eaton estate train which ran from Eaton Hall to Balderton and back. A rare treat indeed.

To commemorate the coronation of George VI we joined in the village celebrations, which included a service of thanksgiving and the planting of a tree at the church by my grandfather. Then every child was presented with a coronation medal followed by sports in Eaton Park and ending with a grand tea and group photograph showing us all waving our Union Jacks.'

GAMES AND TREATS

We made our own fun, games following the seasons and involving very little equipment or expenditure. Many of us had our playground in the street, when traffic was light and slow moving. Treats were, perhaps, few and far between, but how we enjoyed what we had, whether it was a ride on an elephant or a wonderful Jamboree.

THE STREET

'I lived in the town of Macclesfield in the 1920s and 1930s. In contrast to some villages, the street was the focal point in most children's lives there. Although the main roads were becoming busy with cars and buses and lorries, the residential streets running off them were very quiet indeed and the street was much preferred as a playground to a solitary backyard or garden.

My friend and I played endless games of bat and ball in the street outside our houses (later we called it tennis – it wasn't!). If you were lucky enough to be near a street that had a blank wall in it there were a variety of games to play on that, besides simple bat and ball. There were "exercises" for one. These consisted of a rigid system of throwing and catching in diminishing numbers, beginning with ten simple throw and catches, both hands, through throw and catch right and then left hand, nine times and eight times, right down in number but higher in difficulty until you needed just one throw, but you must turn completely round before catching to complete the exercise. If you failed at any time during the numbers you had to start again at the beginning!

The boys played a game with cigarette cards. One team would lean a number of cards against a wall. The other team, standing a required distance away, would flick their cards towards the standing ones. If they knocked them down they could claim them, if they didn't they were forfeit to the other side. Failing all else, these walls were useful for doing handstands at, a feat I could never accomplish. Then there were marbles, a year long game. The great thing here was to avoid the grids!

Some street games were seasonal. Suddenly one day it would be top and whip time. If you could find last year's top and whip, out it came. If not you just had to buy new. Soon children were all out chalking their wooden tops with interesting coloured patterns. When you were satisfied with your artistic effort you put the top in a nick between the pavement flags, wound the slender rubber thong round its neck, grasped the handle of your whip, pulled – and you were off, whipping for dear life as the top spun round and the coloured patterns whirled into vivid life! Then, after a few weeks, tops and whips were out and it was time for bowling our hoops. Girls had wooden hoops, graded in size from very small for five year olds to hoops five feet in diameter for the big girls. These needed really strong whacks to keep them bowling along. Usually you needed a strong stick, but a hand would do if it had to. The boys had iron hoops with iron hooks to guide them along and they made a fearful noise when a gang of boys came clattering by.

There was a game played mostly in the evening called "Rally-o". I was never allowed to play this so I don't know the rules, but it sounded jolly exciting. Lots of children were involved, there was a lot of running about and gathering at the gas-lamp post, and great cries of "Rally-o" could be heard until darkness fell.

Team games at the blank wall included a kind of dance where the children sang "The big ship sails on the Ally Ally Oop" at the same time weaving under each other's arms until they were stuck and then unravelling.

The boys had a much more dangerous game called "Crambo" where one boy bent with his head against the wall and seven others bent down behind to form a chain. The other side of eight boys would leap over the boys' backs, each to land on a chosen boy. If they all got on and stayed on they shouted "Crambo" and they had won!'

'It was safe to play out in the street at Glazebury, for there was hardly any traffic. We played hopscotch, and on early winter evenings in the dark we would play tricks on local people by tying door-knockers together, or by putting a paper parcel on the footpath. When a passer-by stopped to pick it up we would pull it away suddenly by the hidden length of string we held as we hid. Sometimes it was too foggy to be out. The fog in those days was greeny-yellow, sulphurous and choking.'

WE NEVER FELT DEPRIVED

'I was born in October 1941 in a block of flats in Birkenhead opposite the main gate to Cammell Laird shipyard. The conditions we grew up under would nowadays be described as "deprived" – but we never, ever felt deprived.

Our industrial surroundings provided a rich playground. The railway sidings 30 feet from our front door offered a tempting wall to climb and jump from. We would cock a snook at authority by picking up lumps of coal which had fallen from the shunting engines. (Kind-hearted firemen would throw the occasional lump to us for devilment.)

The same railway wall, black with soot, made a solid base for our hide-outs or shelters made from corrugated tin, wood, doors and all the other coveted debris gleaned from the various "bombies" or bombed out buildings.

The large paved area between the three blocks of flats provided a safe place to play ball games. The girls had a large expanse of brick wall, with no windows, to play "two balls" against, while the brick walls became goal posts or wickets according to the season. The paved floor was also ideal for hopscotch, skipping, whip and top, and marbles. The narrow roadway outside our front doors was used for skipping ropes. Often Mums would turn the ropes for us as they had a good "jangle" (chat).

The light summer evenings saw the gang games of hide and seek, "Alleo" or, noisily, kick the can.

On wet or winter evenings, we would congregate in a yard under the sheltering overhang of the upstairs balcony. Here we would play guessing games, sing songs or act out plays. The guessing games usually involved film stars and we were avid collectors of cards and pictures featuring the likes of Clark Gable, Deanna Durbin, not to mention Roy Rogers, Trigger and Flash Gordon.

Bonfire Night, May Queen Day, Duck Apple Night (Hallowe'en), these were landmarks in our childish calendar. Easter was marked with wearing our new sandals, the old heavy leather black lace-ups being joyfully abandoned. Our new snowy socks twinkled for all of three days. I shudder now to think what urchins we looked. Friday was bath night and washing our one pair of socks was my job. I had to darn the holes first!

On May Queen Day some of the children would dress up in old net curtains and other bright garments, plaster their faces with rouge and lipstick and go knocking on doors asking for "penny for the May Queen". In November, it was a "penny for the guy". I was envious of those who did this as it was strictly forbidden by my parents as being "begging".'

WE MADE OUR OWN FUN

'For entertainment at Lymm in the 1920s we made our own fun. In summer we played in Dane Bank and roly-polyed down the slope. In winter tobogganing was popular. At other times we played with hoops; girls had wooden ones with a wooden stick and boys had iron ones with an iron hook. There was no traffic on the roads so we could go where we wanted. We also had whips and tops and would

Family outings were even more fun if we had our own car, but such treats were rare when this photograph was taken in 1928.

stick a piece of coloured paper on top to see the pretty colours spinning round. Tops were more for boys, while it was skipping ropes for the girls. Another thing we did was to stand in front of shop windows playing I Spy with the articles in them. I don't think we made a nuisance of ourselves as the shopkeepers never complained.'

'I was born in Ellesmere Port in 1937 and my earliest memories of school, when I was five, are of making boats of bottle corks with used matchsticks for their sails. We sailed the boats in bowls of water and it was great fun.

At playtime, as we grew older, the girls became very good at skipping games, including French skipping using two alternate ropes, turning inwards. We always sang as we skipped and we also sang as we played ball games against the school walls. Sometimes we played with two balls but the most skilful girls could use three balls. The boys always played football or chasing games.'

'After the Hall was destroyed by fire, much of Carden Park became a playground to Clutton children. To climb the red rock was the highlight of many Saturday and Sunday playtimes. We carved our initials on the soft red rock and sat and talked on the heavy wooden seat fitted on the rock. Rolling down the slope towards the huge beech tree, where we climbed and swung on its branches, was wonderful and chestnuts from the tree nearby an added delight, and to run helter-skelter down Parker's Hill a great dare, often ending in disaster as the pace was too great for little legs. Another "dare" was the cave under the smaller hill which we called "ice hill" because of the deeper cave into which we dropped stones to hear how long they took to reach the bottom. We played in the larger cave, which had a corner in it, around which we never ventured – it was so dark and spooky. A super cave on the edge of the park was a perfect semi-circle with a seat in rock all round and we were always intrigued by the marks on the rock made by the tools used to form the cave – spears we thought! Further along the perimeter was a large cave, big enough to house a vehicle – we knew we should not be in that area but ventured in the spring to pick snowdrops. Woodlands we never entered, we must have been warned not to trespass there, and the lake was visited by only the most daring of trespassers, the mid-lake cottage with its rickety bridge was a great temptation.'

POCKET MONEY

'Pocket money was three pennies a week. I spent twopence to go to the cinema on a Saturday afternoon. The films were silent and always black and white. We could buy four ounces of sweets for a penny, while a comic cost a penny halfpenny. My favourite was Tiger Tim or Tom Mix.

My father would give me a penny to clean his boots. Men's boots seemed to be much shinier when I was a youngster.'

'My earliest memories of childhood in Grappenhall are of being able to go to one of two general shops in the village. Our pocket money of halfpenny and a penny went a long way. A penny lucky bag contained sherbet dabs, liquorice bars, aniseed balls and pepper-mints. Each autumn the shop nearest the school had baskets of apples and pears, with a notice which read "Help yourself". We all did, but not one of us took more than one.

When the Yo-Yo came from America it became a craze, but if any child could not afford to buy one, two large buttons were fastened together and worked very well. I still have mine.

Every Saturday afternoon in the summer, we walked to the cricket field, spending happy hours playing behind the pavilion. Wives, mothers and aunts prepared the teas for the players. For the princely sum of ninepence we could have two small sandwiches, half a meat pie, a scone, a piece of cake or a small iced cake, and a cup of tea.'

'In the summer Mum would take us down to the shore at Egremont and on a hot day the tar would bubble, especially down Church Street. We would pop the tar bubbles in the gutters and woe betide the child who managed to get tar on her clothes. For a treat we could have a penny lolly ice which, if not careful, would stick to your tongue or lips. A thoughtful shopkeeper would dip the lolly ice in water before giving it. We swam or paddled in the river Mersey with no ill effects and would wait for the Cunard liners to pass up or down river so that the wash caused large waves for us to jump into.

The rubber wheeled; ball bearing roller skates had to be saved up for and any pennies we obtained for doing jobs were taken to the shop and the shopkeeper marked it down on the club card and what a great day when they were paid for. Sometimes a gang of us would skate along the promenade from Egremont to New Brighton to the fairground. The penny machines were favourite and the ride where gravity would make us stick to the wall while the floor fell away.

I can remember Mum, who was a widow, emptying her purse out onto the table to see if she could afford to let my sister and I go to the Saturday afternoon pictures. We'd have threepence each for the pictures and a penny for sweets. We would buy a penny chew or sticky lice or a sherbet dab. If we saw Batman or Flash Gordon or Superman we would run home after the show with our coats buttoned under our chins and flying after us like a cape and we felt we were flying.

Our backyard was sometimes used to store the wood for the bonfire and my brothers would stand guard on top of the toilet to make sure the rival gangs didn't steal the wood. The lads used to throw ripraps and bangers and we would stick a potato on a stick to bake it in the fire.

Mum used to do domestic cleaning and wasn't always home for us when we came home from school so we had a key on a string around our neck. This didn't happen often. After the war some Americans used to send parcels of food and clothes and through a relative we were lucky to have these sent usually twice a year. I can still remember the smell as it was unpacked. There were beautiful dresses (they had daughters the same age as my sister and I), toys, comics, dolls and tinned food. Mum was on National Assistance with a widow's pension and if the pension went up, the Assistance went down. The Co-op used to give divvie (dividend) and I can still remember Mum's number – 69577, which had to be given in whenever we did any shopping there.

Kindly neighbours used to allow us in to watch their black and white televisions at five o'clock for Children's Television until we

111

could afford to rent one from the Rediffusion (all the houses were wired and a switch was fixed to the wall with a pointer; there was a,b,c,d,e,f, which included televison and radio stations including Luxembourg). We also had a radiogram when my brother started working and could play 78 rpm records; we would listen to The Goons, Tommy Steele, Bill Haley etc.'

'At Chester Zoo in the late 1940s the great treat for a lot of children was to have an elephant ride. He had an Indian keeper called Saboo, who carried a whip. You climbed wooden steps on to a small plat-form , either side of the elephant, four people to each side, and sat strapped in the seats. Adults could ride with you. When he started to walk, I remember, you swayed from side to side. Great fun.'

'Exciting excursions were made down the river Mersey and Manchester Ship Canal by paddle steamer to Eastham Lock. There my brother and I played ball games on the grassy banks and picked huge, juicy blackberries. Before the return journeys, a visit to the small wooden kiosk for lemonade and ice cream. A real fun day out.'

HAPPY MEMORIES

'Wallasey in the 1930s. Then with all the Wirral a part of Cheshire and, with New Brighton, Hoylake and West Kirby, holiday resorts for many from surrounding towns.

Summer in the 1930s was the possession of a "contract" giving one the right of entry to any of the three swimming pools for the sum of twopence a visit. Guinea Gap, indoors and, in summer, only used when the weather was bad; New Brighton baths, and, the favourite of local families, the Derby Baths at Harrison Drive, where some lucky families also had their private beach chalets. Outdoor pools were not heated, save by the sun and we considered we were very fortunate on the rare occasions that the water temperature reached the luxury of 65 degrees. In memory summers were always hot and sunny and happy days were spent at "the baths", no longer there for today's children.

New Brighton was a popular resort and day out for the people of Liverpool, with a big fairground and ballroom at the Tower, Punch and Judy, donkey rides and paddle boats; fishing from the pier and motor boat trips round the estuary and back. And the estuary was full of shipping; passenger liners and cargo ships from all over the world docked in Liverpool and Birkenhead, not to mention regular ferries to Ireland and the Isle of Man.

There are memories too of cycle rides through quiet country lanes to Leasowe, to the sandstone and heather covered common of

Thurstaston Hill or to Irby, with tea at a farm – two boiled eggs and bread and jam and the outside "netty" was a two-holer with a scrubbed wooden seat and squares of newspaper on a nail.'

THE JAMBOREE

'It is 64 years since the great Scout Jamboree (to mark the 25th anniversary of the movement) was held in Arrowe Park, Woodchurch, but when I find the right piece of "tape" and run it through my mental recorder, all the memories come flooding back. No, the first things I think of are not rain or mud, but sunshine and the sheer jumping-up-and-down excitement of all those wonderful sights and sounds and happenings. Well, I was only seven and with living in one of the Smithy Cottages opposite the Lodge by the green was right on the spot.

Preparations on the park began weeks before the event, but one which remains foremost in memory was the digging of large holes in various places. One place was on the edge of the wood where the bowling greens now lie, between the Lodge and Ivy Farm. This was *our* wood where we children played for hours and was thick with rhododendrons, brambles etc. We inspected this hole every evening after the men had gone home, wondering what it was for. It soon got too deep for me to jump down into it and one of the bigger boys had to lift me down – no mud around then. It was only when the hole was roofed over with planks of wood with holes at certain intervals that the truth dawned and we collapsed in giggles.

As the time drew nearer, our cottages were in demand to display the names of the main newpapers – at first my mother refused, but it was pointed out that one notice saying "Buy the Daily Tale" would bring in the equivalent of a week's wages. Then there was a demand to put a stall in the front garden, resting on the stone wall and again the same reaction. But in the end, it was go with the tide. We had a fruit stall and the neighbours had sweets and biscuits, I believe. The drama nearly turned into a crisis when the vendor's family arrived from Liverpool to spend that first Sunday "in the country" – wife, aunties, grannies and hordes of screaming children. Dad really had to put his foot down!

Newspaper reporters became part of the daily scene – early on one came to ask Mother where he could get breakfast as The Horse and Jockey was too busy with liquid refreshment. She agreed to feed him – with bacon and eggs, toast and home-made marmalade and tea. He paid her twice what she asked and sent along his colleagues. They used to return in the evenings and have supper at the round table in our little parlour, often staying quite late. Dad was kept busy going to the village shop to replenish supplies, especially as Mother

113

finally gave in to demand and did teas as well.

The entrance to the Jamboree where the hospital entrance now comes, had been widened and treated with cinders but was totally inadequate to withstand the heavy lorries loaded with equipment which poured through, and a few heavy showers resulted in a quagmire which could only get worse – and did. Mind you, some people even put this into a positive mode, as hefty Scouts stood by offering to carry young ladies through the worst patches, and finding plenty of takers. (I thought it would be more fun to walk through the mud, but wasn't allowed to do so.)

A tented city sprang up with shops and banks and various facilities to serve the camps. The Midland Bank had a tent and Harold and I opened an account with them, getting a Home Safe in which to save. (It was money saved through our Home Safes which bought us each a bicycle when I was eleven.)

Scouts continued to arrive, some in buses and some in lorries. There was one tragic accident when a young Scout hit his head on the railway bridge over Woodchurch Road and a closer watch was kept on open buses and loaded lorries. The foreign Scouts were young men, of course, not boys. The Hungarians had a large contingent with hats sporting large feathers and wearing romantically swirling cloaks. They regularly marched past our house and we rushed out to wave. There were groups of kilted Scots playing bagpipes and Arabs with their distinctive head dress. One of these called one day asking to leave his muddy boots while he went to town in his shoes. When he returned Mother had washed off the mud – he was so pleased he kissed her hand. More to the point he gave me stamps from his letters from home – Iraq, and I showed him my Woolworth's stamp album telling him it was for my Brownie collectors badge.

On the crown of the hill where the hospital now stands a large wood and hessian stadium had been built and the different nations put on displays and various entertainments. We did not go to these performances as they were too expensive, but people waiting their turn to go on could be seen waiting to one side. I remember being sorry for the Red Indians waiting to do their act, they were clad only in leggings and breech clouts on a day that was damp and chilly.

Crowds of people came to Arrowe from all corners of the earth, it seemed. I had never seen anything like it, Woodchurch was usually a quiet and sleepy place. A fleet of Corporation buses brought people out from town as well as Crosville which had been the sole agents until then. The tide of people was outwards until around four o'clock when the tide suddenly turned and the crowds hurried down for the buses before the queue built up. Before long the queue would stretch back half a mile towards Upton; we children used to kneel at the bedroom window watching the people long after we should have been asleep. Sometimes it was well after midnight before the last of them got away. Scouts would walk along the queue looking for young families or the very old and exhausted and gave them priority.

There was a daily Arrowe newspaper containing articles and photographs; one which delighted many people showed German and English Scouts with their arms round each other. It was still widely believed that the slaughter of the trenches had "bought us peace" and this photo was taken as confirmation of that view. But I noticed that Dad shook his head and seemed more sorrowful than glad.

I suppose the icing on the cake of the Jamboree was the visit of the Prince of Wales and everyone wanted to see him. Our next door neighbour, Mrs Sanders, who was a cousin of Mother's, suggested that Harold and I sit on top of her garden wall, a high one which separated her garden from that behind The Horse and Jockey and had a flat top. From there we could see across the green and would see the Prince's car enter the main Arrowe gates. Large crowds had gathered and lined the roads. In the garden below us was a group who had obviously had a liquid lunch and were trying to see over the high hedge. Chairs weren't enough so a trestle table was put in place and several females lifted on to it. Eventually the cry went up "Here he comes" as a number of large black motor cars swept across the green. A number of men scrambled on to the table which promptly gave way and deposited them all in a screaming heap in the border. Diverted by this, I just had time to catch a glimpse of a bowler hat in the back of one of the cars, a languid wave, and he was gone. That was no way for a Prince to arrive – where was the blue velvet and the coach and six? What a disappointment.

Despite all the excitement I had been missing my friend Betty and her sisters, and Bert, they had all caught measles right at the beginning and were in quarantine. The day after the Jamboree closed I was able to run back to Ivy Farm and meet them all again. What a lot we had to talk about. Right at the top of the wood was a huge mountain of white loaves, surplus to requirement, which had to be taken away in lorries. There was also a tea chest of old bread – and maggots. This was dragged into the hen run and overturned – the hens must have thought it was their birthday.

Beside our hole in the wood a column of smoke rose from the burning hessian and the wooden seating as the hole was rapidly filled in and the turf put back. Soon all was quiet and peaceful once more.

One permanent feature remained from the Jamboree – the statue of the Scout near Arrowe Hall. It stood beside the drive for another 25 years before vandalism caused it to be removed.

With the money which had been raised via teas etc Dad and Mum, Harold and I were able to go to Kent for two weeks in the September to visit friends. The first time we had been away on holiday. Kent in September was lovely and golden – but that, as they say, is another story.'

ON OUR WAY TO SCHOOL

We went to school on foot, or if we were lucky, by bicycle, and the journey there and back was memorable, whether it was for the danger we avoided or the sweets we bought on the way!

CALLING AT THE SWEET SHOP

'We used to call at the sweet shop in Hale on our way to school. There were rows of glass jars with glass stoppers, and a great variety of small sticky sweets, such as mint balls, pear drops and aniseed balls. You could get several varieties for a penny, the only rule was you had to pass the jars to the counter and replace them afterwards before you received your triangular white bag. We bought non-smelling varieties to eat in school so we would not be caught, and saved the nicer ones for later.'

ACCIDENTS WERE LEGION

'We walked about a mile and a half to school in Antrobus every day. We took sandwiches and cocoa and sugar with us, and Miss Pearson, the headmistress, made our cocoa with a kettle boiled over a coal fire. It was like a miracle when we received bicycles in the 1930s. Accidents were legion for a while. At one time Mother was bandaging 14 different places on our arms and legs.'

'COW MORNING'

'I started school at the age of four, walking over a mile with my big sister and her friend. Later when I went on my own I used to leave the milk can at Church Farm and collect a quart of milk in the can on the way home from one of the three daughters who clattered round the dairy in clogs.

I then graduated to a bike and joined my sister when I went to grammar school. Every Monday morning we had to start out early because it was "cow morning" when Crewe cattle market was held and groups of cows were being driven along, with their herdsmen running ahead to stand in the gateways. Other times it could be a flock of sheep with their lovely dogs racing ahead to keep them together, or perhaps a bull on the end of a pole.

My husband's memories are earlier than mine. He was born in 1900, the youngest of six children of the headmaster of a rural school which was five miles from either of the market towns within reach. The school had a large attendance. Many of the children belonged to big families and there would be several going to school at the same time. Often the little ones would be tired out after walking miles to get to school. The school had a system of attendance badges to reward good attendance and I have seen photographs of these children wearing as many as five badges for years of good attendance.'

CALLING AT THE ABATTOIR

'On our way home from school at Norley we often went the long way round and would spend some time at the abattoir watching the killing of pigs and sheep. Other children went to watch the blacksmith shoe the horses.'

DOWN THE LANE

'Before the white railings were put round the lake, Sandy Lane, Redesmere was a narrow country lane. Opposite the lane were watercress beds, where the watercress man came with his big sack to collect the cress to sell.

As we walked to school we would hear the large school bell ringing and we would run to be in time. Lunchtime we had an hour to run home for dinner, then back again, with the bell ringing.

In the summer it was the custom of the people from the cottages, who also had small fields to keep cows, to tent them on the waysides to eat the grass.

Further down the lane we came to Fanshawe brook, which was not covered over. The traffic, mainly horse-drawn, went through the stream. There was a flagstone over the stream about one yard wide, which was a hazard for cyclists who came too fast down the hill and were not always successful in crossing over the flag. There were many tumbles into the water.

One winter there was a prolonged and severe frost, when the lake was frozen over. The vicar came to take all the children out of school to go sliding on Redesmere, to everyone's enjoyment. In the summer Redesmere lake was covered with water lilies. So beautiful and, sadly, now all gone.'

'The village school at Astbury, two miles away, was reached by a country lane lined with grass verges filled with flowers in the spring and summer. We passed only four farms before we got to the village and the school. It remains the same today. On fine summer days or frosty winter mornings field paths could be used to shorten the journey, when hazards such as a herd of cows or a bull on the path added to the excitement, especially if the school bell could be heard in the distance!'

THE ROAD AND THE RIVER

'I did not start school until I was six years old, which was in 1928. We were living in one of 20 houses recently built amongst endless fields along a crushed-stone road. It is still there, that road, but it is wide tarmac now and the endless fields are now an endless housing estate.

In 1928 few had cars, and this road had never seen a bus. The village school I went to was a good three miles away and across the Main Road (note the capital letters). If I was to get to school I had to walk the equivalent distance from Wrenbury to Nantwich twice a day. So I started when six. You may wonder why a parent did not escort me, but my father worked in town and must have left home at about seven o'clock, for I never saw him go, and my mother had my infant brother to care for. Of neighbouring children going to this school I remember none at first, though a couple later. So I walked alone. It did not seem to matter, that was how things were.

I now realise that our houses were just across The River (capitals again) from another village which must have had a school, and only half a mile away. So why did I not go there, crossing The River at the great lock? Ah! but do you not remember that in those days popular fiction was full of hapless children swept away in mill streams and sluices, and snatched from a watery death by the Hero at great risk to his own life? It would be unthinkable for a five or six year old to risk that. Far safer was the three miles of country lanes and crossing the Main Road.'

JENNY GREENTEETH

'We had to pass a pit on the way to and from school at Marton. My mother extolled all of us not to linger by it "as Jenny Greenteeth would get us"! It worked, because I used to approach the pit with trepidation and run as fast as I could past it. Even to this day, I have hideous thoughts about Jenny Greenteeth.'

PLEASED TO SEE THE RAIN

'Until after 1945, children at Norley school went home for their midday meal. My twin sister and I used to make our little sister, seven years younger, run between us all the way home and back. She was always so pleased when it was too wet to go home and Father brought us each a tin box with our dinner in.'

THE FIRST BUS

'In 1934, when I was almost six years old, we had just moved to Croughton. The school was over three miles away at Upton-by-Chester.

There were eleven school age children in the village who started out to walk at 7.45 am and returned home at 5 pm.

I was so tired I would say, "My poor little legs," and go straight to bed. My father would repair our shoes most nights. He bought leather in sheets a yard square, then put the shoes on the last after cutting the size of the sole, then finished with a steel tip on the heel and toe.

My parents had two friends who came one day. One was Dr Griffin, vicar at Dunham Hill, and the other who happened to come was Mrs Faitney who ran a coach and taxi service in Faulkner Street, Hoole.

My mother told them about the children walking to school in all weathers, sometimes wet through, drying our clothes and mending our shoes.

They were both members of Cheshire County Council at the time, so they said they would see what could be done. The result was the first all the year round school bus in Cheshire.'

SCHOOLDAYS – THE BEST YEARS OF OUR LIVES?

Small schools and large classes, strict discipline, little equipment and even fewer modern amenities such as running water or electricity – but we still have fond memories of those country schools, whose teachers worked hard to give us a good, basic education.

THELWALL SCHOOL

'The school, built in 1873, was a small brick building with a porch entrance room and a classroom divided by a sliding screen. It had a beamed ceiling and heating was minimal. In the small playground outside were the pail closets. It changed little over the years, having only cold water taps, an unreliable heating and lighting system and still the pail closets before the last war. It remained in use until the 1970s and although it never did get indoor toilets it did eventually have a proper water system. For over 100 years it was an important part of village life.

The schoolmaster in the 1900s was about five foot two inches but stood no nonsense even from the biggest boys. He was a good teacher, making sure the ablest pupils got scholarships to the grammar schools, giving many a good start in life. He lived with his wife and two daughters in the school house, his wife was an invalid and was wheeled about in a bath chair. They had a pony and trap and the pony grazed on a field opposite the school on part of which the boys were given gardening lessons and grew vegetables for the schoolmaster's family. He was also the church organist. The two young lady teachers walked to and from Latchford each day, one getting the tram to Warrington, making it a very long day but people did have to walk everywhere then and thought nothing of it.

After the schoolmaster retired the coalman's wife became the organist and having had seven sons and five daughters she had a great way with children. She used to coach them for the maypole dancing at the village sports day and for the concerts she organised and ran in the schoolroom. She was a great favourite with all the children, and in fact with all the inhabitants.

There was a pond known as Long Acre pit not far from the school and much fun was had skating on it in the winter; it no longer exists and a shop and houses stand on the spot. We had so many things to see and do in those days and we didn't have to worry about traffic racing through the village as it does now. There was no worry about playing out then and everyone knew everyone else. That did have its drawbacks, your mother always found out if you'd been up to mischief!'

ALLOSTOCK SCHOOL

'I was born on 14th February 1915 on a small farm in Allostock, the next village to Over Peover separated by the river Eye. I went to the village school in Allostock. It was also a Unitarian chapel and was used twice a year for services on Daffodil Sunday and Harvest Festival.

I started school when I was five years old along with my older sister and brother. It was two miles to the school and we used to walk there and back every day in sunshine, rain or snow. I remember we used to wear clogs to go to school and when it was very bad weather we had to take a sheet of paper out of the cloakroom into the school and put it under our feet, especially when it was snowing.

The school only had two rooms, the infants and the big room where you went when you were eleven years. It was heated with two big iron pipes that went all round the school and the head teacher used to let the children that had come a long way, like us, have a warm for a little while before we started lessons.

There were no school dinners so we had to take sandwiches (butties in my day), or sometimes my mother would give us an egg each and we had to write our names on them, take them to the cleaning lady in the school house and she would boil them ready for dinner time. In winter time my mother would make pies of mashed potatoes, meat and bacon with pastry top and bottom, and we would take them to the lady at the school house and she would heat one big pie up and cut it up into how many pieces we wanted. We had cocoa made with boiling water and a little milk to drink at dinner time in winter which we paid a halfpenny each for a cup. In summer we had to help ourselves at the pump just inside the school yard. Sometimes the boys would play around with the pump, throwing water on the girls, then we would be stopped having a drink for a while.

We had a pulpit in the big room and once a month the Rev Payne from Knutsford would come and take a small service, then the big class (over eleven) would be taken for a nature walk by the vicar through the woods. There were a lot of woods around Allostock and I used to like going for these nature walks.

Over Peover schoolchildren in the school garden in 1919. Schools changed very little for village children until after 1945.

We used to have all kinds of games, each in its own season. There would be running with a big round iron hoop, marbles, hopscotch, skipping and the spinning top. We all had our own home-made skipping rope and we used to make marbles out of clay and dry them off in the oven by the fire then paint them. It was only the better-off children that had coloured glass marbles and to be able to win one of these was a big event. We played rounders in the school yard at dinner time and cricket (girls and boys). I remember when the white hawthorn was out, we used to go down the lane by the school and dress one of the girls up with all the branches of may blossom and she would be the Queen of May.

I enjoyed my school days. I can remember at Christmas the day we broke up for our Christmas holidays, there would always be a huge Christmas tree and when we got to school that morning the partition that divided the two rooms would be pushed back and as if by magic, there would be this big Christmas tree loaded with presents, one for each child. There used to be some lovely dolls all dressed up and I would look longingly at them hoping one was for me, but I never got one or a teddy or a gollywog, it was always a book or a box of paints. Maybe it was the most clever children that got the best present or the "teacher's pet".

I went to Allostock school until I was nearly 14 when my parents moved out of the district, and in all that time I had had only two weeks off (that was when I had my tonsils out on the kitchen table by the local doctor and district nurse, but that is another story). I had

122

never been late in all those years and I was presented with a gold bar brooch, and I am sorry to say that the first time I wore it, I lost it and no matter how we searched, we never found it. I was so disappointed because I was very proud of it.

I never went to another school as I was then 14 years old the month we moved, and my father made me stop at home to work.'

THE VILLAGE SCHOOL

'I started at Byley village school in 1919. There were quite a number of children round about. We would gather together about 8.15 am as we had two miles to walk to school and there was no excuse for being late. The school bell would ring promptly on nine o'clock. We formed a straight line and marched into school. If anyone was late, they either stayed in after school or wrote 100 lines "I must not be late".

As infants, we used slates and slate pencils to write with, which could be wiped clean. Later on we were allowed to use a pen with a nib in and ink from wells that were set in the desk. If you used your pen with a heavy hand, the nib would cross then ink would fly all over your book and you would get into trouble.

In those days we seemed to get long hot summers and very cold winters with plenty of snow. When there was a deep snow, I went to school in clogs with steel tips; as I walked along the snow would stick between the tips and I had to keep stopping to knock it off. We called them "clonters".

I remember well how we celebrated Empire Day on 24th May. We made flags of our Empire. We would perform little plays dressed in the costume we thought would represent the nations. The Union Jack would fly from our church tower and we would have a half day's holiday in the afternoon.

We also celebrated Royal Oak Day on 29th May. It was observed by the girls wearing a sprig of green oak. Those who had no oak spray would be chased round the school playground with a stinging nettle and, if caught, would be stung.'

NORTHWICH

'In 1906 a new council school was built in Victoria Road, Northwich replacing the Paradise Street and Timber Lane schools, although there were smaller schools in the villages outside the town. Victoria Road had good playgrounds, separating the boys from the girls. In the morning and afternoon playtimes, also at lunchtime, many games were played. Hopscotch entailed the sliding of a piece of slate into numbered squares chalked on the ground and each little girl hopped to the square where the slate had landed, balanced on one leg to retrieve and after hopping to the end returned to the beginning. Needless to say, if the free leg touched the ground, you lost your turn! Another favourite was skipping – a piece of Mother's clothes line called into play, held by two girls and each child skipped to a rhyme, leaving the skipping when the rhyme ended or when a foot was caught stopping the turning of the rope so that the next child jumped and took her turn. Hide and seek was another popular game, also hand-standing against the school wall and two-ball also played against the walls. Boys played marbles, and both sexes played tag and French cricket, the only requirement for the latter being a piece of wood and a tennis ball.

Children at Tabley school (now the Cuckoo Clock Museum) played whip and top on Chester Road (Watling Street) known today as the A556. They enthusiastically coloured the tops to show elaborate patterns as the tops were whipped. Children attended this school from Pickmere, walking each way down Miller Lane carrying their lunch in little boxes to sustain them until they returned home in the late afternoon. The only drink available was cold water from the tap in the school yard. As the girls grew older they attended cookery classes in Knutsford.

Some children eventually transferred to Altrincham Grammar and had to cycle to Plumley station to catch the steam train. Their cycles were left with Mrs Jones at a cottage opposite Plumley village hall. She charged sixpence a week to each child for this service – a princely sum when it is considered that the average wage was probably only about £1 a week in the 1930s. One of the girls remembers, after leaving their cycles, how they had to run to catch the train and how the engine drivers held up the trains until the breathless children were safely aboard.'

TABLEY SCHOOL

'I attended Tabley school when the Leicester-Warrens lived at Tabley House. They would visit the school occasionally, when all the children stood up at the side of their desks to say, "Good morning sir, good morning my lady."

We had a Christmas party at "the house" each year with presents and another one in the summer, when the highlight was scrabbling for sweets at the end, then finding out on the way home who had picked the most.

My grandmother used to tell me about the Christmas parties at Tabley House when she was a little girl in the 1880s. There was always a choice of presents – an umbrella or a doll. She would have loved a doll but presumably her parents thought this might appear too frivolous. She was under strict instructions that when asked what she wanted, she should curtsey and say, "An umbrella please, m'lady".

The girls in their last two years at school dressed dolls for children in need at Christmas. The dolls came from "the house" with offcuts of material. We each had to take a shoebox to keep them in. These we dressed in part of our dinner hour and in sewing class.

When Miss Margaret Leicester-Warren was married, six girls from the school were chosen as flower girls. We were dressed in long red dresses with white lace collars, and carried gold-coloured baskets to scatter fresh petals on the bridal path.

A country school with only two teachers, but we were well taught. It was a happy school.'

WE HAD NO LIGHTS

'The school at Ince was built of stone from the local quarry, where we used to go and play. The school was surrounded by trees, so in the winter it became very dark. We didn't have lights, so we could not have lessons. The schoolmaster would read to us by the light of a candle.'

HOW DID WE SURVIVE!

'I remember going with my class to Sandbach open air swimming baths, where the water was icy cold and a very dark, dense green. The changing room was a wooden shed and I'll never know how we survived, let alone learned to swim.'

TEACHERS WERE STRICT

'Our Wallasey school clothes were a blue gym-slip – similar to a tabard with box pleats, white blouse, blue serge knickers with black woollen long stockings held up with black elastic, and black lace-up shoes which had to be clean. My grandfather used to polish our shoes each evening ready for school next day. Every morning at school the pupils, a few at a time, would stand in front of the teacher and she would inspect our shoes – "No matter how old they are, they can still be clean," she used to say. Then we each had to produce a clean handkerchief – discreetly from the little pocket in our knickers! If we failed in these, we would have to write out 100 times "I must keep my shoes clean and bring a clean handkerchief to school". We never forgot it twice!

For a ha'penny we used to have one third of a pint of milk every morning – the milk tops were cardboard.

We went home every day for lunch. It was about one and half miles, so in all I walked six miles to and from school every day. My eldest sister had a bicycle, but my other sister and I were not trusted on a bicycle! I can remember all my school teachers, even by name, from when I was five years of age. We were disciplined and had to do as we were told. I enjoyed school and respected the teachers.'

'Teachers at Crowton school were strict and rules were obeyed – there was always the cane as a last resort.

By the time they were nine, the girls had knitted a pair of men's socks on four needles and a baby's vest, and had sewn pillowcases by hand, being very careful to keep all tacking threads to be used again and again. Wasting tacking threads was a dreadful fault. One girl can remember being made to stand on a stool for half an hour with her hands on her head, and that was just for talking! If you went to school without a handkerchief you were provided with a sheet of hard paper to use, enough to jolt anyone's memory.'

MAKING COCOA

'There were many children at Malpas schools who had long walks to school each day in all weathers, and who simply took sandwiches for their dinner. The local Women's Institute organised, during the winter months, a cocoa-making effort. They bought a gas boiler and each day members went to the Jubilee Hall and made the cocoa. At twelve o'clock the older boys and girls collected the cocoa in large cans and it was taken to the three schools – boys, girls and infants. The children could have as much cocoa as was available, all for the charge of a halfpenny a day. This continued until a kitchen was built on the back of the girls school and Mrs Wragg began cooking dinners there for the schoolchildren.'

A COUNTRY SCHOOL

'I attended a very good two-teacher school in a farming area. Discipline was very strict and every minute of the day was spent on routine lessons. However, there were a few special occasions, one being Empire Day, 24th May. The headmistress talked about our proud empire and the men who were responsible for it, and the brave soldiers who fought in the First World War. We knew we had a half holiday in the afternoon and it stretched forward like endless bliss and it was always a perfect summer's day. Before going home at noon we sang *Now thank we all our God* and it is still my favourite hymn!

Another greatly exciting day was the annual sports day held at the local Hall, home of the Brocklehurst family. It was so exciting to have your mother there (in those days parents hardly ever appeared at school because children walked to school by themselves). The amazing thing was the lawn, which was so mossy that your feet sank into it and nobody was able to run very fast. I dreaded the obstacle race because I did not fancy getting stuck in a tyre hanging more than waist high, and on no account did I want to go under the heavy tarpaulin. Afterwards we were given tea at the Hall.

The annual Christmas party was given by the Brocklehursts at their village hall. We could wear best dresses and suits and you could even wear a necklace! Soon after dinner (sandwiches eaten at your desk) we were marched along the road to the party. We always danced the "Grand Old Duke of York" and played The Jolly Miller and Twos and Threes. After the party fathers arrived to take us home and we scrambled for nuts and were each given an orange and a block of Cadbury's milk chocolate.

All Halloween was another special day. We bobbed for apples and tried to bite apples hanging from strings. There was a bowl of mashed potatoes and one or two lucky children found a sixpence in their spoonful.

A day I dreaded was 29th May, Oak Apple Day. If you did not wear a sprig of oak you could be either nettled or tripped up,

depending whether the time was before or after noon. I associate those days with boys because I hated roughness of any kind and dreaded being hurt. The word "hurt" reminds me of the many tumbles we used to have in the rather uneven gritty playground. You had to put your grazed leg up on a chair for the inevitable dab of iodine, which stung so much that your leg shivered like a jelly. Another memory is that we always seemed to be getting colds and earache was the bane of at least four little lives. We put our ears against the hot pipes in the classroom to feel the lovely comforting warmth.

Whooping cough could mean weeks off school and there was the scarlet fever epidemic where the worst happened and you were carted off in the ambulance to the isolation hospital. We were allowed to watch (with a sense of doom), as the ambulance drove along the road with our friends inside.

On one fearful occasion we were taken to the house of a school manager. We knelt by chairs and prayed as he lay on his deathbed upstairs. That sobered everyone up for quite a while! Religion was very important and on one memorable day our teacher diverted from the Bible to give us a lecture. She was disgusted that she had seen a girl who had just left school walking down the lane with her mouth painted with *lipstick*! Oh, the dreadful crime of this Jezebel! Happily she turned out to be very clever and smart and has had a successful life.

One happy day was the Silver Jubilee of George V in 1935. We were each given a mug and we joined in a combined service at the next village church. I don't remember very much except practising singing *All people that on earth do dwell* so that we would be a credit to our school. It was at this time that we had our one and only school trip. The juniors went back to school after tea and were taken on a coach to Platt Fields in Manchester to watch the historical pageant. The trip was more exciting than the pageant, I think.

These two events were exciting but not so the awful visits of the dentist. In those days he came with his dentist's chair and the happy infants room became a torture chamber. Treatment was carried out in school and you hoped you would not shout or cry out. Oh, it was dreadful. Even more I dreaded the optician. I thought he only treated eyes with the letter chart, but horror of horrors, one day the infants room was blacked out and Dorothy had lights shone into her eyes, and I thought she was the bravest girl in the world.

Another regular visitor was the Attendance Officer. A quiet whisper went round when we saw his distinctive yellow ochre car, and we wondered what family he was after, and would the father go to prison?

I must tell you about the concert, the only one I think we had in my primary school days. The seniors acted a very grown up play, to my infant thinking, and Betty was extremely posh in a full length oyster gown embroidered with pearls. I thought it was marvellous and *how* I wanted to be the train bearer. It was between Gladys and me, and Gladys was chosen. Never mind, there were compensations. We infants did a Christmas play about fairies and I was "Wrinkles". (Mother hoped I had not been given the part because of my habit of frowning.) My crepe paper dress was a beautiful lilac with silver scissors on it, and they certainly don't make crepe paper like that in modern times!

One turn at the concert was the band and Ted was taught to conduct us. (Only Ted in the whole concert was allowed to turn his back to the audience.) I think one or two children played on tin whistles, some on combs covered with tissue paper, and we infants sat at the front and banged every so often on a jam jar with a teaspoon. We were each dressed as a nursery rhyme character. I was Hot Cross Bun and a very fat boy was Humpty Dumpty. For some obscure reason we all wore trousers and to my eternal satisfaction my mother bought me pyjamas specially for the concert. They were white with blue edges and I felt really grand. Poor Billy, the fat boy, was not so lucky. He had to wear a pair of the teacher's shiny pale green bloomers which must have reached to her knees! How grateful I was for those pyjamas!'

INTO THE WAR

'Sports day at Lymm grammar school in the 1930s must have been the original family fun day. There were races of all kinds – skipping, sack, egg and spoon and a plant pot race where you moved the plant pots forward one at a time while balanced on the other one, on one foot.

The prize for the visitors' race was a comb in a leather case which I, aged eight, won and treasured for a long time.

Certainly the seniors indulged in great feats of athletic prowess, but the final event, the tug-of-war between the houses Warburton and Domville, was the highlight of the day.

The outbreak of war in 1939 brought out the Cheshire farming instinct in anyone privileged to be born in this lush county. Lymm grammar school staff and pupils set to with a will and some sports fields disappeared under the horse-drawn plough. PE lessons became dig-for-victory sessions, as indeed did religious instruction when there was urgent harvesting to be done. Hen coops surrounded the hockey pitch and geese and ducks roamed the bike shed. Goats and a cow lived under the cricket pavilion. We not only produced all the vegetables needed for school dinners but we stayed behind, on a class rota, at four o'clock to prepare them for the next day. The surplus was sold and after the war the money was used towards the cost of the school's outdoor centre on Anglesey. From school we went out to the farms in the district to help with the harvesting. Here we met German and Italian prisoners of war who came from the big camp near Northwich to do heavy duty farm work. Some stayed on after the war and settled here. Cheshire suited them well.

At the beginning of the war school stayed open all year and the staff took a staggered fortnight's holiday. Pupils were expected to rest in afternoons, lying on mats, if there had been air raids during the previous night. Time spent in the shelters during the day was not wasted, lessons continued. If the all clear had not sounded by 4.30 pm we were allowed to eat the iron rations, biscuits and Horlicks tablets, which were kept in the shelters. I remember well the warm feeling of wartime togetherness.'

THE WORLD OF WORK

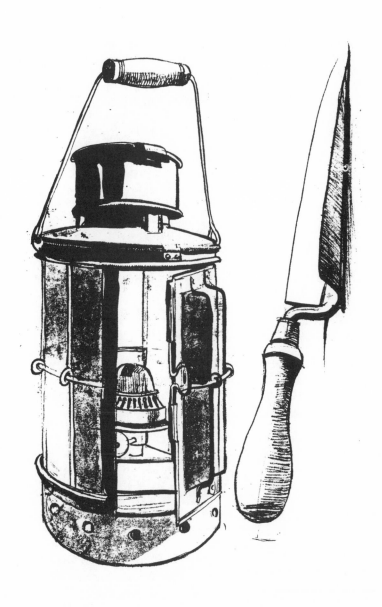

ON THE LAND

Cheshire's rich agricultural land has made farming one of our most important activities, but how things have changed over the last 50 years. Once horses provided all the power on the farm and many farms were small, mixed affairs worked by the whole family. Cheesemaking took place as a matter of course, and many farmers also ran local milk rounds.

THE DAIRY COUNTY

'Towards the end of the last century, Cheshire being the "Dairy County", nearly all the farms made cheese, which was taken, when it matured, to the Cheese Fair where it was sold. Sometimes the factor travelled to the farm and bought it there. This continued until after the First World War, when a change came about – the farmers turned to selling milk. First they had to take it to the station to meet the milk train, which took it to the towns. Then a collecting dairy was built and lorries would call at the farms to collect the tankards, which were taken to the dairy, then poured into large glass-lined tankers and special trains took it to London. This method was used until the Second World War. A few farmers carried on making cheese, but by the 1950s all commercially produced Cheshire cheese was factory made.

The smallholdings kept cows for their own use and made butter with any surplus milk. They also kept pigs and calves. The farmer's wife looked after the poultry and the eggs were taken to market to sell. Geese and turkeys were fattened up for the Christmas markets. Farmers who kept pigs would often kill a pig for their own use. Flitches of bacon and hams were cured then hung from the ceilings to season. They also reared calves.

Crops of potatoes, carrots, mangolds and beet were grown and also cereal crops and hay were harvested, these were all to supplement their income. Work was very hard, as all ploughing, sowing and mowing at harvest time, was done with the help of horses and all the milking was done by hand.'

THE CHEESEMAKER RULED THE ROOST

'Cheshire being mainly a dairy farming county, meant most of the farms were involved in cheesemaking. Whenever a man was taken on to work on the farm he was asked if his wife was able to milk cows. If she could not or would not he probably wouldn't get the job. He was also asked if she was a dry or a wet milker – a dry milker being preferred.

Each farm had a cowman, a cheesemaker, a dairy maid, and other help in the house and on the farm. The cheesemaker ruled the roost, because until the cheese was made everything else had to wait.

Cheese was the staple diet. There was cheese for breakfast, lunch, tea and supper.

At a cheesemaking farm in Guilden Sutton, during the 1930s the daughters of the house kept pet lambs, known as cade lambs. They were a nuisance when customers came to the farmhouse door to buy cheese, as they would butt the unsuspecting person down the path. One memorable day one of these creatures tossed the dairymaid into the cheese vat!

Pigs were always part of the livestock of these cheesemaking farms, as they ate the whey from the cheesemaking process.'

DELIVERING THE MILK

'I lived on a 125 acre farm at North Rode in my young days, where we kept around 60 milking cows, yielding some 80 gallons of milk daily. This was sold to a dairy in Manchester – Dobson's Dairies at one time. The milk was delivered in five or six 17-gallon milk churns and sent by rail from North Rode station. The "milk train" was due at 7.45 am and this was the train my sister and I travelled on to attend Macclesfield High School, so we often had a lift to the station.

Helping us on the farm were three workmen and one woman who all "lived in" and my mother did all the cooking. As soon as the milking was finished in the morning – by hand, as there were no milking machines in those days – a horse would be harnessed to the milk float to take the milk to the station, about a mile and a half away.

I remember one especially severe winter when heavy snow had blocked the roads overnight, so the milk had to be taken across the fields. This was heavy going as one particular field was rather hilly and the horse had a real struggle through the deep snow. Wires had to be cut in the fence separating our land from the next farm so that the milk float could cross the "Cow Brook" at the flattest point. We, as children, found it very exciting, but rather frightening.

In the summer time, when there was a glut of milk, we would

often receive a telegram saying "Keep your milk at home in the morning", then we would have to get busy making cheese. The most vexing thing was that sometimes after we had decided there would be no more telegrams and we had thoroughly cleaned and stored all the cheesemaking equipment in the attic, there would be another telegram and it all had to be brought into action again. Such were the trials of farming in the 1920s.

One farmer we knew was nearly always the last to arrive at North Rode station with probably seven churns to our five, and the guard on the train would hasten to blow his whistle and get the train off so as not to be late at Macclesfield station. This was the businessmen's express to Manchester from then on and we were fascinated to see the smart gentlemen with their briefcases jumping on to the train as it was beginning to move off. Sadly, North Rode station is no longer there.'

FARMING ON THE ESTATE

'I was the second child of a family of five, born to farming parents, who worked a 100 acre farm with cattle, pigs and poultry as a living. In 1918 we moved to a much larger farm on the same estate, my father returning to his home farm as his father retired.

Our milking herd was 70 black and white cattle and we had more than 20 large white pedigree pigs. We reared all our young stock, calves for herd replacements, and piglets into gilts and boars for breeding and to sell, as father was well known in the pig breeding world, having won several prizes at local shows.

I well remember Lord Daresbury and his farm manager coming many times to buy stock pigs. His large black and yellow limousine had his coat of arms painted on the side. They had travelled through the Mersey Tunnel the first day it opened; we could hardly believe it was possible to have a safe road under the river.

The milking was all done by hand and, as we children grew, we had to learn to milk, which seemed difficult at first. The wives of the workmen also came to milk, leaving their prams with sleeping babies nearby while they worked. All the milk was carried in buckets attached to a shoulder yoke by one of the men, from the shippons to the house dairy and poured into the vat ready to be made into coloured Cheshire cheese. The silver cups and salvers won for cheese at the agricultural shows were displayed with pride on the sideboard.

Cheesemaking was a daily job and Mother was in charge of each stage in the process; cream was skimmed from the milk and twice a week was churned into butter. This was hard laborious work, especially if there was a shortage of help. Small cheese presses had

Haymaking at Vicar Farm, Wilmslow in 1939, one of the busiest times in the farming calendar.

to be checked and turned daily as the contents matured in the press room.

In the depression of the 1920s, prices for cheese were very low, only fivepence or sixpence a pound at one time, this not covering the cost of labour and the farm rent. We employed five or six men outside, with two or three maids in the house, who helped to milk, make cheese and do the housework.

I looked after all the poultry on the farm, and hatched chickens and ducks in the paraffin-heated egg incubators, and then reared them for flock replacements. A man called each Friday evening to buy eggs; he took them to Birkenhead market and sold them for eightpence to tenpence per dozen for hen eggs and even less per dozen for duck eggs.

Work on the farm was done by four big cart horses, ploughing, sowing and harvesting with the waggoners in charge; they took great pride in looking after their animals.

We bought a tractor in the mid 1930s; it was wonderful to complete the work so much more quickly and then, with the addition of machinery, life changed on the farm. The big smoking steam engine would bring the threshing machine round the farms in the winter to thresh the corn, usually taking a day or two. The corn was bagged in hessian sacks and stored in the granary; this was used as feed for the cattle, pigs and poultry. Extra men were needed at these times, some travelling around with the threshing box from farm to farm and fed by the farmer's wife.'

GROWING UP WITH FARMING

'From the age of about two weeks (in the late 1930s) until my marriage, I lived at Bollin Hey Farm, Styal. My mother and father were both from families with 13 children, but I had no brothers nor sisters, and only a few cousins.

My earliest memories are of sitting on a half cwt weight in the farmyard with a hen on my knee. It always came to me and I fondly hoped it would lay an egg on my knee, but of course it never did. I was about two years old at the time. I also remember, when our Rhode Island x Light Sussex hens became broody (which they seemed to do very frequently) my father would buy a clutch of duck eggs and set them under a broody hen. About a week or a fortnight before they were due to hatch he checked the eggs to see which were fertile by placing them in a bucket of warm water. If they moved they were fertile, and if not they were infertile, so these were thrown away; when they hatched out they were dried and placed in a box by the fire to keep warm.

We kept Ayrshire cows on the farm, and as soon as I was old enough I used to go out with my mother at five o'clock each morning to deliver milk. Whilst we were out my father would do the morning milking, and then whilst he had his breakfast my mother and I would wash all the milk bottles by hand and my father would do the later round. We used a pony and trap to deliver milk, and shopping when needed was done whilst delivering milk. We were fairly self-sufficient; we grew potatoes, some of which we sold, peas, beans and cabbages. We grew wheat, oats, barley and rye, and we rolled the oats. My mother made all the bread (I loved it straight from the oven) and we made our own butter. I still have two of Mother's butter pats. We kept some pigs which were fattened and sold, but usually kept one for ourselves. After killing it was cleaned and dressed, and one of my jobs was to grate salt from a huge block to salt the pork and bacon which was then stored in the cellar.

We had blackberries, apples and pears, damsons, greengages, gooseberries and blackcurrants, and my mother made jam or preserved them. My father didn't consider a meal complete unless it finished with some bread and jam, and my mother would make at least a ton of jam a year, which was stored in brown earthenware jars.

The fuel we used was coal – and what coal it was. Big, black, shiny lumps which burned away to nothing; no bass in that. My father used to sweep the chimney in a rather unorthodox fashion; he would first remove the hearthrug, then bring in a board, half a bale of straw, and some paraffin. He soaked the straw in paraffin then pushed it up the chimney with a pikel, then put a match to it. He always made sure the wind was blowing in the right direction first! I had to run outside and see all the blazing straw and soot flying away.

We had free range hens which had to be fastened up securely each night because of foxes, and we had to watch out for magpies during the day because they would go into the hen cote and steal the eggs. We had two men working on the farm. One of them lived in a small outbuilding called a shant, the other lived at Moss Nook. We also had an Irishman who worked seasonally, not always the same one. During the war we had 20 Italian prisoners working on the farm; I think they were kept at Dunham. One incendiary bomb fell in one of the fields during the war. We had to have large poles sticking up in the fields to stop enemy planes landing. We weren't supposed to give the prisoners anything to eat or drink, but my mother always gave them a plate of scones, and in return they used to make me toys.'

HORSES AND TRACTORS

'Tractors were very primitive when they first came in. They had coil ignitions which needed to be warmed up in the morning. The steering wasn't up to much either. They were only used for heavy work. Fuel was fourpence a gallon, which had to be bought, whereas a horse helped to grow the oats that it ate and lived on the farm. In fact, they reckoned that you could never cost the price of a horse because a horse ploughed the land which grew the oats which fed the horse which ploughed the land.'

'At the outbreak of war in 1939, when it was compulsory to plough, we decided to buy a tractor. A two month old Allis Chalmers with rubber tyres was purchased but of course, we had no implements so the horse plough was pulled by the tractor with someone walking behind to steer it. People came from miles around to see a tractor with rubber tyres. An elevator had been purchased in 1937 for £50, delivered by rail to Poynton station and fetched to the farm by a horse! This was in use until 1970, and in the 1980s it was donated to the museum at Tatton Hall.'

CHARACTERS

'We all know how the villages of Cheshire have changed over the years with large and expensive houses being built from the two-up, two down farm labourers' cottages. One of these farm labourers I remember as a man of few words but with a talent for weather forecasting. When asked if it was going to be a fine day, he would reply, "Well, it'll rain if thee dinna watch it!" Or for a change, "Well, it'll rain or g'dark before mornin'!" He was never wrong. His day started with milking the cows, next he would muck out the shippon, by hand of course, with a wheelbarrow and shovel. Then, with the evidence of his job all over his hands and arms, he was off home for breakfast. Half an hour or so later, Bill returned to work still in the same state.

And, of course, there were the Irishmen. Throughout the summer some of these ageless looking men, usually alone, would move from farm to farm picking potatoes and doing general farm work, often sleeping in a loft over the shippon. Others would stay in one place for the season and live in the "shant" − a small brick building with a fireplace in it. One particular Irishman lived in such a shant and the farm cat kept him company. His staple diet was boiled potatoes and home-cured bacon; the latter being the end of the flitch which the butcher would almost give away as it was 90% fat − cholesterol had not been invented! After mucking out in the early morning old Tom would rinse off his shovel and use it to cook his breakfast on over the open fire − a couple of bacon rashers and perhaps an egg he had found somewhere in the bales, on one half and alongside a mouse well fried with the bacon fat for the cat. Man and beast at peace with the world!'

'On the occasion of the annual visit of the threshing machine to Well Farm, Adlington, Mrs Potts, as was customary, prepared a large hot-pot to feed the gang of men. Unfortunately, on taking it from the oven she dropped it on the hearth but for the sake of expediency scooped it all back into the pot, including bits of cinder and ash, all stirred up together. According to Mr Potts, "Believe me or believe me not, one fellow on that threshing rig had always had a bad stomach ulcer, and from that day on after he'd eaten that hot-pot as my missus had prepared, he never had any more stomach trouble for the rest of his life."

Mr Potts had a neighbour, another farmer whose fields met his. They were on bad terms for some reason or another. During the war a German bomber returning from a raid jettisoned four bombs. Two exploded in his neighbour's field and two in Jim Potts' field. For days afterwards he would tell everyone, "That there Mr Hitler in Germany must have known we were at loggerheads with one another for he comes over and drops two bombs on him and two bombs on me" '

THE SPRING HIRINGS

'As a very small child I remember my father going to the annual spring hirings in the local market town. There the men would stand in rows waiting to be hired as farm hands. The strongest men were always taken on first, leaving the less robust to be taken on at the end of the sale at a lower rate. A strong man was paid between £7 and £8 a year. These hirings continued until about 1929.'

THE FARMING YEAR

The farming year had its own rhythm, and whole communities looked forward to haymaking, harvest and threshing time. Thanksgiving for a harvest gathered in was given wholeheartedly in the village church.

FARMING IN LYMM

'Life in the late 1930s and early 1940s in Lymm was leisurely and slow. Everyone in the village knew each other, especially in the farming community. Farming was the biggest industry in the area and there were many people employed on the land. The farming calendar never started and never finished. It was a continuous way of life, from dawn to dusk, for all workers. The weather was the law in the country.

As soon as the potatoes were dug in September or October, the land was ploughed – with horses. The spring wheat was sown straight away to lie all winter in the ground. Then came Christmas, plucking turkeys, geese and chickens for the Christmas market. January to February were busy months feeding livestock, as food had to be carried to the fields; hay had to be cut and mangolds sliced for all the cattle. In those days there were plenty of Irishmen living on farms – in shants or outhouses. They came over in March and went back in October when the crops were harvested.

The horseman or teamsman as he was called did nothing but look after his horses. They all had nicknames like "Hellfire Dick", "Gramps" and "Stinker". Dear old Gramps – William Cook – was a delightful character. He had a beard, wore leggings and smoked a clay pipe. He loved his horses and always said his religion was that of the horse – work six days and rest on a Sunday. He used to tell stories of when he was a lad at High Legh Hall of how he carted all the vegetables to the cook and she would hide him in a cupboard and when no one was looking, give him his breakfast. He also carted milk from Bradley Hall down the Cinder Path to Thelwall station. While he worked at Bradley, one morning he met a swarm of rats coming up the drive. He ran fast, for he said they would have eaten him there were so many, literally thousands of them. When they go in droves like that they do not stop, they eat through anything. There were no ratcatchers in those days. His wife was always sick and after he bedded down his horses he would walk to Broomedge for medicine for her when necessary, as the doctor lived there. William was 85 when he died in 1959. He worked at Cherry Hall and retired from there. I can still see him ploughing and the seagulls following. He walked very slowly as he would never rush his horses. Farm workers' hours were from 7.30 in the morning till noon with an hour for dinner and finishing at six in the evening.

Haymaking was a happy time with plenty of rides on the cart into the field and a ride on top of the load coming home. Harvest time was busy with all hands on deck as the corn had to be put in stooks and if it was tall it had to be hooded. The sheaves were carted in after ten days in the field – depending on the weather – and then built into neat, oblong stacks.

Threshing time was heavy work for all. During the war each bag had to be counted and the chaff was mixed with the horses' feed. People were up to all sorts of tricks to get food as it was so scarce. I remember a farmer who was ill in bed. He had killed animals for a butcher and somehow or other sheep disappeared. The authorities got suspicious and he got a whisper in his ear that they were coming to his house and so that they would not find the sheep which were slaughtered ready for cutting up or skinning, he put them in bed with him, and they never looked there. Each worker who had a farm cottage could keep a pig by giving up his rations. It was fed on all sort of things – potato peelings, crusts and any scraps one could get hold of, but the Ministry of Agriculture claimed half of the pig. On the farm one also managed to churn a little extra butter and try and make bread.

German prisoners were brought to work on the land and they were glad of a dinner even if some days there was no meat, just vegetables. They enjoyed being on the farm and several never went back to Germany. There was a lot of swapping of labour. A farmer always helped his neighbour and he in turn helped him; even if there were a shortage of foodstuff for cattle and the meal waggon had not come, he could rely on his neighbour to lend him a bag until the waggon arrived. At harvest in particular, they helped each other. When there was a sign of rain one felt obliged to save all the harvest whether it was your neighbour's or your own. This sense of sharing and caring has nearly disappeared. We will never see the beautiful stacks of wheat, oats and barley in the farmyard again.

To build a stack was an art in itself. It was started by standing two sheaves together in the middle of the stack "bottom" and building round those until the oblong stack bottom was ready for placing the sheaves in the order of the stooks in the field. By being slightly uneven at the bottom, the progress of the stack was impossible unless the sheaves were placed in a certain way, locking each other. The stack was narrow to start with, then bulged a little, then wider up to the eave where it was brought in a bit and gradually up to a point. This was to prevent the rain from penetrating the corn as it ran off the eave, and the stacks were kept dry all winter. After the stack was built it was thatched with rye grass and roped. If there was rain in the air the thatching and roping was done after dark, as heavy rain might damage the top of the stack. This work was rough on clothes. By the time the harvest was over there were no knees in trousers, no sleeves in jackets and sometimes one was wearing a clog and a shoe, or odd wellingtons.

There was also a big risk of fire so no one was allowed to smoke near the stacks. Many years ago there was a fire at a farm in Cherry Lane. The fire engine at that time was kept by the old council office in Whitbarrow Road and firemen were ordinary working men who just went to a fire when they heard the fire bell. The fireman in charge was in Blackpool for the day, so someone had to go down into the meadows near Lymm bridge and catch the horses to pull the engine. By the time they arrived at the blaze the corn stacks were well alight, so the farmer told them to concentrate on the midden – the rest was insured.

There is no beginning to a farming year and no end to the stories it contains.'

IT WAS ALL SO DIFFERENT

'Farming in the 1930s and 1940s was vastly different from farming today. Nowadays most farms specialise in one or two enterprises, but in the old days most farms were mixed. That is they kept cows, sheep, a few pigs, some hens and ducks and grew some corn and an acre or two of potatoes, turnips and swedes and mangolds, and of course the grass to make the hay for winter and summer feed for the cows.

The farming year really starts in the autumn when the ground is prepared for next year's crops. The ploughing was done with a small plough pulled by one or two horses, the man walking behind the plough holding it steady and at the same time holding the reins from the horses to guide them. Pride was taken in making a very straight furrow and markers were put at each end of the field as a guide to make the first one correctly. Later the ground would be worked down ready for the crops – always working with the horse. We had our first tractor in the late 1930s. How much easier life became, although I do remember grumbles that they were too heavy and squashed the ground down too much!

When the grass was cut in June to make the hay for the winter it was left in swathes which had to be turned and shaken up after a few days to make sure it was all dry. Then it was raked together in thicker lines with a big horse rake. After this the men came with pikels – a long-handled two-prong fork, and put the hay into small stooks all over the field ready to be lifted onto lorries when it was taken to the farm to be put in stacks in the hay sheds. I remember the relief when a new method came out in the 1940s and the hay was left in the long swathes and a man came with a stationary baler and the hay was baled in the field and then brought home.

The grass was brought to the baler with an implement called a "sweep". This was a large wooden pronged thing like a great big fork which was fixed onto the front of the tractor to gather up the swathes. What joy to a young girl – you could drive a tractor at any age – to be whizzing around the field picking up the grass to take it to the baler. I did not turn quickly enough one time and caught a wooden prong on the hedge top and broke it off. As the years went on, into the 1950s, silage started to take over, because it was not so dependent on good weather.

The corn harvest followed in August. Before tractors took over the binder was pulled by two horses. The binder was a machine which cut the corn and the flail flipped it on to a flat canvas which rolled it along and up between two more canvases to a platform where it was automatically divided into sheaves and tied with string and then flipped out onto the ground. The driver sat on a seat on the binder and guided the horses and watched that everything was working properly, especially the string which tied the sheaves. Two men were needed when the tractor was used, and the one on the binder needed a good voice to be able to shout for the driver to stop if anything went wrong. You could go the length of the field with no sheaves tied because the string had broken and the driver did not hear or bother to look back. Work was often carried on until dark and the knives had to be sharpened and the machine oiled about three or four times a day.

The workers followed putting the sheaves into stooks – oats were usually in eights in a line with the grain leaning together. Wheat was usually in a cross of twelve sheaves with four fastened up upside down on top to protect the grain. This was then left for a few days to dry and harden before being put into stacks at the farm. As children we were always in trouble for playing hide and seek inside these stooks and sometimes knocking them over.

The potatoes and roots were lifted in the autumn and put into hogs. These were shallow trenches and the roots were mounded up in them and then covered with straw and soil to keep out the frost.

In addition to all the field work all the animals had to be looked after and kept clean. Milking was done by hand, sitting on a three-legged stool and having a pail between the knees to catch the milk. That was until we had a milking machine installed in the late 1930s. The milk was poured into a Dend container and cooled down in a refrigerator. This looked like an old washboard, but it was hollow and cold water ran through it as the milk slowly trickled down either side into a sieve on top of the tankard. Before the Milk Marketing Board was set up in 1933, the tankards were taken to the local dairy. After 1933 they were picked up by waggons and taken into dairies often in large towns. Sometimes children were given a lift to school on the milk waggon.

Another job in the winter was to cart out the manure to the fields. This was put out in small rucks and then spread with a fork.

Christmas was a time for plucking the chickens, ducks and geese, to sell at the local market. This provided housekeeping money for the farmer's wife, as did the eggs throughout the year. It was her job to look after the poultry. How much times have changed.'

ONE JANUARY DAY

'The alarm rings – it is 5 am and time to get up. It is a January morning in the "olden" days! Helpers live in at the farm – three men, and a girl who helps in the dairy. Father comes down first, lights the kitchen fire, drinks his glass of milk and eats two marie biscuits and one ginger (must be exact) and then goes out to the shippon to milk. He takes a couple of paraffin storm lanterns to illuminate the buildings. Cans are collected from the dairy opposite and four men start to hand-milk all the cows. Each man sits on a three-legged stool next to the animal. The milk is carried to the dairy where it flows over a cooler filled with water. The churns are quickly filled and it is time for the "lad" to go and harness the horse and put it into the shandry. He takes the milk to Plumley station for the 6.30 am milk train to Manchester. The station yard is full of others bringing their milk. These come from three to four miles radius. Two porters are on duty to help. Empty churns which had contained 12, 15 or 17 gallons are taken back home.

Breakfast is a substantial cooked meal which Mother and the girl have prepared ready for six adults and four children. The waggoner goes to feed and groom the horses and, if not too frosty, harnesses two horses to the plough. It takes weeks to do all the fields, ploughing one furrow at a time. Cheshire farms are mostly "all round" farms, which means growing hay, corn, mangolds, turnips and kale to feed animals, and early potatoes to send on the train, in hampers, to Manchester market. A merchant receives them, sells at the best price he can obtain, takes his commission off, and pays the rest to the farmer. In winter the "milk-horse" is shod with shoes capable of having studs screwed into them to help on icy roads. In winter months all animals are kept warm and bedded with straw indoors. At this time of the year field hedges are cut by hand with a bill-hook. A favourite job is to have a bonfire with the trimmings.

Poultry is fed out of doors – the girl usually takes charge of this. Each morning she lights the boiler fire and carries the hot water to wash and scald the dairy utensils. Can lids have brass nameplates which have to be polished. All the indoor and outdoor lamps are filled with paraffin and the glasses polished. Twelve noon sees ten persons ready and waiting for a cooked dinner. Second course is often milk pudding, cooked in the iron oven and served with fruit pie. Probably once a week steamed suet or apple dumplings may make a welcome change. Afternoon is a repetition of feeding poultry and animals. The "turning out" field has a brook, so animals are put outside to drink water – there are no water bowls in the shippon.

Sometimes in the long winter evenings rag rugs are made from secondhand used cloth. This is cut into strips and pegged on to hessian – nice and warm to stand on.'

THRESHING DAY

'The day before threshing was to commence the "engine" arrived. It chuntered its slow, ponderous way into the yard and was settled a suitable distance along the hay shed. Lots of blocks of wood were positioned around its wheels and coal was deposited on the ground nearby.

The next morning at about 5.30 am the "men" arrived to fire the engine and at about 8 am the farm men and the extra hands arrived.

I was too young to be allowed out near all the dust and noise but when the men were to have their "baggin" I was allowed to carry a can of tea out to them.

The threshing machine was fantastic. A man stood in the barn throwing the sheaves of corn with his pitchfork (pikel) on to the top of the machine and another man cut the string and scattered it into the centre of the machine where it was agitated along a conveyor belt. At one side of the machine a bag was attached where the grains of corn fell into it; further along another bag was positioned where the chaff was discharged. The whole machine was driven by huge (unguarded) belts which took their power from huge wheels driven by the engine. The noise was horrendous, the dust appalling, but the excitement . . .

The men (many of them Irish staying on after the potato picking) used to wear corduroy trousers, always tied just below the knees to stop the rats which they disturbed, running up their legs!

Threshing usually lasted two or three days and oh, how quiet and dull life became when everything was packed up and they puffed off to another farm, leaving me despondently scuffling the pile of ash left on the ground in the stackyard.'

IN SERVICE

For many young girls, going into service was the only employment open to them when they left school. Right up to the Second World War, it was common for farmers and professional people, as well as those in the 'big house', to keep servants.

LIFE FOR A PARLOURMAID

'When I was a young girl in the 1930s, I worked as parlourmaid at Bolesworth Castle for the Barbour family. The staff then consisted of one cook, one kitchenmaid and two scullery maids. There were three parlourmaids, and also three housemaids who were responsible for the cleaning of all the reception rooms and bedrooms.

The parlourmaids cleaned the dining room and were responsible for cleaning all the silver. Glassware was always washed carefully in a wooden tub so that it would not get broken. We would also have to serve meals to the family and their friends.

There was additional staff of one lady's maid, an odd job man who would take care of cleaning shoes and boots, bringing in logs and coal and also the cleaning of windows, and a governess to look after the Barbours' children.

Each little department within the staff kept to themselves but would all meet after the duties were complete at meal times, except for the governess who would eat with the family.

Meals during the day would be served at the following times. Breakfast was laid up in the dining room at 8.30 am, coffee would be taken at 10.30 am, lunch at 1 pm, afternoon tea at 4.30 pm and then the evening meal at 8 pm. A normal working day started at 7 am and finished at about 9.30 pm to 10 pm.

During the dinner the housemaids would tidy the fireplace in the drawing room. They would turn the bedclothes down and if it was winter, fill the hot water bottles and put them in the beds.

When guests arrived at the castle the door would be opened for them by the head parlourmaid, their hats and coats taken and then they would be announced in the drawing room.

When the Barbours had friends and family visiting, staying lady guests would have assistance from the housemaids unpacking their cases, unless they had brought their own maids with them. The gentlemen guests had their luggage unpacked by the parlourmaids. We were responsible for the care of all their clothes during their stay.

The parlourmaids worked extremely late if there was a dinner party taking place, which usually meant about ten or twelve guests. On occasions such as dances or the Hunt balls, we would require the help of "Bollands of Chester", who specialised in catering.

We worked hard, but had a lot of fun as well, which included outings and dances, but on half days if we were in any later than 9 pm that was it, we were locked out by the head servants. The whole Barbour family were great to work for, they never talked down to any of us and we were always appreciated. It was the head servants that we were always wary about!'

THE UNDER-HOUSEMAID

'My experiences of domestic service in the late 1930s and early 1940s varied from the "upstairs downstairs" households to living as one of the family.

I was first employed at 14 years of age in a household where the family consisted of "Sir and Madam" and their two small children. The house itself was very tall – six floors including the basement. There were five servants and a nanny living in, plus a daily help.

I was under-housemaid. My day started at 5.30 am and my first task was to scrub the white marble floor of the very large hall, continuing through the front door to do the wide front steps down to the pavement. Time then to clean the lounge before a welcome break for breakfast.

Next it was the turn of the study, bedrooms, bathrooms and all the staircases which were of polished wood. Each room had elegant large Indian carpets surrounded by wood which had to be polished every day except Sundays. There was also a servants' staircase. It was my task to scrub the stone steps here twice a week.

Uniforms for mornings were print dresses and large white aprons;

The indoor staff of Heawood Hall, Nether Alderley in the 1920s. Many young girls found that going into service was the only work available to them.

afternoons we wore dark dresses with frilly aprons and goffered hat bands. We changed after lunch – if we were lucky we would get an hour's rest at this stage.

Our day finished around 11 pm. There were 99 steps from the basement to our bedrooms. The hundredth step into bed was always taken with a sigh of relief. Time off was one half day per week, with a half day every other Sunday. We had to be in by 10 pm. My pay was £2 per calendar month.

Later I was employed by a couple who treated me almost as one of the family – what a contrast! It was from this post that I was eventually married.'

'My father was head gardener at Norley Bank. He had eight under-gardeners, and the families of the outdoor staff were invited into Norley Bank's dining room at Christmas to receive presents from Mrs Pilkington. I can also remember being sent to the back door of the "big house" with a basin to get it filled with dripping by the resident cook.

When I was 14, I left school and went to "help out" at Norley Bank. My first duties were to carry up the meals for the nanny and children on the nursery landing. I went to live in at the "big house" when I was 15, packing a tin trunk with my clothes and crying bitterly on my first Sunday in residence. I was under-housemaid and my duties were to clean the entertaining rooms and to follow behind the housemaid as she served tea in the mornings, emptying the overnight "potties".

The servants' hall was where I had my meals with the other servants. The butler at one end of the huge table and the cook/housekeeper at the other. There was also a kitchenmaid, a between maid, parlourmaid, and head housemaid.'

MY FATHER THE CHAUFFEUR

'My father was a very handsome man and looked splendid in his navy blue chauffeur's uniform with peaked cap. The "Kollars" man called every week with the special cardboard box containing seven thick, white, stiffly starched collars in exchange for the box of used collars from the previous week.

The chauffeur's duties included one or two week-long trips a year to Harrogate or Bettws-y-coed with his employer and wife. My father would stay in the chauffeur's quarters at the best hotels there and eat, gossip and play cards with the other chauffeurs. During the other weeks of the year the "old lady" might wish to go shopping or visiting friends. Most of the time my father would be cleaning the cars or doing repairs wearing his blue boiler suit.

Our house was a beautiful place which went with the job. Tucked into the bend in the main road on the way down the hill into West Kirby, it had a wonderful view of the Welsh hills across the Dee. It had a strange design, being purpose-built only a couple of years before my parents went to live there. Downstairs was all garage with room for three or four cars (many years later the royal car was parked there while the Duke of Edinburgh visited Hilbre) and my father's workshop. The long wall of the house was completely filled with high folding wooden doors which concertinaed back to allow cars in and out on to the large concrete wash area.

Our flat was upstairs with large bedroom, living room and kitchen on the south side and bathroom and two smaller bedrooms off the central hallway on the north side. Except when we had visitors my sister and I had a bedroom each. They were rather dark, damp and noisy even in those days but we didn't really notice this. It was the steepest part of the hill and the double decker buses always changed gear on the corner just outside our windows, the noise echoed off the high sandstone retaining wall on the opposite side of the road. More exciting was the sound of several fire engines clanging past at great speed to deal with the inevitable hill fires every summer after a dry spell. By peering upwards from the windows we could often just see the smoke and flames. We longed to go and get a closer look but this was one thing we were not allowed to do.

The garden was huge and part of a much larger estate belonging to my father's employer. My father grew quite good fruit and vegetables in the poor, sandy soil and also kept hens.

All our neighbours lived in large detached houses with big gardens and as we were of a lower social class we didn't mix with them. There were no children living near us anyway and our friends were made at school. We are still friends 60 years later. Our employer's grandchildren were a little older than us and although the whole family were kind, considerate and friendly we just didn't mix socially. They went to a private school and later boarding school. We went to St Bridget's Church of England school and at the age of eleven passed the scholarship.'

SO MANY STAFF

'At the age of 14 I came to Heswall, entering into service with a shipowning family in Dawstone Road. It was a large house and had a very large garden. I was a between maid. It was hard work, up first to light the boilers and fires and to clean the kitchen and pans – in fact, I was a dogsbody. On the under-nanny's day off I had to help in the nursery too. The household servants were a nanny, an under-nanny, a housemaid, a parlourmaid, a between maid, a chauffeur, and there were two gardeners and an under-gardener. The family even had its own skating rink outdoors, but it was rarely used. I had half a day off a week and my wages were six shillings and eightpence a month. I stayed there for two or three years.'

'When the estate workers finished at Peover Hall, it was like a factory emptying, there were so many of them.'

STRAIGHT FROM SCHOOL

'I was born in 1898 and I left school at 13 and went into service nearby as a nursemaid to three children. There was Baby Alfred not a year, Nancy three and Lucy four. I was paid one shilling and sixpence a week. My mother used to come and do the washing. At other houses her washing was done by kneeling on the yard and scrubbing white coats and overalls (white was often worn in Crewe Works).'

'I am now well over 80, and I started work at the age of 15 as an under-housemaid at Thornton House, one of eight indoor and eight outdoor staff. I obtained the position through the Madame Emily Service Agency (signing on fee two shillings and sixpence). As well as looking after the little girl, one of my jobs was to look after the bathrooms – all seven of them. Brown's of Chester would make a special visit to the house at Thornton Hough to measure the staff for very smart uniforms; pink linen for the morning and maroon for the afternoon, with organdie cuffs, collar and bib apron.'

THE RAILWAY WORKS

The Works at Crewe employed many a local man, as did the railways throughout the county. Indeed, there was a time when a job at the Works was seen as 'bread for life', work was so secure.

A WORKING LIFE AT CREWE

'My interview with the Chief Clerk was held in the lovely ornate building known as the "General Offices". After being vetted by the doorkeeper, I proceeded down a long corridor (accompanied by my mother) to the room where the Chief Clerk operated. At that time I was still wearing short trousers, and I recall the clerk saying, as we were leaving his office, "You will, of course, be expected to wear long trousers and overalls when you commence employment in the workshops." The Second World War had started by the time I commenced my apprenticeship in this very large railway works, then known as the "LMS Loco Works".

On this first day of my working life, I was now classed as an adult, but not yet very confident. Entering a works which employed 7,000 people was a bit frightening, meeting so many types of people with different temperaments. Women were employed in the works during the war years; they were more pleasant to look at than the machinery and made life more interesting. My first job was in the Machine Shop, which was full of machines driven with flat belts from pulley wheels revolving in brackets along the walls of the shop. Imagine the noise from all these, plus the rattle of revolving bars in the lathes etc. I worked a nut tapping machine, which became rather boring after a while. My next job was working at a bench, using proper tools – like hammers, chisels and files. Burr filing, too became a little monotonous. As time went on the real skilled job came along, making face to face joints for steam valves, using red raddle, a face plate and a scraper. This work was done in the Fitting Shop, where it was a little quieter.

I was then moved to the Erecting Shop, commonly known as the "Madhouse". This massive shop housed all the steam engines which came in for repair, as well as building new ones. Two runways for overhead cranes spanned each bay, a ten ton crane on the lower runway and a 50 ton crane on the higher one. A permanent feature of this shop was the smoke from the burning metal, oil and soot, which crane drivers breathed in daily. It was amazing how they survived. The noise from the rivet guns and chisels was ear splitting. Hence the term "Madhouse", you were either deaf or daft after working in here!

Stripping steam engines was an extremely dirty job; at the end of the shift the only clean part of one's anatomy was the eyes and teeth. Washing facilities were not available when I started my apprenticeship, these came at a later date in the form of a long pipe with a series of holes in it, fitted to a wooden trough which had hot and cold water pipes and taps attached at one end. We were issued with a piece of soap but no towels. This situation improved a little when the women were employed.

All through the war years we had to work with artificial lighting in every shop. This affected our eyes when coming outside into the daylight, making them rather painful. The windows and sky-lights were blacked out.

When working on steam engines we were given a "duck-bill lamp", which had a wick protruding from a spout that was immersed in cleaning oil (turps). This wick would burn like a candle, emitting a lot of smoke. As well as providing light, this lamp was also used for warming tools during the very cold weather, and for heating rusty nuts on bolts to assist the removal of same, which were saved and re-used whenever possible.

Crewe Loco Works was self contained. Practically every part of the steam engines was made there. There were furnaces making steel, cast iron and brass, but copper was not manufactured. It was thrilling to see the wonderful machinery which made the various parts of the steam engines, such as hydraulic presses and rollers, plus massive steam driven drop hammers. The skill and teamwork of the men shaping a white hot block of metal under a steam hammer into side rods that linked the engine wheels together, was something to behold. The hydraulic driven rollers could shape a complete engine boiler from a flat piece of one inch (or more) thick sheet of cold metal.

Army tanks were also built in a small section of the Erecting Shop during the war time. This section was out of bounds to anyone other than the fitters employed on this work.

The age of steam came to an end in the late 1960s. The change over from steam to diesel traction and electric locomotives meant reorganisation of the works. The material used in the building of electric and diesel engines was purchased from other manufacturers, this meant an end to a lot of the machinery and equipment used in the making of steam engines.

The locomotive works starting in Crewe meant the whole town was built to accommodate workers for this industry. The skills of the railway workers were so great that Rolls Royce set up a factory in Crewe with the view to acquiring some of the skilled work force into their factory. The morale of the railway workers was good, they were conscientious and hard working.'

BREAD FOR LIFE

'Most men at Shavington in the early years of the century worked at the Crewe Railway Works, which was said to be "Bread for life and cheese for everlasting", work was so certain. My father worked in the country on a farm before going into the Works.

To get to the Works he had to walk about four miles to be there for 6 am. A buzzer sounded for breakfast at 8.15, back to work for 9 am, dinner of sandwiches from noon to one, then work until 5.30 and walk home again. There were no canteens so sandwiches were prepared at home, women rising early to pack bags with food and drink for their men. On arrival home at night there was a hot dinner before, perhaps, gardening. In winter it was just work and bed, with perhaps a game of dominoes. My father only earned £1 a week, bringing home 18 shillings.

The only transport at that time was Parton's brake, which some of the older men used from the Works in West Street, Crewe to Shavington post office. The brake held about twelve people. On a Friday night, late night shopping, some women from the village went back in the brake to Crewe, but had to walk home with their bags of shopping. It was a great occasion to ride in the brake.'

WORK ON THE LINE

'I was born in Shavington and my father worked for the railway. In January 1908, on a foggy morning, he and two other men were working on the line and all three were knocked down by a train and killed. His wage at the time was 17 shillings and sixpence a week. As compensation, the first year my mother was paid 15 shillings a week to keep herself and three young children. The second year this was reduced to ten shillings and the third year to five shillings – after this no payments were made. I clearly remember the day I came

152

home from school and was told my father had been killed. He used to have a straw bass (a basket) on his back to carry his work things and I would run to meet him as he often had oranges and apples in it for me.'

IT BELONGED TO THE LMS

'Nearly everyone, at some time in their life, has gone through or stopped to change trains at Crewe station. Perhaps not so many actually came off the station to visit Crewe, the uncrowned queen of railway towns. Nearly everything and, it seemed to me when I was a child, everyone, belonged to the LMS (London, Midland and Scottish). They owned the streets of tiny houses where my grandmother and aunts lived and where my mother was born. These had been built to house the employees of the company. Nearly everyone was employed in the railway works.

Their weekly comings and goings were dictated by "the buzzer" which blew at ten minutes to eight then five minutes to eight every morning to warn the men that it would soon be time for them to clock on for the eight o'clock shift. Then again at quarter past one and half past one dinnertime. This in the days when "dinner time" meant midday and not evening. Then again at half past five came the final buzzer of the day when it was time to knock-off. At half past five in the evening West Street would be filled with workmen in greasy overalls and flat caps walking or cycling home. The people of Crewe set their clocks and watches by that buzzer, more important to them than Big Ben. On alternate weeks my father went on the "two till ten" shift which meant we had to be very quiet when moving around the house as he slept during the day.

Way up the social ladder were the firemen and train drivers, who had to be wakened at all hours by the "knocker-up" employed by the railway company. It was his job to go round and either knock on the door or tap on the bedroom window with a long pole.

Of course, there were privileges for the ordinary workmen. My father was allowed one free pass or three or four quarter-fare passes a year, which meant we could travel to such exotic places as Bournemouth or even more exciting, Blackpool, for a week's holiday. Dad's outings were carefully planned for a day to the Tower of London or London Zoo. It was so exciting to be waiting on the station and to hear the oncoming train and see the clouds of cotton-wool steam. On my way home from school I had to go over one of the railway bridges and we children used to run like mad when we heard a train coming, so that we could get lost in the steamy clouds.

The LMS owned the electricity works, the gas works and the water works, and the baths where I almost learned to swim but was held back by the heavy orange and brown woollen bathing suit my mother had knitted for me. At least I always blamed it on the bathing suit!

The railway also owned The Crewe Arms hotel opposite the station. Willing porters whisked away the luggage of the more affluent passengers, leading them through a tunnel underneath the Nantwich Road bridge and straight into the hotel. Perhaps they still do!

Our one boast was our beautiful Queen's Park. The best in the North with its huge lake where we boated on Sunday afternoons and the colourful beds of flowers and black and white lodge at the front gate. There were banks of daffodils and standing amongst them Wordsworth's poem *I wandered lonely as a cloud* on a plaque. At the main entrance was a monument and a glass case with a model train that would set its wheels turning if we put a penny in the slot. The park, opened by Queen Victoria, was presented to the council by the LMS company.

Whenever New Year's Eve comes around I think of lying in bed as a child and shivering with excitement as on the stroke of twelve all the trains in the station would hoot. Then I knew that by kind permission of the LMS Company, a New Year had begun.'

THE INDUSTRIAL SCENE

Remember the days when everyone cycled to work and it was hard to cross the road when they all came out of the gates together? Just one of the things that have changed in our industrial scene over the years, of which these are a few glimpses, from silk to salt to ships.

AS I SAW IT

'I came to work for ICI in mid-Cheshire in January 1940, arriving at the height of the blizzard on the 27th which caused many roads to be closed, and the likes of which has not been experienced since. I joined the Winnington Research Laboratory and did not leave it until 1972. It had the flavour of a university about it. We worked late into the night and weekends, if the research needed it; and we had experts in many chemical fields. The job looked secure but people often spoke, in corners and hushed voices, of the many redundancies of "the slump" in 1932. Nevertheless, by 1940, the

154

view generally was that, once you were in ICI, you had to do something very wicked to be given the sack! There were lots of characters around and lots of extremely able people. Winnington Laboratory had long been able to outbid almost anyone else for the particular chemists, engineers and mathematicians they wanted; and it showed in the brilliant development work following on Gibson and Fawcett's discovery of polythene in the lab on 27th March 1933. In only two or three decades, polythene was to become the world's biggest selling plastic.

A big thing in research when I arrived was to do with the method of extracting salt out of the earth by "solution mining": earlier pumping of "wild brine" had given rise to extensive subsidence and the wholesale collapse of buildings in some areas. A number of the old people were able to relate from personal experience and in graphic and possibly exaggerated detail how an old pub "The Witch and Barrel" had sunk quite quickly one Saturday night into a hole that eventually became Ashton's Flash, a big water area (now filled by alkali waste). Not that I could follow their story easily; they spoke a rich Cheshire dialect which those from outside the county would find almost impossible to understand. That dialect has now gone.

The pioneering work on solution mining to avoid subsidence (now used world-wide) was most interesting to a bystander like me. Some years on, another great benefit of it became evident. One of the big worries in my early days at Winnington was the ever advancing area of the Weaver Valley covered by ugly lime-beds. Plainly, disposal of the inevitable lime-bed waste would take up enormous areas of farm land by the 1960s and 1970s and something had to be done. Ideas of sending it to sea proved unacceptable and, in the end, an elegant possible solution was researched and found good – the mud would be sent to the worked-out cavities in the rock salt layers beneath Holford Brine field. Some were bigger than St Paul's cathedral so there was plenty of room!

These were the days of works' buzzers which blew at accurate times of each day – to summon people to work or remind them to hurry. You corrected your watches by them! These too were the days of bicycles: at the lab and at each works there were sheds full to overflowing with hundreds of them, and they needed no locking! After "knocking-off time" there was a positively frightening stampede of them down Winnington Hill – a sight never to be forgotten! Traffic was thin: petrol rationing saw to that until after the war ended.

Meanwhile alkali manufacturing at Winnington and Wallerscote thrived, as it had done since Brunner and Mond started the factory in 1873; and being profitable, the gardens and the generosity of the company made life in ICI Alkali Division, as it was then, very pleasant. The company had what we'd call today a paternalistic attitude, providing employees with good dental, medical and other facilities, and many were the free concerts and "Sportsmen's Evenings" when prizes for all sorts of company sponsored events would be distributed. Perhaps the most persistent memories for all of us in the war years and soon after were the blackout and the shortages and the not-infrequent instances of "bad news". Few bombs fell on our area except from German raiders returning from Liverpool with a few bombs still to be released.

Polythene interests, except the historical, left mid-Cheshire in the 1950s; but most older people will recall the very loud explosions which characterised the operation of the polythene plants when they got out of control – the little pioneering one at Wallerscote and the bigger one at Winnington. This went on until polythene manufacture finally left the district. Perhaps we've forgotten too easily that the elegant research at super-high pressures in the 1930s which went on right through (and in spite of) "the slump" was to give rise to the world's biggest selling plastic – something worth celebrating!'

EVERYONE CYCLED

'In our area everyone, both boys and girls, thought they had done really well if they got a job at ICI, and everyone cycled to work, or walked if they lived close enough. At the research department where I worked, there were rows and rows of bicycle racks at the back of the building. In the crescent-shaped area at the front there was room for about eight or nine cars but never more than three or four were parked there. If you were late in the morning you could not find an empty space in the cycle racks. I believe it was quite frightening for the people of Northwich, as hordes of cyclists, riding four or five abreast, came sweeping down Winnington Hill and over the Town Bridge on their way home to the villages on the other side of town.'

THAT RUSH OF HUMANITY

'My father designed ships at Cammel Lairds, Birkenhead, so there was always excitement when ships like the *Mauretania, Ark Royal,* or *The Prince of Wales* were launched. I recall being taken on board the *Mauretania* and admiring all the different woods of the Empire lining the walls of the main lounge.

We used to meet Dad at the shipyard gates sometimes, and once the hooter sounded the rush of humanity would stream through the gates and you felt quite panicky in case you couldn't find the person you were looking for.

Living close to the Mersey, there were often dense fogs and the ferry boats sounded their foghorns as they signalled to one another. Another familiar sound was the one o'clock gun at Morpeth pier, which was a regular signal for the shipping trade until 1969 (except during the war, of course).'

'Most men in the area worked at Cammell Lairds shipyard, on the docks or the ferries, with others going to Lever's Port Sunlight and Shell at Ellesmere Port. Every morning at 7.20 we would hear marching. It was the men on their way to Lairds. They all walked and they all wore hobnailed boots. They came home at noon and back at one o'clock (marked by the gun), and home again at six.'

SILK MILLS AT MACCLESFIELD

'Machinery in the mills was driven by steam. It was the boilerman's job to keep the fires going under the boilers, throwing shovels of coal, by hand, on to the fires. About 80 years ago there were still some children working in the mills. At about the age of twelve years they would work mornings one week and afternoons the next. This was called "half timing". These children would go to school for half the day. They would start work at six o'clock in the morning with a break at about 8.30 am when they would either eat sandwiches which they had taken with them, or go home for breakfast if they lived nearby, returning to work until dinnertime. Full time workers' hours were 6 am to 6 pm. In the cotton mills and silk mills a "shade" was a room about 80 yards long, where thread was twisted. There would be two "twisters", men who twisted the thread on a twisting wheel. Each would have a "helper" – a boy runner, whose job it was to run from one end of the room to the other, all day, carrying the thread on bobbins. These helpers always ran barefoot. In the dye works all the dyeing was done in open vats by hand.'

SALT AT WINSFORD

'There were several salt firms in Winsford at the beginning of the Second World War, amongst them Hamletts and the Salt Union, later to be ICI. The Salt Union stretched along the side of the river Weaver from Winsford to Meadow Bank. The rock mine head was situated at Meadow Bank and below ground was a huge cavern.

During the war, paintings, important papers, etc, were brought from London for storage here, as the atmosphere below ground was very suitable for their safe keeping.

The salt was made by pumping up brine and then boiling it in large pans situated along the roadside between Meadow Bank and Winsford; the resulting salt crystals were used to produce table salt,

Stripped to the waist because of the heat, a cart is loaded in one of the salt mining "sweatshops".

cattle locks, etc. The rock salt was not as pure, so was used to spread on the roads in winter. The salt was taken by boat down the Weaver to Liverpool and then distributed abroad.

Men worked, stripped to the waist, in the steaming hot conditions. Their children were allowed to leave school early at lunchtime to take "baggin" to their fathers.

At one stage, "bass houses" built from the clinker produced in the ovens where the brine was boiled, were used to house Polish workers brought over to work in the salt industry (perhaps because of local troubles). These houses were very basic and full of cockroaches and other vermin.

Winsford was a very working class town with many chapels. The Co-operative Society was extremely strong, with grocery, furniture, shoe, butchery and funeral departments. There was also a "Zan" shop in the High Street selling ironmongery of every sort; this business was centred at Wheelock, where they made dyes, polishes, soft soaps, brushes, mops, dusters and other cleaning agents. There were 16 Zan shops in all, variously in Middlewich, Winsford, Crewe and Sandbach, with large vans touring the rural areas regularly selling items such as paraffin, soft soap, galvanised buckets and mops.'

SUBSIDENCE

'It is well documented that many buildings sank because of salt mining in the Northwich area, but one road vanished almost overnight and that was the continuation of Chapel Street, across Ollershaw Lane, Wincham and is known now as Witton Flashes. Along this stretch two public houses sank, one being the Townsend Arms but known locally as The Old Wytch or sometimes The Wytching Devil. However, the washplace from there was saved and brought by tractor and horse to the back of a two room cottage and re-erected. The cottage was on Lennards Lane at Wincham, adjacent to Rayner's shop, the owners of which were the only people at that time to have electricity because they owned their own generator.

Mr Walter Boon, the publican, built the two houses known as Warren's Lake Cottages and a previous resident remembers her father telling her that all the doors came from The Wytching Devil.

Because of subsidence a "lifting principle" was found and one could go down steps to a shop one week and after the property had been lifted, go up steps thereafter.

In 1915 children were taken to see the first subsidence caused by the pumping of brine, the land falling in and then filling with water. It became known as "The Old Hole" and as the chemical industry needed more brine, pumping up went on, the ground subsidence worsened and the hole widened and deepened. Boats were moored at the back door of houses to enable a quick getaway, especially those buildings close to the hole.'

OTHER WAYS WE MADE A LIVING

There were of course dozens of other ways we made a living, from traditional crafts such as the wheelwright, to salmon net fishing, to running a shop or fustian cutting. Villages were often self sufficient and industrious places, where trades and services were carried on for the local community. Here are just a few jobs from the past.

FUSTIAN CUTTING AT LYMM

'My grandfather, Henry Daniels, introduced fustian cutting to Lymm. At 14 he went to Manchester to learn the trade. He then bought a "piece" (a roll) of fustian and tried out the cutting on a frame at his home in Booths Hill. He set up a shop in the side road at the back of the house, an area at that time called "the rookery". The pieces, oatmeal coloured, came by packet boat and steamer along the Bridgewater Canal from Manchester and were put off at Statham. One steamer was named the *Duchess Countess*.

After cutting, the pieces were returned to Manchester for dyeing and finishing. My mother helped him by doing business for him in Portland Street, Manchester, which was easily reached by train from Lymm. She also used to cut. I can just remember being taken by her as a little child to the cutting shop and being laid underneath the tables. This custom was not unusual for women with babies.'

'I was born in 1896 in Clay Terrace (Cherry Lane) and like my parents and grandparents have always lived in Lymm.

I was 16 when I started fustian cutting. My father didn't want me to go out to work at all, but my mother taught me how to cut and then she gave up working herself. I was apprenticed to Mr Cowper in Cherry Lane for two years. He employed about 14 people. We had to walk along a table called a frame, on one side and back down the other, cutting as we went. I used to get paid 35 shillings a week. The men got a little more and they earned extra if they worked all Saturday. I worked 77 hours a week, from 8 am to 7 pm. We had an hour for dinner and half an hour for tea. On Saturdays we went from 6 to 8.30 am, then from 9 to 12 with half an hour for dinner, finishing at 2 pm. I went home for dinner as we lived near. We were then renting one of Mona Villas, West Hyde, owned by Mr Moston.

He asked Mother if she would like a bigger house and she said she would. His cutting shop was next door and I could watch the workers there before I ever learnt to cut. I remember a Mrs Smith who was able to cut with a knife in each hand, which was exceptionally skilful. The shop was by the canal and the pieces from Manchester were unloaded there.

If you only had one length to cut you had one candle, but if you were on the long run you had two. Candles were the only light in the shop and we had to bring our own. We bought them from Harry Mort, one of many grocers in Booths Hill Road. We also provided our own aprons. These were of white cotton with big bows at the back. The girls took great pride in their aprons and looked very smart. At bonfire time they used to tie rip-raps on the end of the ties, for a bit of fun. The women took their babies with them to work and laid them down under the tables until dinner time and again during the afternoon.

Sometimes we made mistakes in cutting by making a hole with the knife and guide, but the piece wasn't wasted, the men used to come and have a look at it and get us round it and we would go on again. However, if we made a long mark with the knife we were reprimanded. If you were cutting a piece you went on till it was finished. I remember Maggie, she hadn't finished hers and she had two lengths to cut, which meant two hours' work, but she had been paid for it so it had to be done. I said, "Never mind some of us will stay with you while you finish," and we did. Maggie said to me, "You know Elsie, see this money, it will all have to be turned over," and I said mine would also. We had to give all our money to our mothers, there was no holding a little bit back. If we wanted anything Mother would buy it, or give us the money, but we were very poor. Normally we shopped at the local shops, but went to Warrington for anything special. It cost sevenpence on the train.'

THE WHEELWRIGHT

'My father, Albert Glover, was a wheelwright working for Wallasey Corporation in the 1940s and 1950s (all Wirral was in Cheshire then). The yard was in Mill Lane where the fire station is now and also Mary Mount convent school; it covered a large area and all the various tradesmen had their own "shop", where they kept the tools and materials of their trade. Each would have labourers and at least one apprentice commonly known as the "can-lad". He would have to make tea in cans, which were usually enamel with a wire handle and a lid which served as a cup. Because sugar was hard to come by after the war the tea was sweetened by condensed milk if they were lucky enough to have some.

My father made wheels for waggons, many of which were still horse-drawn, handcarts, and wheelbarrows that the workmen used, also ladders. His workshop resembled a blacksmith's shop with a fire in the centre of the floor where the metal for the wheels was heated and shaped with much hammering. The metal was then given a wooden rim and spokes. My strongest memory is the smell of wood shavings and the glue which was always kept warm in a pot on the fire. It was made of cast iron. My father took great pride in his tools which were always kept sharp and clean. As an apprentice most of your wages would be spent on tools as none were supplied by the employer.

My brother's godfather, George Clark, worked as time-keeper at the yard. He had a small office which was just inside the gates and nothing passed him unnoticed. Men came and went all day going to various jobs in and around the borough, all duly recorded in a ledger. He wore a watch and chain across his waistcoat and he was always checking the time with this and the large clock which was on the wall outside the office. He was the person who rang the bell at midday for lunch. The signal for going back to work was a hooter which was blown at 12.55 pm down at the gas works in Gorsey Lane, which you could hear from a long way off.

I also remember the lamplighters. Street lights were gas and were switched on and off by a hook on a long pole which the experienced lamplighter could manage without getting off his bike! He would also, for a "bob", one shilling, knock on the window to wake you up for work.'

'My Grandad was the village wheelwright at North Rode. When he made a farm cart the wheels had to have an iron rim round them. It was looked on as a great day when this was done. We called it "hooping day". We lived by the river Dane so we had to collect water from there and fill every available old bath, bucket, dolly tub and anything else we could find, because when the hoop was placed on the new wheel it began to blaze. My Grandad and two more men had "dogs" to hold the hoop, while we poured water on to it. They went round it knocking the iron into shape. My Grandad used to get very worked up about it!'

'At Comberbach there was a wheelwright who was also the local undertaker, and it was said that when he went to the public house he always had a tape measure in his pocket!'

BUILDING UP A BUSINESS

'I have vivid recollections of a much admired and loved grandmother who was widowed at an early age and left with four young children, the oldest girl twelve years. In much reduced circumstances, Elizabeth Thursfield settled down to earn money and bring up her family. Her parents had been haberdashers from Swansea. She built up a trade in socks, stockings and underwear, first on market stalls and then in shops. Elizabeth had a sister, Ada (Auntie Redboots, who used oxblood polish on her shoes) who had been a cook in Wales and who came to Crewe with her husband, Uncle Arthur, a confectioner, who came to work at the new Co-op. Crewe was the fast growing railway centre.

Grandmother Elizabeth was successful. She sold to farmers' wives who came to market. She was a little lady, five feet tall. She had samples of material and was prepared to make milking bonnets, maids' dresses and aprons, open drawers, chemises, underbodices, pinafores, nightshirts etc. Time went on and she acquired a new machine for knitting stockings (presumably an American or German invention) – the latest thing. She took orders one week and had them ready the next. She worked through the night on occasions. As she sewed, her young daughter (my mother) would iron the seams flat and the boys would trim the seams. She developed a good trade in knitting replacement feet on old worn stockings. This was not popular with the local man who started a new knitting factory! Work was strictly for cash. She was able to found a business which kept my mother and her brothers, and educated them until interrupted by the First World War, invest in five houses and then other properties, and set the daughter and sons up in business.

At first stock was moved from market stalls by handcart and railway to Nantwich, Sandbach and Market Drayton and then a Ford van was bought. Later a glorious Arrol-Johnston c1922 open tourer car with real leather seats and ivory handles was acquired.

As a little girl, I learned to count sorting out the "takings" from the stalls and shops, counting the halfcrowns and pennies, threepenny bits and farthings, putting the old white five pound notes in rolls with a paper band. I can remember gold money, sovereigns and half sovereigns, being brought in by farmers. They had to be put in leather bags. Much bargaining went on and was settled with a handshake.

Granny employed girls to help in the home. Lizzie was engaged to her chap. He was in "Hafrica" and was going to marry her when he got home. She had a link of "Hamber" beads to prove it. Like thousands of others he never did come back.

In winter Crewe market was lit by kerosene lamps. People would come to buy at the market on Friday and Saturday evenings. My father took over the stalls that Grandma had had for over 25 years. The mass of the people came after tea, ie after 6.30 pm, purchasing carpets, shirts, bloomers, blouses, jumpers, anything and everything. In the outside market people sold patent medicines. A lady with long hair (she would sit on it) sold hair restorer guaranteed to make a bald man's hair grow. Mrs Laycock sold fish, rabbits, ducks and chickens.

My job was selling in the shop. We sold virtually everything: millinery, dresses, mantles, children's clothes, schoolwear, blankets, rugs, macs. Twilfit, Vyella, Wolsey, Bear Brand, nightwear, dusters, rugwool. There was a showroom upstairs and a cash dispenser from downstairs which took cash upstairs on a wire in a series of balls of wood which opened and disgorged the change.

The shop opened at 9 am sharp and remained open until 8 pm and 9 pm on Saturday. There was a room for the staff, with a pot-bellied American stove. Tea and lunch were taken in shifts. I went home for tea and ran all the way there and back. The rush started about 5.30 pm. Friday and Saturday we stayed open until the takings from the market stalls were brought in, left the shop about 10.15 and then home to supper.

Customers became friends. They had a routine to come at certain times. The Dabbers (Nantwich people) came in Friday and Saturday evenings. Coppenhall folk came on Friday afternoons and early evening.

Christmas Eve we stayed open as long as anyone was there to buy. Once it was nearly midnight. I remember one very "jolly" farmer driving his great horse up to the shop door, the metal hooves raising sparks from the pavement, shouting for his missus to come now or, "I bin goin' without ye!"'

UPHOLSTERING

'In 1933 I was a 14 year old starting an apprenticeship to become an upholsteress, a part of my life which I look back on with great pleasure. The apprenticeship was for five years, which started at the age of 15.

The first twelve months I did all sorts of jobs, the first one being darning the boss's socks. Every day I had to brush the workroom floor, make the tea three times a day for 20 of us, and go shopping every morning for whatever the women wanted for dinner time. The list was very long to me at that time. The shops included the market butchers, for a chop costing fourpence was a good sized chop too, and if the person that asked for it didn't like it I was sent back with it for another one. Then if it was anyone's birthday, they bought everybody a cake and up Grange Road I would have to go to Sayers for those, all different of course. When I eventually arrived back at work, I had to go to the mess room which was at the very top of the building, up five flights of iron stairs, where there was a cooker and I cooked whatever the women had brought for their dinner, chops, chips, boiled potatoes, roast potatoes, and an assortment of vegetables.

After my first year was over, I began to really serve my time. That was very different but I still had to brush the floor after five o'clock when the women had gone home. It meant I could be taught how to sew carpets, that was quite a tough job. In those days, carpets were all sewn by hand, seamed together and cross stitched all round with steel rings sewn on every six inches apart. There was a two inch turn-under all round too.

Another year on I was sewing loose covers, making curtains and bedspreads. Most of the work was for shipping, so we had bags and bags of repair work to do, mostly table linen, table napkins and bed linen; also loose covers and carpets and curtains. One job I really used to hate was having to go up to what we called "the feather room" to sew up 500 or 600 feather pillows. Two of the boy apprentices used to fill them and that meant we used to lark about up there and they would throw us girls in the feather bin and we'd be covered in feathers, of course, and we'd spend ages trying to clean ourselves up before we returned to the sewing room, hoping the forewomen wouldn't notice.

A few more years on, when I had become proficient at the work, I was sent with an upholsterer to ships when they docked to do repairs on board. I used to like that. I felt very important being sent on a ship. I also went to private houses to sew carpets. The men would lay and fit them, then usually two of us would sew round them and sew the rings on. I still loved my job in spite of it being a bit tough at times.

Now the war came and I was called up to work at Broughton at Vickers Armstrong, where they made Wellington and Lancaster bombers. I did a variety of jobs there, using spanners and electric drills and riveting guns. It wasn't bad and we made the best of things. I did the night shift for four years. It was there I met my husband, and left there to marry in 1945.'

THE PRODUCE ROUND

'I remember when I was three years old learning which days were village days. My parents had a produce round in the local village of Alderley Edge and straight after breakfast on Tuesdays and Saturdays there was the business of getting the horse harnessed to the cart and taken round to the pinky-puce coloured "shop", which was a shed with a corrugated roof. It got this name because long ago when my aunts and uncles were at home, produce was sold from here to the locals. Here were all the vegetables, weighed out the day before into small sacks. They held either one, two or three lots of potatoes, peas etc, depending on whether they were in two, three, six or even twelve pound lots. At this age I liked to help with the weighing and it was impressed upon me that after the scale had gone down a few extra pods etc were thrown on, as these kinds of vegetables particularly, lose weight, and the customer must always have an ounce or two extra for his money than less weight. How often I think of this nowadays.

My parents were very fair to their customers and wanted to keep their good name for first class produce and honest business. I can remember my mother snapping a runner bean every so often when weighing to make sure they were not overgrown and stringy.

There was a fine art of loading up the cart. Baskets of eggs and chickens were put carefully out of harm's way under the high seat with larger hampers of vegetables at the back. Potatoes were thrown in the front where it didn't matter if your feet rested on the bags.

My father often walked up the steep hill near our house to save the horse from being over-burdened. How I loved to sit safely between Mum and Dad for the two and a half miles to the top of Alderley hill, which was considered dangerous to traffic in those days. I cannot remember actually going with them until I was school age, but even then I realised how very much pleasanter it was to survey the countryside from the high seat of a float than in a low stuffy car.

One day they came home and told us about their amusing journey that morning. On reaching the main road they had seen the tail end of a circus travelling to Macclesfield and had seen several elephants. On the way to Alderley they knew that the enormous piles of droppings at intervals along the road were made by elephants. No oncoming motorists knew this, of course, and each one in turn registered wonder and amazement, and my parents had many a laugh as some looked so amazed it seemed they couldn't believe their own eyes, and kept leaning out of their cars in disbelief.

All the houses and farms around here are built of red bricks and I remember being quite surprised the first time I saw some of the really big houses down what we called the front and back hills into Alderley Edge. These had been built at the time of the big cotton boom in Manchester. Mum said she believed that at one time there were more millionaires living there than in any other place (perhaps London excepted). These houses were made of yellow bricks and stood in huge gardens.

Sometimes at the bigger houses there was no one to answer the back door if the servants had gone to the shops. My father told me exactly where I would find the dish for eggs or a bowl for vegetables, and stipulated that one did *not* look around or touch anything else. I was so careful to do as I was told that I don't think I would have seen even the most exciting toy in another part of the kitchen!

When I was smaller and went with my father I had more chance to look around while the cook was ordering for next time. At home we did all our cooking over the fire in our living room, and I remember being struck by the really big kitchens with their huge cupboards and cooking ranges, and the complete lack of workaday clothes hanging behind doors or drying over chairs.

Some people used to envy my parents riding round in a horse and cart, but it was extremely tiring once they started delivering, and many times they got cold and wet.'

SALMON NET FISHING

'The oldest surviving industry in Chester is salmon net fishing. In 1960, I was 14 and I can still remember many of the old-time netsmen from Greenway Street, Handbridge. They were a breed of men which has now vanished from society – all society. Charley Davies (Chango), Johnny Spencer, Peter and Dickie Walsh and many, many more, all now gone. I began to fish at the age of 13, and many of the fishermen I got to know well were old men then; I must say that they seemed ancient to me!

Nylon nets were unknown then. Everything was hand-knitted from hemp string and then tarred to preserve the twine and stiffen the net sheeting to help reject twigs and sticks, which tend to cling to a limp net.

The boats were all made of wood – 16 to 18 foot long, larch on oak, and all made to a set pattern by Taylors of The Boatyard, Whipcord Lane, Chester. These boats were very weatherly – shallow of draft, beamy, very estuaral boats. They were also, as I soon found out, very heavy to row. I nursed many blisters until my hands hardened up. Before my time there were sails on the boats and long trips down river, sometimes lasting days, but that is another story.

I can vividly remember my Grandmother Bellis – strongly independent and fair, having raised four sons, all salmon fishermen, living in a cottage in River View (up the Broad Entry) off Greenway Street. These cottages have gone now – they were two up and two down, with a flagged yard at the rear. I can remember wandering around that small yard as a tiny boy – the smells of tar and hemp twine, the mustiness of netting hung in the lean-to for storage. The

Salmon fishing in the Dee at Handbridge, Chester. One of the oldest local industries, the old fishing communities are now gone.

old galvanised bath, used for tarring the net, hanging from its nail on a wall. Bits of leather, old fishing needles, waders, coils of rope, new and used, corks to float the net hung in garlands inside that lean-to. Spare anchors, large and small, oilskin coats, black and stiff, mud still clinging to them. And a cat who watched, curious yet uncaring.

In the summer, the old ladies would sit on their doorsteps in the sun, all in shawls and long skirts. They had a fine view. Facing them, the Croft or Craft, always containing some horses, rolling down to the Stakes, rows of wooden posts lining the river bank. Maybe eight or nine ranks of them, there since before anyone could remember, where nets were hung, or repaired, or tarred.

They would see some boats riding at anchor and down river the imposing Grosvenor Bridge. All gone now – the site levelled and nothing built on it – weeds and tall nettles with perhaps a brick here and there and maybe that cat . . .

Greenway Street is still there with its sharp cobbled incline. Most of the fishing cottages have long gone – and with them the fishermen. Salmon netting, in decline though it is, must surely be Chester's oldest industry and possibly the most unappreciated.

I can remember going fluke (flounder) fishing with my uncle and a friend of his when I was 15. We motored down to the vicinity of

Flint Castle, in the boat, on a very cold night in October and fished our way back upriver on the morning tide.

The run of the tide took control of our nets and we became entangled with some marker poles or "perches" as we swam the nets upriver. We freed ourselves with difficulty and some bad language, made even worse when the fouling of the nets caused many flukes to escape as we drew the nets aboard, flying free to fall back into the water like white enamel dinner plates. It was bitterly cold and we were tired and hungry. I seem to be able to remember that trip in more detail than things which happened last week.'

THE BOILED HAM SHOP

'My parents purchased with their life savings a boiled ham shop in Macclesfield. The year was 1937. This shop was situated on Park Green opposite the fountain, a landmark in Macclesfield but which was demolished for scrap iron during the war.

They sold only home-boiled ham, ox tongue and pickles. My father had a big boiler in a shed at the back of the shop, and boiled about eight to ten hams in one boiling. The hams were cooked, drained, trimmed and garnished with breadcrumbs and parsley. I seem to remember the boiler reminding me of a witches' cauldron, always bubbling. Three hams were always placed in the window on very large stands, the others kept ready for cutting. Mother and Father stood behind the counter in white coats, with carving knives at the ready. Even now I can smell the lovely aroma of the fresh cooked ham. This sold at ninepence a quarter, and tongue sold at tenpence a quarter.

There was quite a lot of cutting on the discarded ham bones and they were in great demand. You could put your name down for them – sixpence to ninepence each. One particular Saturday, two ham bones were ordered for a wedding reception. They were to be collected on the following Saturday morning. A man called to collect them and remarked to my mother, "No need to wrap them up missus . . ." – but of course my mother insisted. On enquiring how the wedding went, it appeared at the end of the "do" the bride hit the bridegroom with the bone.

Alas, the war took over and as a consequence of food rationing no more hams were available. So we had to close the old ham shop. Its friendly customers gone who were always prepared to wait and chat while the ham was cut. This was the end of an era never to return.'

INDUSTRIOUS VILLAGES

'When our family moved into Rainow in 1948 it was still a real old-fashioned village. There were two schools, Church of England and Methodist, and both church and chapel were active. We were among the earliest "outsiders" to reside in the village and one of the earliest questions was, "Are you church or chapel?" We, being Quakers, caused some curiosity and surprise. Early on we learned to be careful in speaking about any resident in the village since most were related and inter-married.

The parish (Rainow with Saltersford) is one of the most extensive in England and was, in 1948, predominantly agricultural. There was also quarrying and great logs of stone would go to the local sawmill to be sawn into slabs. Sheep grazed the higher land but the village farms were mainly dairy and the 18-gallon churns of milk would be taken to the lane ends to be collected. There were only about ten cars in the village when we first arrived and travel was largely by bus, the first at 6.30 am and the return fare fivepence. Horses were still in use and the tractor a rarity. I recall an old Fordson (in regular use) with steel wheels instead of tyres.

Many people were employed in farming, for apart from the horsemen, all the milking was done by hand. Often a school lad would work on the farm before and after school. Hand milking affected me professionally for as an oculist I had to attend to corneal injuries from flicking cows' tails and from cows' horns. Other farming casualties were from scratches to the eye from straw and from husks of corn sticking to the cornea. Hedging could be a source of eye injury, for goggles were not worn. Other eye injuries came from quarry work, with flying bits of stone or a metal chip which might penetrate the eye with serious consequences. Prior to my appointment in Macclesfield such casualties would travel to Stockport Infirmary or the Eye Hospital in Manchester. Villagers with such eye troubles were welcomed at our back door and this saved much time and unnecessary travel.

The village had its own builders, plumbers and decorators, many of the families still in existence. Other workers went to the mills in Macclesfield and to Bollington (reached by a flagged footpath across the fields to Ingersley) where silk and cotton were still worked. Some outworkers made trimmings etc at home. The villages had five shops (including the post office). Milk was delivered from the farms by horse-drawn floats or on foot.

The roads of the village were kept in order by lengthsmen. The work was all hand done with brushes, shovels and a wheelbarrow and the verges of the roads were always beautifully neat and tidy. The gulleys were emptied by using a long-handled scoop. Piles of grit left by the roadside would be spread by hand with a sweeping motion from a shovel.'

'The post office at Thelwall was also the bakery and general shop. It was quite a small place and if you went in with a couple of mates to spend a halfpenny or penny you had to make up your mind quickly which sweets you wanted or you were told to get out and stop "cluttering up" the shop. One son was the baker and he and his brother took over all the business when the parents retired. It was quite an occasion when the carrier bike was replaced with a Ford motor van for the deliveries. Of course, women expected the daily orders of food to be brought to the door, and sometimes it was ten or eleven o'clock at night when they got to our house when they only had the bike.

The letters and parcels were delivered and collected by horse-drawn mail van from Warrington. Telegrams were phoned through from Warrington and if the man was out on his bread round a schoolchild would deliver the telegram, being rewarded with a few sweets. The postman lived nearby and it would take him all day to walk round the very large area he had to cover. Local mail was sorted at the post office and cards posted on Christmas Eve were delivered on Christmas Day (those were the days). The postman's wife was the school cleaner but most of the dust landed on our desks

A typical village high street complete with ironmonger's shop.

171

or the wooden beams instead of her dustpan. As boys we used to gather in the space between the post office and her garden wall to play but if the ball went over the wall we never saw it again, goodness only knows what she did with them!

The four farms by the post office no longer exist but then the milkman had one of them and he used a pony and trap to carry the big milk churn and would ladle out the amount you wanted into your can or jug. There were no milk bottles in those days. The milk was delicious, quite a different taste to now.

The coal was brought in waggons to the station and there it was put into one hundredweight sacks. It was hard and dirty work shovelling the coal into the sacks, weighing each one and carrying it on your back to load the horse-drawn coal cart ready for delivery. The coalman's sons also ran the evening paper round delivering the *Manchester Evening News* and the *Liverpool Echo* which came by train.

The muffin man used to come from Warrington by tram to Latchford and then walk to Thelwall with a huge basket filled with muffins on his head. He would do his rounds throughout the parish and then walk back to Latchford.

The cobbler worked in a wooden hut and it was a favourite place for boys of my age to go and watch him at work. We were all fascinated by his treadle stitching machine but never allowed to touch it. It was most interesting to see him carry out a complete repair on the boots, clogs and shoes. He could also make boots and shoes. Another favourite venue for us boys was the smithy, where as well as watching the horseshoes being made and fitted on the horses' hooves we would see farm implements being made and repaired. The most fascinating was the making and fitting of the red hot iron tyres on to the rims of the wooden wheels which had been made in the wheelwright's shop around the corner. After the smithy closed down one smith worked for a Warrington firm until his retirement. Just before he died, some years ago now, he was commissioned to repair and restore the stocks in the next village of Grappenhall; he was considered to be one of the last men of his craft in the district.

The wheelwright's shop still exists but is now used for another business. Then complete farm carts and lorries were made there and also, to the morbid fascination of us small boys, coffins, for the wheelwright was also the undertaker.

The men who worked the pontoon ferry across the Ship Canal had both been in the Royal Navy. One had been a ship's tailor and he kept a sewing machine in the ferry hut and besides doing repairs made fancy dress costumes for girls and boys, for fancy dress dances were very popular at that time.

Further along the canal bank stood the huge wooden shed where many men were employed making the huge lock gates of greenheart wood for the Ship Canal. It is very hard, water-resistant wood from the tropical swamps of South America but if you got a splinter in your finger you could not pull it out, the wood just breaks up and causes a septic infection. It was a great sight watching these huge gates being launched down the slipway into the canal and then towed away by tugs and cranes. The gates are now dealt with at Runcorn and bungalows were built on the site here in the late 1950s.'

THE MILLER

'I was a miller's daughter living in Bate Mill, and married the son of a local competitor and became a miller's wife living in Siddington Mill at Marton. I had two maids – in those days labour was cheap and the tasks of running a home and the associated entertaining before modern conveniences such as electricity, were never ending.

Siddington Mill employed six men and corn was used as barter against debt with local farmers and businesses. Any corn over was taken to Handforth by horse and cart and was sent for sale to Manchester with the corn merchants who came out to collect it. My father regularly rode a bicycle with a Gladstone bag on the handlebars which contained the proceeds of the sale – approximately 100 guineas in sovereigns and guineas – from Handforth to Siddington in complete safety!'

GATHERING HERBS

'One memory is gathering herbs as children in September. We gathered these on Kerridge, being the best source. We then took them down on the Saturday morning to Pleasence Street, opposite Hurdsfield church, where a man who had a donkey and cart paid us. He weighed them and we had to keep them separate. There was a different price for each – burdock, feverfew, yarrow, comfrey, ten kinds, even nettles (although the price for them was very low). We used to try all ways to bump up the price, wet them or add a few stones, but I don't remember getting away with it much. As I remember it, we probably got about two shillings or so each. It was not much for the work involved, but there was fierce competition for the work. I remember one boy who was persuaded that the man paid for thistles for his donkey (so he was really unlucky that week).

I think these herbs were taken to Cecil Woods at Hazel Grove. The pills and powders were on sale at all the small shops and were for every ailment known, almost, and they were used a lot. It must have been quite a large business.'

WAR & PEACE

THE GREAT WAR 1914–1918

Though the fighting took place far away reminders of the conflict were ever present, from the occasional Zeppelin to food shortages and, of course family tragedies. Then it was over at last, with joy and with sorrow.

LIFE WAS NEVER THE SAME AGAIN

'Came 4th August 1914 and the First World War began. In Crewe all social activities stopped and many sad things happened to our community. Life was never the same again.

A company of soldiers called the Crewe Artillery practised with horse-drawn carriages in the fields near our home. All tradespeoples' horses were commandeered to pull the gun carriages, if the horse measured the required height. By this time, our old horse Jessie had died and my father had a chestnut mare called Dolly. He was terribly sad because he loved horses. However, Dolly was one hand too small for army needs, so happily she did not have to go.

We watched the boys and the artillery go away, waving and saying, "We'll be back for Christmas!" They thought it was a sort of Boy Scouts' jamboree. None of them came back. Their group was wiped out.

My father and brother were not eligible for the army but I will never forget that when we saw a youth on a red telegraph bicycle he was usually bringing a telegram from the War Office. Who was it for this time? It meant tragedy for some family, and he did not always call only once. All my life, I have never liked telegrams.

There were posters everywhere with Lord Kitchener pointing and saying "Your Country Needs You". Conscription had not been brought in at that time. A lot of our local young men dashed off to join a regiment called the Liverpool Pals. This group were pretty well wiped out. My best friend at school was called Emma. She had an uncle who was a skilled engineer in the Royal Navy and had served on the same ship as George V when a young officer. He was a hero to us girls at school. One dreadful dark day we heard that the ship he was serving on, the *Hampshire,* had been torpedoed with Lord Kitchener aboard. There was no hope for "Uncle Matt" as it was his job to stay below decks and keep the engines turning for as long as possible.

However, it was not all doom and gloom. When you are young you manage to find enjoyable activities in spite of troubles.

On 11th November, 1918 the Armistice was signed. At 11 am all the works' hooters and train whistles were sounded. People came rushing out of workshops and offices. The whole country was delirious with joy!'

SADNESS AND SHORTAGES

'The First World War was well on and everyone was knitting hats, gloves and socks. The large vicarage at Witton was now a hospital. We used to see the soldiers on warm days sitting or lying in their cots on the lawns. Some who could walk to the shops could get "cigs" and sweets. They were dressed in bright blue suits with red ties. One day my mother took me to Runcorn to see her aunt. When we got there we found her very upset, and then she told us she hadn't heard from her son for a long time. Mother had a little weep on the train home and, as she said, he was one of her favourite cousins. Later on we heard he was safe and that he had won the Victoria Cross. This was the first VC won by the Cheshire Regiment in the First World War. His medal is in the museum in Chester Castle and in Chester Cathedral in the Regimental Chapel is a brass plate with his name on, Tom known as "Togger Jones" or "Todger".

Coming home from school one day I saw what I thought was a silver balloon flying over the chapel. At night I told my father about this and he agreed, but not the kind you could play with. It was indeed a German Zeppelin sent to bomb the chemical works but because the smoke and mist over the river was so thick the "Zep" passed over. Wigan was not so lucky. The bomb came down near the river and store buildings. Unlucky Wigan pier.

We were very sad one day. Father told us that Mr and Mrs Heine, a German couple who had a butcher's shop, had killed themselves. They were such nice people, but they couldn't stand the jeers and damage done to their shop from the people around.

One day we heard the fire engine bells ringing and the horses galloping up the street with the firemen hanging on. Later we saw all the girls running home shouting, "The factory is on fire." They meant, of course, the munitions factory. We thought how lucky we were that it was built in a field away from the town. We never saw the damage, it was too well guarded.

During these war years when vegetables and potatoes were in very short supply my two elder brothers and sister would get up early on Saturday morning and walk three miles to a farm and then carry a bag each of at least five pounds of potatoes and anything else that would help my mother to feed us for the next week. One thing we children did enjoy was to come home from afternoon Sunday school to the smell of potato cakes browning at the bottom of the old oven. These were soon demolished with either syrup or treacle, especially on a cold winter day. My mother was always trying to make wartime rations into good meals. When father's fishing tackle came out we hoped he would be lucky. If he caught a pike it was boned and stuffed with anything to make it tasty, like sausagemeat and herbs. It was then roasted, again at the bottom of the old oven. Where my father did his fishing lived a kind gamekeeper who sometimes gave him a rabbit. This was cooked with bacon ribs and finished off with suet dumplings. The gamekeeper's wife was a dear lady. She used to tell me lovely stories of her childhood. Her father and grandfather were coachmen to the Duchess of Marlborough and when she was old enough she started work as a "tweeny" at Marlborough House. The cook gave her strict orders never to let a little fat boy called Winston get near her pantry as he would eat everything there. As she was the same age as him it was a very tough job. She lived until she was over 90 years old so she lived to see him as the Prime Minister.'

PRISONERS AND SOLDIERS

'I was eight years old when the war ended. During the war we used to watch the German prisoners being marched on to the marshes to clean ditches. The recreation hall at Helsby had been turned into a hospital for wounded soldiers, complete with operating theatre. I can remember seeing wounded soldiers in basket wheelchairs, drawn by donkeys. There was a nurse in attendance and they drove round Carriage Drive on Helsby Hill.'

RATS AND SPARROWS

'At Dodleston school the boys started collecting rats' tails for a penny each and also sparrows' heads. They were paid for this as a way of preventing damage to crops.'

THE PLAGUE OF CATERPILLARS

'An event which occurred in 1917 or 1918 was a real calamity for a few farmers in Saltersford, centred on Greenstacks Farm, which was then farmed by the Hill family. This was a plague of caterpillars and these devastated an area of about one square mile. I was only about nine years old then but the reason I recollect it so well is that the vicar who came to Rainow from St Peter's was a great naturalist and also he took a great interest in the Boys Youth Movement, which was pretty universal at the time. He came on a temporary basis as the Vicar Hugh Davies was in the army in France. He had rooms at Round Meadow Farm, but lived mostly in a tent in the garden. He was very popular and could often be seen working in the fields with the farmers. Due to the war much had to be cultivated and it was mostly manual work as many of the horses had been commandeered by the army.

On a Saturday afternoon the vicar took a party of us boys up to Saltersford and the idea was to establish the approximate number of caterpillars. We concentrated on the road which was through the centre of the affected area, the number of caterpillars killed being calculated to a given area. I do not know what his calculated number came to but it must have been in millions. He also brought some back in a cardboard box with the object of finding what they developed into, but I do not know if he got any results.

All kinds of theories were talked about as to the reason for this plague, including one that the Germans had dropped germs from the air. Actually one Zeppelin got this far inland. It dropped one bomb at the rear of Hammonds Brickworks, but this failed to explode. They were probably guided by the glow from the kilns. It was an exceptionally bright moonlight night. Ingersley Vale Bleachwork was working a night shift and all the workmen, including my father, were watching. It was very low and I understand it was the only one to penetrate this far inland. It was shot down before it reached the East Coast.

The strange thing to me is that the plague of caterpillars does not seem to have been mentioned in the local papers of that time. Shortly before he died I discussed this with Leslie Hill who lived in the centre of the disaster and he said that what he remembered was how they invaded the home, so that his family walked on them and if they sat down they sat on them also. They took precautions to prevent them getting upstairs, and from getting on to the food by hanging it up from the ceiling. He also remembered that thousands of crows appeared and gorged on the caterpillars, to such an extent they could only fly up onto the wall and the walls became white with their scourings. The Hills took what animals they managed to keep to graze on the road verges on the Buxton Road down in Rainow and even to Pott Shrigley. As to what the caterpillars developed into, he said they simply died off at the end of the summer. Leonard Stubbs' parents farmed Burton Springs at that time. He told me that they often talked about it. All the surrounding areas were clear with the exception of one small area at Billinge Side Farm about two miles away occupied by the Kirkhams. Mrs Kirkham was my father's sister, and there the caterpillars devoured one small field only,

179

possibly two acres in extent. However these events are considered it was certainly strange and I would think one of the strangest things ever to have happened in Rainow.'

WHEN DADDY CAME HOME

'I was three years old at the end of the war. It was a beautiful sunny morning and I was dressed in my best party frock and sent to play in the garden, when suddenly a man, dressed in what I later learned was army uniform, complete with a kitbag thrown over his shoulder, came walking up the path. He said "Hello" – and I turned tail and rushed to the end of the garden where I hid in an old henhouse. After a short time my mother came to retrieve me and I was informed this was "Daddy", a fact that did not impress me at all. Little did I know that 25 years later the same thing would happen to my own small daughter.'

ARMISTICE DAY

'I remember well the day when I was a child staying away from school with toothache. It was a Monday and Mother and Lizzie were doing the washing. The date was 11th November 1918. It must have been announced in the morning papers that the Armistice was to be signed. Lymm church clock struck eleven and the church bells rang a joyous peal.

There must have been sounds of rejoicing nearby, for my mother sent me down the road to see what was going on. I obediently trotted down Elm Tree Road – toothache forgotten – and in Church Road there were groups of people talking excitedly. The wounded soldiers in their hospital blue were dancing around with a group of land girls. The large Victorian house opposite to where Dr Sissons' surgery once was, just behind where the Welfare bus stop is today, had been commandeered as a Red Cross hospital. The soldiers in wheelchairs were brought to the gate to join in the fun. I stayed and watched the jollification for some time and then made my way home. In the open space behind the cottages I noticed one woman was calmly hanging out her washing. I told Mother of all that I had seen and I remember saying, "What do you think? Lizzie's mother went on hanging out her washing as though nothing had happened."

That evening I went with my parents and grandmother to St Mary's church to a thanksgiving service. I shall never forget it. The church was packed, with about everyone in the village there. I remember the organist playing the 23rd Psalm and the National Anthem with gusto. I cannot remember any more. I suppose I was tired out with the excitement of the day and went home with my parents when the service was over and then to bed.'

'One thing I remember from my childhood is Armistice Day between the wars. There was a genuine two minutes' silence throughout the land. People stopped talking to each other, buses stopped, trains stopped, horses pulling carts stopped, the wireless went silent, bus drivers got out of their cabs and took off their caps and cart drivers stood by their horses with their hats off. There wasn't a sound or a movement. So different from today.'

BETWEEN THE WARS

Within a few years of the war ending, the 'land fit for heroes' had become a land of unemployment and hardship for many in Cheshire.

HARD YEARS IN BIRKENHEAD

'Between 1925 and 1936 the years in Birkenhead were hard. This was the time of disarmament and it affected Cammell Lairds badly, which reflected in the town's well being.

Saturday night was a family outing, starting from home at about 6.30 pm to walk down Grange Road. The Salvation Army marched down followed by Jehovah's Witnesses. Their goal was the Haymarket, which is now the site of the tunnel entrance. This large square of ground was the venue for lots of free entertainment. Each group had its own patch, the Salvation Army in one corner, Jehovah's Witnesses in another. There was a man claiming cures for baldness and hair troubles. Another man, clad only in vest and trousers – summer and winter – selling a tonic. Tucked away was a small shop where you could buy herbs, and this had a couple of benches where you could sit and have nettle beer, dandelion and burdock or sarsaparilla at a penny a glass.

Then when you had exhausted all that the Haymarket had to offer it was up the steps and into the Market Hall, where the country stalls from around Heswall and Barnston sold cheese, butter, black pudding and brawn, and eggs. These were the days before deep freezes and at about eight of the clock, all the butchers sold off their stock. For most people going home from the market meant the best meal of the week; a fry up of sausages and chops and liver. The fishmonger also sold up, and my mother bought a whole cod one Saturday night. Our cat and dog thought Christmas had come that week. It was cooked and kept in a meat safe in the yard. No tins of shop meat for animals, then, just the scraps off the table.

As I said before, Lairds were the main employers, and they closed down for the first week of August when all employees had their week's holiday.

Then came the General Strike followed by riots in the town. The whole of the shop windows in Grange Road were smashed and very ugly scenes occurred. Those were the days of the "means test" to see if you needed assistance. One man, fed up with nothing to do, bought for twopence a box which had contained margarine, and then made a simple child's chair out of the wood, which he sold for sixpence. He was reported by a neighbour to the means test as being employed. However, the committee saw the human side and his dole was not stopped.

There were various schemes to help the unemployed, notably on New Brighton promenade. An estate of houses was built near Tranmere Rovers' ground by the Corporation. These were built for sale and lots of council workers bought at very low prices with a mortgage rate around two and one half per cent. Rates were less than a penny in the pound and discount was offered for early payment. Later on there was a little light relief and great excitement to see a full eclipse of the sun. Many people trudged up to Bidston Hill to view it through a piece of smoked glass. Another spectacle was the Hindenburg airship flying over the Mersey, so low that office windows were darkened and the passengers could be seen in the gondola. As this was before the Second World War many comments were passed during the Liverpool blitz that during this visit the whole of Liverpool docks had been photographed for future reference.

A big loss to Liverpool was the demolition of "the Docker's Umbrella" – the overhead railway. This was a unique landmark and a trip on it during Civic Week was a school outing. During this week Liverpool was an open city. The Royal Liver was open, and I with many others went to the top and stood looking out from behind the clock across to New Brighton, watching the ferry boats calling at the pier. This was demolished after the war.

The climate changed in Birkenhead during 1938. Laird's order book was full and preparations were being made to adjust the balance of disarmament. Birkenhead prospered and things began to change. We now had a wealth of electrical appliances and life was easier, but with people moving out to suburbs like Woodchurch and Bebington the close neighbourly atmosphere of the terrace house was lost.'

SOUP KITCHENS

'In 1926 came the miners' strike. A soup kitchen was set up at Burtonwood so that each person could have one meal a day. The farmers helped by giving produce and concerts were held to raise funds.'

'I remember soup kitchens at Saughall for children whose fathers were on strike. On one occasion I gave a child a penny for her ticket. My father being a mining official, I did not qualify and thought it would be lovely to have dinner in the church hall with my friends. Not quite such a thrill when I was handed a bowl of very watery pea soup and a wedge of rather stale bread. It taught me a lesson I have never forgotten.'

A BRIGHT SPOT

'We lived at Sandbach and I remember one day my father coming home to say Brunner Monds had closed down. No redundancy money in those days – poverty was at its worst for many families. Then, just to brighten things up when they seemed so dark, Foden's Motorworks Brass Band won a competition in London. All the town turned out to watch them walking down the High Street playing their wonderful music.'

THE JARROW MARCHERS

'I saw the Jarrow marchers when they spent a night in a disused factory in Crewe on their way to London. They had a meal in Coppenhall church hall, the food being provided by local shopkeepers. I had never seen such poverty-stricken people. There were both men and women, very thin and poorly dressed – their faces were expressionless.'

'WILL YOU COME TO MY PARTY?'

'The 1930s were a time of great deprivation, with thousands unemployed. This is a little verse I remember from those days:

Will you come to my party, will you come?
Bring your own bread and butter and a bun
'Cos my father's on the dole and my mother's picking coal
Will you come to my party, will you come?'

I BEGAN MY NURSING CAREER

'In 1933, before the outbreak of the Second World War, I had begun my nursing career.

Many of our patients came from the poorer areas of town where life was so difficult for them. Babies would be brought in suffering severe malnutrition due to lack of food and poor hygiene conditions. I saw many a man in casualty who, when stripped of his clothes, would have only a worn out jacket and trousers with brown paper underneath to help keep him warm. Many women didn't know what it was like to own a warm coat, they wore a large black shawl to keep them and possibly their babies warm. Also, beneath these garments, they would wear a long black apron with a large pocket in, in which they kept all their "worldly goods".

Poverty and unemployment caused much depression. Many an attempted suicide was rescued from the river Mersey.'

THE SECOND WORLD WAR
1939 – 1945
THE BOMBING BEGINS

Once again we were at war and this time Cheshire suffered nights of bombing as German planes searched out industrial and military targets.

A DANGEROUS PLACE TO LIVE

'Some local farms, namely Ringway Hall, Firtree Farm, Grange Farm, and part of Manor Farm, were purchased by Manchester Council in 1935 for the building of Ringway Airport. The airport was opened in July 1938, but in 1939 it was closed to commercial traffic with the outbreak of war. At this time I was eight years old – already milking cows morning and night, before and after school. The airport became a paratroop training centre. Fairey Aviation and AV Roe had hangars there for the assembly and maintenance of military aircraft. All the roads to the airport had blockades and passes had to be shown to get to and from school.

Clough Bank Farm became a very dangerous place to live during the war. We had quite a few near misses. Early in the war a Lockheed Hudson bomber ditched into the woodland on the farm – known as "the clough". This was approximately 60 yards from the house. Also a bomber crashed into the orchard at the front of the house when a parachute and its container caught on its tail. The plane missed the farmhouse by some 30 feet. Then a Mosquito exploded in mid-air over Ringway, and two Whitley bombers collided on the airfield; they had just returned from manoeuvres over Tatton Park, dropping paratroopers there. This happened during the hours of darkness – I can still remember the fire being so intense it lit up the whole of Ringway. The most scary event for us during the war was when a Sterling bomber towing two gliders took off from a short runway situated in front of the farm. As they came over the house they skimmed us, just missing us by inches. The noise was colossal. After the war a squadron of Spitfires was based at Ringway. One of these ended up upside down in the field bordering the airfield. The final plane to crash near us was an AV Roe York which was used on the Berlin Airlift. This was coming into Ringway for servicing when it swerved off the runway across Wilmslow road, hit a sand waggon and finished up in our field minus one wheel. It had to be towed back onto the airfield.

When the airfield first opened there were no actual runways, the aircraft landed on grass. The Ministry of Aircraft Production (MAP) built three runways at the beginning of the war. With these the planes could land and take off in six different directions. The main runway of today is one of these runways, obviously widened and lengthened for today's aeroplanes. Buildings at the airport were pretty basic. There was an officers' mess and barracks for the RAF – the paratroopers lived on Outwood Lane in Nissen huts.'

A NIGHT OF TERROR

'Just over 50 years ago, on 28th November 1940, Cheshire experienced a night of terror. Liverpool was attacked by hundreds of German bombers which came in from the Irish Sea. Many overflew the city to drop their bombs over a wide swathe of the Cheshire countryside, causing many casualties. I was just 14 years old at the time and living at the lovely old Nook Farm with my grandparents. The farm stood on the outskirts of Weaverham village.

Air raid activity started very early that evening, but because of the very cold weather, we decided to stay in the farm kitchen rather than go to the air raid shelter we had made in the orchard. As the raid progressed, the noise of falling bombs and heavy anti-aircraft gunfire became almost unbearable and very frightening. Chandelier flares hanging in the sky and hundreds of incendiaries exploding over a

Nook Farm, Weaverham after a night of terror in 1940. Though injured and dazed, the Moss family survived the bombing.

wide area lit the countryside up like day. Overhead we could hear the German planes with their unmistakable drone. Suddenly at 20 minutes to eleven, there was a vivid blue flash and a mighty roar as the old house shuddered and split up, disintegrating around us. We were hurled about by the terrific blast and severely cut by flying glass. A tremendous fall of soot covered us from head to foot. A parachute mine had exploded in the farm gateway to cause this terrible devastation.

My grandfather remained remarkably calm and got us out one by one into the debris-strewn garden. There had been six of us in the house and also a small fox terrier, Rip, who although slightly injured and badly dazed like the rest of us, had survived. Cattle were trapped in the shippons and later villagers came and put their own lives at risk to release them.

Meanwhile, it seemed like an age as we waited desperately in need of help and bleeding profusely from our injuries. When that help came we were taken to casualty first aid stations and although I recall only fleeting moments of these journeys, I remember the feeling of great relief when we were eventually brought to the warmth and security of the Red Cross Emergency Hospital at Hefferston Grange, where we received wonderful attention and were nursed back to recovery by the skill and devotion of the hospital staff, many of whom were Red Cross volunteer nurses, living locally. This was certainly a night never to be forgotten by many Cheshire folk.'

A PRIME TARGET

'Living not far from the docks and flour mills of Wallasey as we did, we were a prime target for the German bombers. Many a night in our reinforced brick backyard shelter, we heard land-mines swishing overhead on their tiny parachutes and prayed that they would miss us. In the morning we would soon hear whether they had fallen on a strategic target, on a nearby field or in a residential road. The latter, sadly, happened on several occasions and many familiar faces were lost to us forever.

The closest shave we had was when an incendiary bomb fell in the yard next to the shelter. I was in the outside lavatory at the time and, although it seems funny now, I really did get a shock. Fortunately, my uncle managed to put it out safely with some sand. The family dog was always out in the shelter minutes before the siren went off, and he was never wrong.

Later, when the bombing got heavier we decided to move away from our home shelter to a public one at Seacombe Ferry. It was really little more than a large area surrounded by sandbags. But every night, at about 5 pm, we trailed (on foot, of course) the three quarters of a mile down there with our sleeping things. This arrangement did not last long, however, as one night a ferry-boat at the landing-stage got a direct hit, only 100 yards or so from our refuge. We were all quickly ushered out and into a large brick shelter over the road. My father, however, was not too happy with its situation so we all hurried back home through the guns and the bombs in the pitch darkness − which resulted in my sustaining a badly bruised head through crashing into an unseen and, of course, unlit lamp-post.

Later again, a huge shelter was opened in the basement of the Wallasey Town Hall and we spent most of the rest of the blitz there, and felt pretty safe. As a child, I quite enjoyed the jollity and bonhomie of that period. Someone was always willing to sing a song or to entertain us. And we slept soundly at last.'

IT WENT ON ALL NIGHT

'My family were bombed in 1940. I was working late in Wallasey when the sirens went; our shelter was underground by the dock. After a time it went quiet. One of the boys said he was going home, so I walked with him part way. Shrapnel started to fall, he went one way, I went the other, running by now. When I reached our house everyone was in the shelter. Just as I sat down there was a mighty bang, and next morning we found the bottom row of shops had gone. All that was left was a huge crater. The bomb had missed me by a few minutes. Our windows were blown in so we moved house.

My next memory is of 12th-13th March 1941. My mother, father and I went into the air raid shelter next door. Not long after that bombs began to fall. We were not far from the gas works and one of the tanks was hit. The bombing went on all night. Crawling out next morning, what a mess, the roof and windows had all gone. People were wandering about with rubble everywhere. One of my brothers, who had gone to night school, arrived home but as time went by we became worried about my other brother. My father and mother went to find out what had happened. When they came to the road where my brother had gone to stay with a friend there was not much left of the street shelter. Thirty people had been inside. A land mine had fallen on it. All were killed, but three days later men clearing away found a baby in a wooden crib, alive!

Later that day we went to West Kirby, Wirral, to stay with relatives. The next morning my father and brother went back to Wallasey to our house, only to find a huge hole in the dining room. When my father looked down there was the fin of a bomb. They left quickly to find a warden so they could rope the house off. Later the army moved in to explode it. It weighed 1,000 lbs. In those two nights 651 people were killed, 603 seriously injured and 668 slightly injured.

In May 1941 there was a raid which lasted eight days. This was at the time when we were living in West Kirby and we could see Liverpool burning.'

WE WERE ALL SO TIRED

'In Birkenhead we had the full force of the blitz between 1940 and 1941 and all the family slept in our reinforced basement for some weeks. After the May blitz in 1941, we were offered accommodation in Willaston and as we were all so tired from lack of sleep, this seemed a good idea. Unfortunately, the planes still came over and we found the ack-ack (anti-aircraft guns) firing near the house just as disturbing to sleep as the bombs. Also we missed the security of the friendly barrage balloons which Merseyside had to prevent enemy planes flying in too low. After a week in the country we decided we preferred our cellar and moved back home!'

'The bombers flew over Acton Bridge on their way to bomb Liverpool and my mother used to put my brothers and sisters underneath the dining table and in the pantry, which had the staircase above it, having been told they were the safest places. We were still sent to school the following day, no matter what kind of night we had spent.'

'We had cleared out the cupboard under the stairs and put in a small mattress and, when the air raid warning sounded, the baby was put in this cupboard for safety. My sister and I also sat in there on many a night. We had a particularly bad night at Little Budworth when the enemy bombers were turned from Liverpool and unloaded their bombs just anywhere. One bomb dropped at the top of the Coach Road and another one in Mr Foden's field. There were several fire bombs on the Coach Road, which were speedily dealt with. On another occasion a bomb was dropped on the ruins of Oulton Hall.'

GAS?

'I was twelve when the war began, and Pa joined the Local Defence Volunteers, later called the Home Guard. Because of Fairey Aviation at Ringway and Wilmslow's proximity to Manchester, we had ack-ack guns at Morley, quite near our house. We did have one large bomb, which fell one night in Water Lane, and everybody took cover. My father and two others, either Home Guard or ARP wardens, were patrolling our road, conveniently near to home, and when it

189

fell they instinctively flung themselves down. When all was quiet, they became aware of an odd smell. Most of them were old soldiers and immediately thought of gas. As it turned out, one of them had fallen in the border of thyme, with which Pa used to edge his flower beds. They trooped in, amid much laughter, and we all came out from under the dining room table. We girls were sent to bed, but I dare say the grown ups had tea laced with a little something.'

THE FRODSHAM FIREMEN

'One night when a German bomber on a mission over Liverpool was hit by gunfire, he hurriedly left the Mersey area and while travelling over Frodsham chose to lighten his load by dropping his cargo of bombs on the village. One killed an occupant of a house on Belmonte Road.

Frodsham had its own fire brigade, who were kept very busy during the war dealing with incendiary bombs. The fire brigade before the war had its headquarters in a small hut in High Street. When the siren sounded the alert for a fire, the firemen, who were at that time all part time, used to run or cycle from their places of work to the headquarters to collect the fire appliance. This was a large hand cart laden with hoses, standpipes and other equipment which they would have to run with, towing it along to the scene of the fire. Invariably they would be followed by lots of children.'

TOWNS AND VILLAGES AT WAR

Towns and villages changed almost beyond recognition as the war got under way, some never to be the same again. Houses and other meeting places also found uses that would have seemed impossible only a short time before.

LIFE IN CREWE

'I was nine years old when war broke out. I can still remember listening to Neville Chamberlain's speech on the radio. Almost immediately, my mother produced a large roll of cellophane and rolls of brown sticky paper. These were stuck on the windows, the sticky paper in a criss-cross pattern, to reduce the risk of flying glass caused by bomb blast. Most other people's windows were treated in the same way, including schools and public buildings. As it turned out, it was many months before the "phoney war" ended and the bombing started. And in fact, there was very little bombing of Crewe itself, in spite of the large railway works and the Rolls Royce factory which made Merlin engines for bombers during the war. After the war, it was found that Hitler had ordered Crewe to be left unscathed because of the Basford Sidings, railway marshalling yards just outside the town, in those days a large, important railway junction.

We did have a lot of alerts and could see fires raging at Liverpool and Manchester. Brick air raid shelters were built in all the streets. Gas masks were issued to everyone and we had to carry them everywhere. They were issued with a case made of thick cardboard, and a cord for over the shoulder. Some people bought decorative covers for their cases and some had cylindrical tins in place of the boxes. Special coloured gas masks were issued for toddlers and large ones for babies which the baby could be put inside and air pumped in. I remember my young cousin was terrified of his "Mickey Mouse" one, so thank goodness it was never needed.

On a huge wall of Crewe Works in West Street, mock houses were painted as camouflage and these can be seen faintly today. Whether they would have fooled the enemy is anyone's guess.

Almost everyone had an Anderson shelter in their garden. It consisted of curved sheets of corrugated iron over a square hole dug about three feet into the ground. The summer of 1940 was lovely, weather-wise, and my mother would put milk and butter in the shelter to keep it cool. We later found that Dad, a keen fisherman, kept his maggots in there before a fishing trip! When the winter came, the shelter filled with water. The shelters were erected mostly by the householders, if able bodied, but the council workmen came round and lined the sides and floor with concrete in an effort to keep out the water, but to no avail. In fact the water could not drain away in spite of a sump in the corner. Finally, we abandoned the Anderson shelter and bought a strong metal one for the living room. This had two bunks and we were able to stay put during a spell of air raid warnings every night, instead of having to come down and shelter under the stairs. Many people had similar shelters indoors, in the form of a large table.

Every neighbourhood had a barrage balloon based on a suitable open site, sometimes a children's playground. These were winched up on strong wires after inflation, from a specially designed lorry. They very occasionally broke from their moorings and were as dangerous as the bombs. I believe they were flown over the town when news came of enemy bombers heading our way. We learned to tell whether a plane overhead was British or German from the throb of the engines. In daylight, of course, we could see black crosses on the German ones. For a spell we had a smoke-screen in the town; a series of burners, a bit like old-fashioned room heaters found in village halls etc. They had tall chimneys, about shoulder height and when raids were imminent, the stoves were lit, exuding a revolting smell and thick black oily smoke which played havoc with clothes if anyone happened to be passing. They were placed at intervals along the pavements.

Everyone had to black out their windows, usually by making curtains of black material. Air raid wardens who had their own shelters/offices in each neighbourhood, would patrol the streets to ensure that no chink of light showed. "Put that light out!" became one of the many catch phrases bandied around during the war. Among others were – "Dig for Victory", ie grow vegetables in your garden or allotment; and "Walls have ears" meant don't disclose information you might have about factories, gun emplacements, army, navy or air force bases etc. On this theme, posters said, "Be like Dad, keep Mum"!

Food was rationed and everyone had a ration book. Living near the Cheshire countryside, there were plenty of local vegetables and fruit. Housewives bottled fruit and preserved eggs when they could get them in the laying season, to use when they were less plentiful. Eggs were stored in buckets in a solution called waterglass. Women's Institutes made jam from local fruit and it was sold in the shops and market. Ladies who could knit made socks, gloves, scarves, balaclava helmets and pullovers for members of the armed forces. For this purpose khaki, airforce and navy blue wool was available without coupons. Otherwise, clothing, knitting wool and dress materials were rationed as were furniture and furnishings. Gardeners "dug for victory" and one or two of the flower beds in Crewe's beautiful Queens Park were planted with onions. Bananas were no longer imported and oranges were allocated only to toddlers. We did have to tighten our belts but I never heard of anyone going really hungry.

Church bells were silenced with the grim warning that if they were rung, it meant an enemy invasion. From time to time George VI would call a National Day of Prayer and people would flock to the churches to pray for an end of the war.

Crewe did come off lightly compared with most cities, in the air raids, but we did have some skirmishes. A day-time raider hit the Rolls Royce works. Many said he had been a premium apprentice in Crewe Works before the war but this had probably been a rumour. However, I believe the authorities thought he had found his target via the Queens Park lake, which was almost next door to the factory. After this, the lake was drained and filled with prunings from trees and bushes. Another tragic bombing killed several people including a little boy and his dog. One other case was almost a miracle. A very old pair of detached houses was hit by a bomb. One house was gutted but the lady living there was safely in her Anderson shelter and her husband was at work. Next door, the family did not get to their shelter, mercifully, because it was lifted from the ground and bowled up the garden. Both families lived to tell the tale.

When war first broke out, school was suspended for several weeks. When they reopened we children had to learn air raid drill. Fortunately we had very few day-time raids, so school was not disrupted. My mother was appalled when we were taught what to do if we were out of doors and were machine gunned or bombs were dropping but again, in our area we were lucky and the drill was not needed. There were shortages at school; pencils were made of horrid hard wood and paper was very short. I suppose we had very few of the items of equipment to be found in schools today but nevertheless we had a good education. One effect of the paper shortage was that all the fly leaves of my children's books had been used for drawings. I fancied myself as an artist in those days. Sweets were another of our delights that were rationed and ice cream was non-existent. We all used to munch raw carrots in those days and felt a little deprived but it was much better for our teeth.

I noticed the effects of the war much more when I went to the Crewe county secondary school (later to become the grammar school). Our school uniform colours were black and gold and we were expected to adhere to our uniform, which had to be bought with clothing coupons. The headmistress was a single woman who did not seem to realise that at that stage of our lives we girls were growing quickly and it was a real struggle to keep to the school uniform and still have something to wear out of school hours. It was a co-ed school but not having a brother I never knew whether the boys had the same problems.

There were air raid shelters on the school field but I do not remember going into them, the air raids must have abated by that time. The school hall had a glass roof with large blinds which could be pulled across when the lights were on. Sixth formers used to "fire watch" with members of staff at night, on a rota basis, in case the school was hit by incendiary bombs. There were no young men members of staff, they were serving with HM Forces.

From time to time the school would have a fair in the school hall. The classes had their own stalls, organised by members of staff and the resulting profit went to the war effort. One summer, the grass on the perimeter of the school field was allowed to grow long and was harvested as hay. Another time a herd of sheep spent the summer months on the school field and the cricket and rounders

193

teams had to look where they were putting their feet.

The music department had a gramophone but only two records, or maybe it was only one. If the music lesson finished early, we had a rendering of *Greensleeves* or perhaps for a change *Nymphs and shepherds*!

I well remember the headmaster coming into the classroom to tell us about the D-Day landings. We were very young and it took time for the significance of this to soak in.

Just as the war was drawing to a close, we began to hear aeroplanes overhead making a "screaming" sound we had never heard before. Rumour had it that it was a new secret weapon to intimidate enemy ground forces but, of course, it was the jet planes from De Havillands factory at Chester. Little did we know at the time that these were heralding a tremendous revolution in air travel.

Victory came to the Allies while I was still at school. First, in May came Victory in Europe. Then came the dropping of the atomic bomb on Japan. To this day I can still remember my feelings of horror at the thought of the terrible thing that mankind had unleashed with this bomb. Then, of course, the Japanese surrendered. The silent church bells rang out all over the land amid great jubilation. There was a bonfire and firework display in Crewe Park and all the little streets of terraced houses were decked out in red, white and blue. Tables were brought out into the streets and everyone had a party.

The war ended but shortages lingered much longer. Meat, the final item, was taken off ration just before I married in 1953. Consequently it took me a long time to learn to cook meat, my mother had just not dared let me loose on our precious rations. The first banana I tasted in six years was a dried one, when everyone at school was given one.

I suppose, because I was young, the years 1939 to 1945 loom large in my memory. When it all ended, the church bells rang, the lights came on again in the streets and shops, husbands and fathers came home and families were reunited. For a short time I saw the world with rose-coloured spectacles and looked forward to a peaceful future.'

WE BECAME A BUSY VILLAGE

'In late 1939 and early 1940, a flying field was quickly made in Byley, billets went up and young men who had been called up for the Royal Air Force were stationed in them and did their air training there. Byley became a very busy village. I remember well the sad day when nine airmen lost their lives: the plane carrying them, returning from a mission in Scotland, was about to land when it got in an air pocket and crashed. I remember attending their funeral, which took place at Byley church, and eight of them lie side by side in the churchyard, along with other airmen that lost their lives while flying from Byley.

As the war went on, the training field became the home of 96 Fighter Squadron. The air raids became worse over Liverpool and Manchester. The air raid sirens would sound and the squadron would take off. We could stand outside and watch the fighters in air battles. Our homes had to be well blacked-out with dark curtains. I remember one night seeing one of our fighters shoot an enemy plane down very near to Byley.

I was married in 1938 and our home was in a little lane which led up to the airfield. We had to have a pass to get to our house and anyone else that was visiting us had to show their identity cards and book in. There were always guards at the entry to the lane. I, along with other ladies in the village, helped at the Church Army canteen, bringing a bit of home comfort to the airmen, serving them with cups of tea and snacks to eat.

At the end of the war, the GIs were billeted at Byley. The girls from as far afield as Liverpool and Manchester flocked to Byley, especially on a Saturday night. I dare not report all that went on, but it certainly opened one's eyes! They used to rely on a lift to get to Byley and I think that is how the first nylons arrived around here.'

CHESTER

'I was born in White Friars, Chester in 1935. I started school in 1940. Everyone had to be fitted with gas masks and rubber earplugs were supplied. The gas masks were simply dreadful to wear. I can still recall the smell of rubber, and the tightness and weight of them on my face. They had a bright turquoise, thin plate on the nozzle end. We carried them around with us everywhere but as time went on and the threat of a gas attack diminished, the rules about carrying them were relaxed. Air raid shelters were dug out of the ground at the back of our school and in the early years of the war, we were shepherded into them quite regularly when the Luftwaffe staged a daylight raid. Barrage balloons flew high above and the night sky became alive with the beams of searchlights trying to pin-point enemy aircraft. We soon became familiar with the sound of German aircraft flying above, usually making their way towards the port of Liverpool. Their engine sounds were quite distinctive and unlike our RAF aircraft.

A few odd bombs fell in the Chester area and I remember the shop area next to Marks and Spencers in Chester (formerly Burrells) was just a crater for a number of years. We counted ourselves lucky that doodlebugs and V2s did not reach the North West, as was the plight of the unfortunate people living in the London area. Our pantry at

195

home was used as an air raid shelter, and my sister and I found it quite amusing and exciting to hide in there when the sirens sounded – too young to realise the danger of the situation.

As my mother worked, my sister and I used to help with the shopping on Saturday mornings. We would go into Chester and stand in various queues to purchase food that was off ration. A queue used to wind down the steps at the top of Watergate Street, leading to the shop directly below, in order to buy tripe and cowheel. I was given that job usually and my sister used to stand in Blake's queue above for bread. I can remember in the early 1940s a family used to come to shop in Bridge Street on a Saturday morning in a pony and trap. What a commotion it would cause today!

An American Servicemen's Club was situated near The Cross in Eastgate Row and crates piled high with food used to be taken in there, much to the chagrin of the locals. Food such as bananas, of which I had no recollection, were carried in. American servicemen based near Chester were a familiar sight. Their manner was always genial and they wore smart uniforms, which made their ordinary servicemen look like officers – in sad comparison to the rough khaki our soldiers had to wear.

During the later years of the war, German and Italian prisoners of war were detained in this country. They walked the streets and joined the cinema queues quite freely. Not unsurprisingly, they appeared quite happy to be here.

One event that sticks in my mind is that of a very hot Saturday afternoon when a Polish aircraft came down in flames on the old King School field on Lache Lane. Local people ran out to see if they could help, but they could not get near the blaze. Three airmen lost their lives. The playing field is now a housing estate and it is probably unlikely that the occupants of those houses know what a sad event took place there some 50 years ago.

A shopping trip to Liverpool was a regular event for Chester people in the 1940s, despite the extensive bombing that was going on there. Lewis's store outside Central Station was a blackened shell during the war. When I visit now and see what an attractive city Liverpool has become, I cannot help remembering what it looked like in those days.

Our lives revolved around the radio then, particularly when we heard the sonorous chimes of Big Ben and the latest bulletins from the front were broadcast. Cheery radio programmes like *ITMA* kept people in good spirits.

Whenever we visited relatives up the North Wales coast, the train and its corridors would be full of servicemen, either going on or returning from leave. Often they would sing together whilst one of them would play a mouth organ. Songs like *We'll meet again* or

I haven't said thanks for that lovely weekend would echo down the train. The beaches along the coast were deserted during the war and a wall of barbed wire would stretch down each one of them.'

BRIDGEMERE CHAPEL

'On the main road from Nantwich to Woore between Doddington Park and Bridgemere Garden World, stands the little Methodist chapel of Bridgemere, rather forlorn looking as there is very little population around. But for a few years, one could say it had its finest hour, for the chapel's war effort commenced in 1938 one Sunday evening when three young men in uniform were in the congregation. They were Czechoslovak airmen who when hearing on their radio that Hitler was taking over the country, had rushed to their planes and under the very noses of the Germans flew them to England. These three were Protestants, followers of John Huss and they and the boys who had come with them were sent to Doddington Park; they were entertained to supper before returning to camp and so the idea of opening a canteen was put into action to cater for any personnel stationed at Doddington.

Under the leadership of Mrs Cissie Lee of Wheel Green Farm, Bridgemere, a rota of helpers from chapel members and their local ladies was organised. I would like to pay tribute to the wonderful work of Mrs Lee; she was a big woman in every way, a gifted organiser and businesswoman, musical and great-hearted. With her husband, Ernest, they ran a business taking the cheese and farm produce direct to the markets. Mrs Lee did all the buying in and obtaining permits for rations such as tea, sugar, sweets, chocolate, cigarettes and coal; crockery also had to be bought and she always paid tribute to her friends on the market who helped in any way they could. If she couldn't buy cake, she made it. The soldiers affectionately called her "Connie" or "Mother Superior". She came down most nights with her cycle weighed down with stores, and her motherly figure with her knitting brought a lot of comfort to the young servicemen.

You will be well aware of the size of the Sunday schools of these little chapels, with an open fire which had to be lit (take your own sticks) and the kettle on ready for opening time at 6.30 pm. We had two primus stoves and on these we cooked eggs, beans and tomatoes, and made a mountain of cheese and spam sandwiches. There was a table in the corner where we washed up in an enamel bowl, first having to heat the water on the fire or the stove. By 6.30 there was usually a queue outside the door and when the schoolroom was full they sat with their butties and tea in the pews. Some would play the organ (or Mrs Lee would) and there would be

197

Peover Hall, where General Patton was stationed during the Second World War. The American flag still has pride of place here.

a sing song; we also had given to us a gramophone, records, dart board, dominoes etc.

In 1940 France surrendered to the Germans. Part of the French Fleet was stationed in French North Africa at Oran and to save that part of the fleet falling to the Germans the British got in first and took it over, with the result that 2,000 French sailors, naval and merchant, were sent to Doddington Park under canvas. A certain French General, de Gaulle by name, came to England and formed the Free French Units which continued the fight with us. Not all the sailors were for de Gaulle; those that were, were allowed out of the camp, the others were restricted. Those that came out soon found the way to the canteen. The camp was guarded by the 5th battalion of the South Staffs regiment; what a great bunch they were and so appreciative of what we were doing, they were always the last to leave the canteen and would help us to lock up and escort us home if necessary. At this period we were packed out every night.

The War Office continued to use Doddington after the dispersal of the French sailors and there were soldiers stationed there until the end of the war.

In 1943 the Americans came to Doddington under General Patton, who in turn was visited by General Eisenhower, and so we had an American invasion. One of the most moving Sunday evenings took place before the Americans went south for the D-Day landings. Their ministers held a communion service in the chapel; the boys were queuing up outside to come in and take communion. For some it was probably their last.'

198

ADLINGTON HALL

'During 1944 a friend of mine had her first baby in Adlington Hall. During the war Mrs Legh lent Adlington Hall to St Mary's maternity hospital for the benefit of the wives of officers of HM Forces. As many wives were on their own, their husbands being either overseas or great distances from home, it was a comfort for them to know that their wives could be cared for when the baby was born. The wives were able to stay in the Brew House at Adlington Hall for up to two weeks before the baby was due.

My baby was due in October 1945 and my friend suggested I go to Adlington as she had been very comfortable there, so I was duly booked in. At that time my husband was a Met Officer in the RAF at Cottesmore and was managing to get home every other weekend, but, of course, the baby made its appearance on the weekend that Dad was not coming home! However, all went well and word was sent to Cottesmore. This was how he heard the news.

"It was a beautiful autumn day and I was exercising with some members of the rugby team when I noticed a large balloon rising from the roof of the control tower. As it was not time for the hourly weather record I returned at some speed to the Met Office. The senior WAAF Met Assistant met me with a beaming smile, and when asked, "What is going on?" announced, "We are celebrating the birth of a son to Mr Churton." I was grabbed by the team and rushed to HQ where the CO immediately gave me leave. I was bundled into the station waggon and rushed to Oakham railway station, all on the understanding that the baby's head would be "wet" when I returned. I eventually arrived at Adlington Hall and was escorted to the great hall and asked to take a seat. After a while a nurse approached me with a baby in her arms. The little fellow had a touch of jaundice. He had a mass of dark hair which had been oiled and slicked down, and his arms were folded and tucked into the sleeves of his nightie. The nurse stood in front of me and as I rose announced with a smile, "See Fu Manchu." Only then was I allowed to join my wife."

At the Hall we were looked after like royalty and given full and detailed instructions on how to look after our baby when we got home, and one could not have asked for more care and attention from the nurses – and all for seven guineas a week!'

THE STRANGERS IN OUR LIVES

'By the beginning of the Second World War my parents were at Park Farm, which is close to Peover Hall. Some of the United States army were stationed there along with General Patton. The drive to the

Hall ran through our land and we used to see General Patton being driven in his car by his black batman. To us village children, this was the first coloured person we had seen and we were in awe of him. They introduced us to chewing gum which was great because sweets were rationed. When General Patton went overseas he promised that if he survived, he would come back to Over Peover church and give thanks. This he did and the American flag still has pride of place there today.

The village also had its quota of evacuees. These town children didn't take very kindly to being stuck in the middle of nowhere and caused many problems for the teachers, Miss Ingram and Miss Sherwin, at the village school. The first morning one group marched out of school and headed for the nearest town, which was Knutsford, only to be brought back again, complete with apples which they had picked on the way. It was very difficult for them to adapt to a whole new way of life away from their parents and it was equally difficult for the people who took them in and tried to help them settle down. The village children had their education extended by the evacuees, learning new games and tricks amongst other things!

Later, army families were billeted at Peover Hall so after the evacuees had all gone home, the village school again nearly doubled in size. It was as if these children had arrived from another planet, as they had been to many foreign places, some of which we village children had not even heard of and many of us had not travelled above about 20 miles from home. They were good storytellers, probably romancing as well, but we knew no better and were impressed and thought (at least for a while) that our lives were very mundane.

There was a prisoner of war camp at Toft and prisoners were brought out to farms in the big army trucks to help pick the potatoes. About 15 to 20 a day used to come to Park Farm, usually the same gang and the truck would pick them up at night. Trestle tables and forms were set up in the "cart house", a brick building with one side open to the yard. Each day at dinner time, they peeled potatoes for the next day's dinner and these were put in a wash boiler, kept specially for the job. My dad tried to explain that the more they peeled the more they got to eat. Language proved rather difficult so the first day they didn't peel many but after that the boiler was always full to the brim! A baker would call at the farm once or twice a week and they would buy loaves off him, cut it into thick shanks which they would then hide in their clothes, so taking it back into camp for them to either eat later or for their mates who, for various reasons, were not allowed out. They were several nationalities, most of them very decent hard-working young men who had been forced

200

into the war when their countries had become involved. They made the children presents of slippers, pecking hens and a ship in a bottle, which my brother still has.'

'German and Italian prisoners of war worked on the farms at Worleston. The Germans came daily by lorry but the Italians lived in. There were two Italians on a farm near to us. They wore brown uniforms with coloured patches on and they were allowed to cycle in to Nantwich. One of them had a lovely tenor voice and we could hear him singing as he worked in the fields.'

'A Mrs Alltree, who lived in Acton, organised dances on Saturday nights. There was a four-piece band who were very good. Soldiers were camping at Dorfold Hall park, English and American, and at Wardle was a small aerodrome, most of the airmen being Canadian. Needless to say, the hall was pretty crowded and there was no shortage of partners!'

'Northwich became host to many thousands of Allied servicemen. There were large camps of American personnel at Delamere and Marbury and a large RAF base at Cranage, where the well known bandleader Jack White was stationed. I was involved in many concerts at the American camps and was always well chaperoned by my mother!

At the weekend Northwich would be virtually packed with Americans, but apart from the wolf whistles, no young lady felt threatened or intimidated.

Everyone seemed to dance and the Victoria Baths Hall was a popular rendezvous for young people – there was a dance held there almost every evening, often sponsored by a wartime charity. No alcohol was ever served on the premises and on the rare occasions when sailors appeared rather the worse for drink or spoiling for a fight, the dance was immediately closed down.'

'I can recall seeing the "Passion Wagons", as they were called, travelling from the Wirral to the American camp at Burtonwood, near Warrington and also from Chester to Tattenhall where there was another American camp. These were full of young ladies being taken to social events at the camps.'

'The location of a searchlight battery near the Knobs, on a field belonging to Moors Lane Farm near Darnhall, created much local interest, especially among the local girls. However, its presence was less welcome when the lights were switched on at an inopportune moment!'

LIFE GOES ON

Life had to go on regardless, as we brought up families on rationing and 'make do and mend'. It was amazing what could be done with a little ingenuity!

HELPING OUT IN BURTON

'There was a Mothers' Union, a Women's Fellowship and a Women's Institute in Burton. I had joined the latter some time before. We knitted khaki socks and seamen's stockings and I collected Red Cross pennies every week. Then another girl and I collected waste paper. It was funny the things we found out about people doing this, one family must have had Shredded Wheat for breakfast, dinner, tea and supper, there was such a mountain of packets, then at another house we got buckets of Oxo cube wrappers. Then we started making felt flowers and leaves into button-holes. We charged one shilling and sixpence or two shillings each, and with the money we made up parcels for all the young men of the district, writing paper and envelopes, a packet of cigarettes, perhaps a piece of soap or a few sweets, a paperback book, a pencil, sometimes a pair of socks, and always a tin of Zambuk in case the Army boots had rubbed their feet sore.

We laughed with Gert and Daisy on the wireless and their brother Jack Warner, and Rob Wilton and Tommy Handley, and felt sad when we heard of someone losing a son or husband and when our armies suffered yet another defeat; but I well remember D-Day. I was outside when the NAAFI girl came running to tell me there had been a successful invasion. We felt very excited as we listened to the news, but none of us ever doubted that we would win. Of course, it was only the beginning, there was a lot more fighting to do, a lot more lives to be lost and why, oh why, do we forget so soon?

We listened to Dr Charles Hill giving pep talks, saying not to creep about keeping quiet if you had a new baby because they slept through any amount of noise, and not to be afraid of hoovering around them because they wouldn't wake. Another thing he said was, "Let Grandma go out and catch pneumonia if she wanted to, rather than take away her independence."

Our food was still rationed and we listened to Mrs Buggins, a mythical grandmother living with her pretend family, always coming to the rescue with sound commonsense, and meals made with food we all had, rather stodgy menus, which filled us up.

We put soaked bread with the mince, which made more of it. We made honey with sugar added to the water the parsnips had been boiled in. A small ripe marrow and one orange, with carefully saved sugar made quite passable marmalade.

I had chilblains on the backs of my heels and up my legs due to not enough vitamin C. I used to cut a potato, dip it in salt and rub the chilblains, painful, but a sure cure. We had mosquitoes in the summer, great brutes that sang around your head in the night – not many insecticides used then like there are now.'

SELF SUFFICIENCY

'My overriding memories of the summer of 1940 are a mixture of sunshine and apprehension. I was twelve years old and my family lived in Nether Alderley. It was a summer of the most marvellous weather, week after week of hot sunny days and blue skies, which seemed to compensate for the uncertainty of what the next day might bring. After the evacuation of Dunkirk, we seemed to be living on the edge of an abyss.

My parents decided to become as self sufficient as possible and we had hens, ducks and a pair of geese called Hansel and Gretel, until Hansel laid an egg, so we had to swap their names over. My pony's paddock was turned into a vegetable garden and she took up residence on the tennis court and enjoyed the luscious grass there.

During the long, hot days of June, July and August, the problem was keeping the vegetables alive, and we spent many hours watering the field. As this field was quite a way from the source of water, the water had to be brought from the house in a "dandy" – this was a large galvanised bucket on wheels, which creaked and groaned its way along the uneven paths; it took two of us to push it but all this was well worthwhile as we had the most marvellous vegetables, vast cabbages, enormous white cauliflowers and long straight carrots.

My father was away a great deal; he worked for the Ministry of Food. My mother was an ambulance driver and she and I, during the school holidays, took a mobile YMCA canteen round to the army camps, barrage balloon sites and ack-ack emplacements, selling cigarettes, razor blades and many other items, including tea and the most delicious fruit cake.

My outstanding memory of this memorable time was a day in August when my brother and I were helping to stook corn at a local farm, when the church bell started to ring and I can remember vividly a stab of fear in the pit of my stomach and everyone in the field looked up as though they were expecting to see German

203

paratroopers descending from the sky; as we know now, it was a false alarm and who rang the bell was never discovered, although it was assumed to be boys playing a joke, as in those days churches were never kept locked.

My father had an air raid shelter dug in the garden and the clay subsoil was piled on the top. My mother wondered how she could cover what she called this "unsightly mound" and decided to plant roses, as these were her favourite flowers; this proved to be an inspired choice as I have never seen such marvellous roses since and they gave us much pleasure during the dark days of that summer and for many years to come.'

CAMOUFLAGE NETS

'During the war the billiard/playroom of the Victorian house in which we lived was turned over to the weaving of camouflage nets. Once a month a huge army truck arrived bringing spools of three inch hessian in shades of brown, sand, olive green and khaki; it took away bundles of the completed nets which had been woven by teams of WVS ladies – and others – who came every weekday afternoon for two or three hours. The nets had to be woven to a definite pattern and one of the husbands had rigged up a pulley system in which the sample net hung between two unworked nets which were raised as the work progressed. Two teams worked, one on each side of the sample net and there was considerable competition to see who could do the work the fastest! Over the years definite team leaders emerged – each team did one day a week – and considerable rivalry grew between the different days. My mother kept a daily record of how many nets were worked and the log book was the first thing the workers looked at when they arrived – to see what their target was. I cannot remember how many were woven daily – perhaps eight or ten – but I know that the pile of finished nets stored in the old stables was quite impressive and the monthly truck took away as many as 200.

I remember the dusty, throat catching smell of the hessian "ribbon" and the creosote of the basic netting. When I came in from school almost the first thing I did was to go to the playroom to see how the work was going and sometimes I was allowed to weave a bit of the net. The "ribbons" were cut in six foot lengths and woven according to the pattern; corners had to be correctly folded in a special way so that they lay flat. It seemed difficult to me then but I felt very proud that I had done my bit of war work.

The Manchester blitz is another memory: although we had spent the night in the air raid shelter under the house I recall being taken up to the attic at about six in the morning and looking across the country to Manchester some 15 miles away. The sky was vividly red and orange and even at that distance it was possible to see the debris in the flames. Searchlights probed the sky but by then the planes had done their damage. It was an incredible sight and I only wish now that I had been old enough to understand the terrible, awful sight that it was.'

THE WI AT WORK

'As Audlem was a reception area for evacuees, members of the WI were involved, along with members of other organisations, in the reception and welcoming of the evacuees. Some time before war was declared, billets had to be found for the children with families who were willing to receive them and who had the necessary accommodation. Where there was more than one child from a family, we tried to keep them together. We had to make sure that they had sufficient beds and bedding. Where they had not, we appealed for gifts of unwanted bedding and loaned beds, where beds were needed.

Later on in the war, we had more children and their teachers from Guernsey. They came when the Channel Islands were invaded by the Germans and they stayed until the war ended.

Members were involved in many other wartime activities. One was the War Savings Campaign. This was a Government scheme to help the war effort. An organiser was appointed who enlisted members to go round and sell savings stamps from house to house on a weekly basis. The whole of the Audlem area was covered and it proved to be very popular, as several thousands of pounds were saved in this way.

Another activity was the Penny a Week Red Cross Scheme. Members again went from house to house and hoped to receive a penny at least from each house. All this money went to help the Red Cross carry on their good work at home and abroad.

Another scheme was the Rural Pie Scheme. We took over a small disused shop situated in the Square between Halliwell's and the Co-op which belonged to an old Audlem man, Mr Lawton, who lived at Stafford House. Each person who wanted a pie ordered and came and collected it on a Friday afternoon. They cost two shillings each and were much sought after. We made a profit from selling these pies and it was given to charities such as the Nursing Association, Red Cross, NSPCC and St Dunstan's.

Before the war started, a St John's Ambulance Brigade had been formed. Members attended classes in first aid and home nursing and were required to pass exams to show that they knew the theory and could do the practical work. When war came, we were asked to man the first aid point in Audlem. Our depot was the old church rooms in Church Fields. Some of the lady members became full time VAD nurses at Stapeley Hospital for soldiers.

In November 1943, the Child Welfare Clinic was opened in the Methodist schoolroom. This was run by members with the doctor and district nurse in attendance. Members did the clerical work and sold the baby food and vitamins. The clinic operated on alternate Tuesdays and has continued until the present day.

Another scheme was the knitting of comforts for the Forces. Suitable wool was bought with money raised from donations and events such as whist drives held in members' houses. Gloves, socks, mufflers, pullovers, mittens, gumboot stockings and helmets were some of the garments made.'

'During the war Acton and Reaseheath WI had a Jamming Centre in one of the outbuildings at Reaseheath college. My mother was a member and very quickly became involved in the centre as it was only just down the road from where we lived.

I was only eleven when the war began, but during the holidays I would cycle with my mother to help to make jam or to can fruit, whatever was in season. The fruit was bought locally and if anyone had a surplus of pears, plums, damsons, strawberries, raspberries, rhubarb, gooseberries or tomatoes, they were all gratefully canned or jammed. There were very strict rules for the jam making which had to be perfectly set or it was put back into the pan and boiled up again.

The grocers' shops in Nantwich and Crewe were always very keen to buy our jam or canned fruit as it was of a much higher standard than the factory made jam. The canning of fruit was also to a very high standard and tomatoes were skinned and packed into cans with just one teaspoon sugar and one teaspoon salt – no water and they were delicious. We were not allowed to can vegetables as they required pressure cooking and we were not geared for that. We were given an allowance of sugar to begin with and then the more jam we made the more sugar we were allocated. I think my main job was sticking labels onto jars and cans and even these had to be put on exactly right. And of course there was washing up. All the jars had to be washed and dried and the cans scalded before use.'

RATIONS AND MAKE DO AND MEND

'When commodities were scarce a consignment would arrive at a certain shop and the news would spread. Before long a queue would form. These goods could be anything from cigarettes to nylon stockings to food. Thus, it is said, the British public learned to

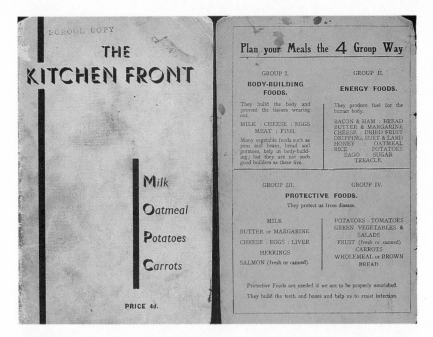

THE

KITCHEN FRONT

Milk

Oatmeal

Potatoes

Carrots

PRICE 4d.

Plan your Meals the 4 Group Way

GROUP I.	GROUP II.
BODY-BUILDING FOODS.	**ENERGY FOODS.**
They build the body and prevent the tissues wearing out.	They produce fuel for the human body.
MILK : CHEESE : EGGS MEAT : FISH.	BACON & HAM : BREAD BUTTER & MARGARINE CHEESE : DRIED FRUIT DRIPPING, SUET & LARD HONEY : OATMEAL RICE : POTATOES SAGO : SUGAR TREACLE.
Many vegetable foods such as peas and beans, bread and potatoes, help in body-building; but they are not such good builders as these five.	

GROUP III.	GROUP IV.
PROTECTIVE FOODS.	
They protect us from disease.	
MILK	POTATOES : TOMATOES
BUTTER or MARGARINE	GREEN VEGETABLES & SALADS
CHEESE : EGGS : LIVER	FRUIT (fresh or canned)
HERRINGS	CARROTS
SALMON (fresh or canned).	WHOLEMEAL or BROWN BREAD

Protective Foods are needed if we are to be properly nourished.

They build the teeth and bones and help us to resist infection.

'The Kitchen Front' was typical of the government booklets that exhorted housewives to use home-produced food economically and imaginatively.

queue. There were many funny stories, some actually true, about red faces when someone had queued for the wrong goods.

Of course one of the scarcities was coal. Most people had coal fires, there was very little domestic central heating in those days. People supplemented their coal rations with wood, and there were "brickets and egglets" made from coal dust and something more solid, I never knew what, and shaped into rectangular or egg shapes. They made a warm glow when added to a well burning fire and the warmth lasted well. Poor-burning coal such as anthracite, not meant for open fires, was sometimes delivered and was not satisfactory at all.

With a scarcity of luxuries, people resorted to substituting things. My mother would mix butter and margarine, which in those days tasted nothing like butter. My friend's mother used to beat butter, water and I think gelatine to eke it out for a growing family. Sometimes these ideas were rather bizarre. The same friend's mother coloured a blancmange for a birthday party with red ink and we did not know until we had eaten it. Whether she had researched its contents I never knew but we all lived to tell the tale. Not everyone was so lucky. There was a case where a mother had added washing starch to the icing on a birthday cake. It was poisonous and several children died as a result.

Clothes, furniture and possibly other items were made to a specific standard called "utility". This was to ensure, I think, that people got fairly good value for their money but at the same time there was no waste of valuable or scarce materials. There was a "utility" label bearing a special mark attached to most manufactured goods. Housewives were asked to turn in their iron cookware to be recycled and turned into guns, planes, tanks etc. Many people had ornate iron railings on top of their low front garden walls. These, as well as metal gates and full length railings, were removed and taken away for the war effort. There have since been conflicting rumours as to whether these were, in fact, ever used. These walls still have the stubs of the railings supports showing today.'

'Clothes were rationed (40 coupons per person per year) and every single dress or coat had a second lease of life in a different colour. Dyeing was "de rigeur" and for four shillings and sixpence you could pretend that the coat or dress was new again. Good leather shoes were difficult to find and for a period shoes were made with wooden soles and heels.

Stockings were rationed (three coupons for two pairs) and nylon hadn't reached us, so they laddered rather quickly. During the summer we all went bare legged and painted our legs with flesh coloured powder mixed with water, "Leg Tan" bought from the chemist for about sixpence. Some daring, steady handed souls drew "seams" down the backs of their legs with dark crayon. Make-up was difficult to obtain, but "lacto-calamine" lotion was quite a good base and I remember making a face mask from milk and salt! The lipstick that we all seemed to chase had the name "Jean Claude" but this brand disappeared from circulation at the end of the war.

Food was scarce during the war, although you could always buy a meal in restaurants. "Vienna steak" was usually available on the menu, but you never enquired about its contents! Everyone had a good recipe for cake made with dried egg – there was even an egg-less sponge cake that went like rubber if you didn't eat it the same day. I remember one particular cake made with liquid paraffin, but I think it was discouraged by the Ministry of Food.

To eke out the meat ration, whale steaks were sometimes available (and something called "snoek") and the butter ration was made to go further by being mixed with a can of evaporated milk. Bread was made from National flour and of a grey appearance: jokes flew around on the subject and all kinds of ailments were said to be "caused by the bread".'

'I think many servicemen came home at the end of the war to find their civilian wardrobe sadly depleted. I can remember my mother making me a skirt from a pair of trousers which belonged to my eldest brother. When we washed our hair we used to make a setting lotion out of sugar and water. We spent the next day hoping it would not rain and reduce us to a horrible sticky mess.'

'Magazines carried articles on how to cut down adult clothes to make items for children, and on how to renovate old clothing. Later in the war we were lucky enough to acquire some parachute material, which made excellent petticoats and nighties (and needed no coupons). Do you remember hand-knitted "costumes" for swimming, which stretched with the weight of the water, and as you waded into the sea your costume would be a couple of waves behind you!'

A CHILD'S WAR

Children grew up accepting war as a normal state of affairs, though for some of them, the evacuees, it meant upheaval and sometimes unhappiness.

BORN INTO WAR

'I was born in St Catherine's Hospital, Birkenhead on 28th October 1940, during the Battle of Britain. The air raid warning sounded as Mum was being taken to the labour ward and during my birth she listened to gunfire from the gun outside the ward. As the all clear was sounded, the midwife announced my arrival.

Though so young through the war, I can remember people saying, "You're all right, it's one of ours," as planes were heard overhead, or being pushed under the stairs or table if they were German. A large drawer from a chest was made up as my cradle as it was easy to move with me asleep in it.

Most of my toys were home-made. My scooter had wooden wheels and the front wheel had to be renewed as it became oval! My aunt would cut out dolls from cardboard and paper dresses with fold-over tabs for me to colour, and newspaper was folded and cut into trees, animals etc, all joined together for me to paint.'

PART OF CHILDHOOD

'When the war broke out, we moved to the centre of Hale, as my father had opened a new chemist's shop and money was in short supply. A vivid memory is the sound of the sirens which often went in the evening or during the night. The public air raid shelter was under the shops on the opposite side of the road, so all those living on our side used to quickly make our way there carrying blankets, cushions and bags of valuables and gas masks. Each family had its own bit of a bench and these spots were guarded jealously. When the all clear siren went we would all troop home and try and get some sleep before it was time to get up. Sometimes we had two or three trips to the shelter each night. As the months dragged on, we were all so weary that we, like many others, had our cellar reinforced, and our beds made up in the cellar, so at least we did not have to get up and go out when the siren wailed. I recall if we had had a disturbed night we could be late to school next day, 10 am instead of 9 am.

At school we each had to have a bag in the cloakroom containing iron rations, a thick jumper and a book and a torch. When the siren went, the whole school of 500 had to make their way quickly and orderly to the dugouts across the Devisdale where two forms shared an underground shelter. Lessons were carried on. Needless to say we broke all rules and immediately started eating our iron rations, as it was fairly dark with only two oil lamps and the teachers could not see us.

Troops were stationed in Hale in the large empty houses on the outskirts. These soldiers used to march down to the drill hall carrying billy cans for their main meals. Many families including ours used to offer these lads hospitality – their greatest treat being a bath in hot water. In return they would bring us the odd bar of chocolate and cake of soap.

Our local Congregational church hall was turned into a British Restaurant, where canteen-type meals were provided quite cheaply. This helped to eke out the rations. I also remember on Fridays, we used to have what was known as Post Office Pies. These were sold by a sub post office and people came from far and wide for a treat of potato, carrot and a little meat encased in pastry. We occasionally received food parcels from friends in Canada – tinned butter and pork, also in a tin with a supply of fat which could be made into a pork pie by the addition of water – a great treat and always reserved for special dates. My friend and I were to be evacuated to these friends in Toronto but the ship, the *City of Benares*, was torpedoed and so my father decided it was safer in England!

From school we used to have days off to go potato picking or corn stooking. We travelled in the train to Knutsford and were met at the station by the farmer with a tractor and trailer who took us to his fields. We received four shillings a day. Once I lost mine and he kindly replaced it, for he said you could not work all day for nothing.

An occasional treat during the war was a car ride to Tatton Park where we would watch the parachute troops practising their jumps. We used to have special days with parades through the streets with collections for the different troops. One I remember was "Wings for Victory" when local organisations joined in the procession with much cheering and playing of bands. On VE night bonfires were lit everywhere and lights were ablaze. The church bells rang and people danced in the streets until the early hours of the next day. The parades that followed were superb with flags and bunting everywhere.'

WHEN THEY CAME TO PLUMLEY

'On that warm September day, the evacuees from Lostock estate, Stretford, arrived at Plumley chapel schoolroom – no village hall in those days – about 150 children, labelled and carrying a few belongings in a bag, came into the room. Mr J Leigh was the billeting officer and, at that time, I was the Sunday school superintendent (and younger in those far off days!) As you probably know, it was compulsory to fill all the rooms at each home. A local farmer started the exit by saying, "Give me a couple of likely lads," and off they went.

Gradually the children, some excited, some tearful, were taken to homes. Those left looked sadder and sadder. Identical twins of nine years old were among those left, so I popped them in the car and took them to Mother at Brookhouse Farm. We were not really scheduled to take any because, although we had five bedrooms, we had helpers living in who worked on the farm. These included land girls. Back to chapel to find the numbers reduced to about a dozen, so it was decided to take six to Ascol Drive in one car and I took the others in our car.

One call made was where elderly people lived but, nevertheless, were down to receive two children. Going to the door, I tried to explain the circumstances when the man said "Where are the children?" One was in the kennel of the chained "savage" dog but quite happy patting the animal without fear! J took them – the six children – back to the car, which had a sun-roof, when one said, "Jimmy's on the roof," and, sure enough, he had managed to climb on top. Next stop Mrs Leigh's, who would have three. Unfortunately, Jimmy would not get out – never been in a car before and never getting out any more! We coaxed for ages and ages but no result – until a cow came to the gate and loudly moo-ed. "What's that there?"

211

says Jimmy, and hopped out to investigate. Immediately I was gone – to our final port of call and happy to have helped to rapidly place each youngster.

Within a week many had returned home but those left settled in quite happily. Our twins, Mae and June, were lovely children. They had to walk to Lower Peover school except when we could spare a little petrol to help on the journey, but petrol, of course, was rationed. Many of the children came from poor homes – ours only possessed the clothes they were wearing. Their father had been out of work for the previous two years. Mother knitted their clothes and arrived the following week with new jumpers etc for each child. They were nice folk and we were glad to know them. Christmas with our extended family was one of the nicest we ever had!'

THE SEASONS CAME AND WENT

'I was five years old at the start of the war. Living in a Cheshire village I was unaware of the terrible events taking place in Europe, Africa and other war torn places, though we *did* sing songs about a man called Hitler which described what we would do to him should he have the effrontery to cross the English Channel.

Air raid practice meant a visit to the school air raid shelter. I hated this dark, damp dungeon-like place, home to frogs, slugs, woodlice and goodness knows what other unspeakable horrors. The air raid siren was located at the salt works near my home and, if that wailing noise was heard, my mother would wrap us in blankets and put us under the sturdy kitchen table for safety. This all seemed very exciting to us so my mother must have been very good at hiding her own considerable fear.

The seasons came and went with comforting regularity. In the wintertime we had the blackout, when even the tiniest chink of light was met with the stern warning from the air raid warden, "Get that light out." In the summer we had double summer time. This entailed putting the clocks forward in spring for two hours and, in the height of the summer months, it would still be daylight at eleven o'clock at night.

I remember, with particular clarity, one such summer night. The weather had been really hot for what seemed like weeks. I would have been seven or eight years old and my sister four or five. We were always put to bed at eight o'clock but, as soon as Mum was downstairs, we two would creep out of bed and over to the window. Once there we would carefully open the window and stand drinking in the cool evening air, looking at the beautiful sunset and listening to the sounds of the dying day. Mr Johnson would be going to lock up his hens for the night and we could hear the clump, clump of his clogs on the brick path and smell the pungent aroma of the tobacco from his pipe. Another neighbour whistled as he tended his vegetable patch. On the back field the village boys played football and our vocabulary was considerably widened by the boisterous comments floating up to our window. When the match was over the young men would sit around the field and sing. If I close my eyes on a balmy summer evening I can still hear them harmonising – *Home on the range, Don't fence me in* and *White cliffs of Dover. Coming in on a wing and a prayer* was particularly poignant. How evocative these tunes are when heard occasionally today.

One day a German pilot parachuted into a field close by our home and everyone ran out to see what kind of monster would be there. A very frightened young man cowered on the ground with a broken leg, convinced that he would be tortured or shot on sight. If only he had understood that the fierce looking ladies rushing towards him with large scissors were anxious to get their hands (and scissors) into his parachute. In these times of austerity and clothes coupons, the silk was in great demand for underwear and many a wartime bride walked down the aisle adorned in the remains of a lifesaving canopy. I often wonder where that man is today.'

GUNS AND BOMBERS

'My memories are of the war years when aged between seven and 13, I lived in Poynton near to the boundary with Adlington. Down the road, just over the Adlington boundary was an anti-invasion road block – huge round blocks of concrete set four deep across the road, with a staggered channel for traffic to pass through. All the children used to try and climb on to them and jump from one to another. These were removed, I suppose, when the threat of invasion passed. There was also a pill box nearby (which is still there) that the Home Guard used to guard the road. Further along the road down Street Lane was a heavy gun site. I only remember the gun, known locally as Big Bertha, being fired once – it broke a lot of windows nearby. We had several cracked windows at home until the end of the war.

There was an American army camp in Adlington and girls used to come from far and wide to visit the camp. When the buses reached Poynton the conductors used to call out "Poynton USA" and girls would stream off the buses. As children we had a lot of fun with the Americans, following them and spying on them with the girls. On the whole they took it very well and often encouraged us in a friendly way.

Another memory is of walking across fields with a friend to Woodford aerodrome where the Lancaster bombers were made and getting inside the airfield perimeter. An RAF Flight was having their photograph taken and we ran across and sat down in front of them and had our photographs taken too. We had a lucky escape one day, when Woodford was divebombed by two Junker 88 planes. They completely missed the aerodrome, but as our house was very near to the runway they were on to us before they could pull out of the dive properly. Fortunately, we had three tall trees in the back garden, which the pilot saw at the last moment and he managed to hop over them. We think the trees saved our lives, as the planes machine-gunned a boys' cricket team at a school a few miles away and killed most of them. The planes were shot down near the coast on their way home.'

'When the war started I was nine years old. Life went on in Heswall. My dad became an air raid warden. He was too old to fight in the 1939 conflict, so he did the next best thing. Dad had fought in the First World War and was wounded three times; his face was full of iron filings. The Germans had run out of filling for the shells towards the end of the war, so they used iron filings. When he shaved you could hear the sound of metal on metal, and it was my job to pull the offending piece of metal out with a pair of tweezers, they were very fine and difficult to see among his whiskers. One day we counted 30 pieces. He also carried a piece of metal at the corner of his left eye. It was embedded, and by the time he got back to the hospital from the front line, three days had elapsed and the skin had grown over. His sight was unaffected, so the metal was left alone.

I attended St Peter's school and we had air raid shelters built in the field next to the school. We children had to take sweets and a bar of chocolate in a tin box, to leave in the shelter in case of "emergency," the emergency being an air raid. We did have to use the shelters on several occasions. Our schooling was interrupted quite a lot. We had to share our school with children from Wallasey, as the raids were heavy that side of the river and on the Wirral. One week we would go in the morning and they in the afternoon, the following week we changed around. In 1941 the Germans bombed the Heswall side of the Wirral; it lasted for one week in May. Our school lost three classrooms, the headmaster's house, and his daughter and her fiance were killed. A boy in our class had his home bombed and his mother, father, sister and her friend, were all killed; the rest of his family survived. My father and grandfather went to Heswall shore on the Sunday at the end of the week of bombing. It was littered with shrapnel, and dud incendiary bombs. My grandfather brought me a dud incendiary home as a present. Believe it or not it sat on the window sill in my bedroom for quite a number of years. Mother had painted the fin black and the base silver. It was heavy to move. In the end it was put out for the bin man to remove!

214

After St Peter's was bombed classes were arranged in the parish hall, three infants classes, with a large curtain separating each one. The four other classes went down to the remainder of the school that was still standing, after it was cleaned up.

Evacuees from Wallasey came to stay in Heswall. We had one for half a day. Mother went to the Methodist church one Sunday morning, where the evacuees were gathered waiting for people to collect them. A young girl around my age came home with Mother. We had breakfast and then it was time to go to church, off we went, as soon as she saw her friends she burst into tears so that was the end of our evacuee, she went elsewhere. We could only take people in if we had a spare room. Some of the people had very sad tales to tell. Most of them had lost everything. One young mother was holding her baby in her arms, the blast from a bomb killed her baby as she held it.

One of our relatives in Wallasey was bombed out. When the family went the following day to view the ruins they found the canary still singing in its cage among the ruins.'

WHAT A SHOCK IT WAS

'I was eight when the war started, an only child living with my parents in Stretford. Because of the close proximity to Trafford Park, it was decided to evacuate the schoolchildren to a village in Cheshire, away from the expected bombing.

The children duly arrived by coach; we all spilled out on to a pub forecourt, where all the officials and deputy mothers were waiting to take us in. After a lot of sorting out, myself and two other girls and one rather sour lady and the officials were left. The lady, who looked very old to us, was arguing with the officer that she wanted three boys, not three girls. "Girls have too much washing," she said.

Eventually she took us in under protest. What a shock life in the country was to us townees; for a start, we all had to sleep in the same bed, there was only a cold water sink in the kitchen for washing, and the toilet was an outside privy with no flushing facility. Breakfast every morning was a very small egg and a wedge of bread. They kept a large battery of pigeons in the back garden and she told us that's where the eggs were from.

We had a long walk to school and we had to go under the canal at one point and the walls of the tunnel were always wet and we used to run like mad, convinced the canal was going to collapse on top of us.

Every day she gave us sago pudding, which we all called "frog spawn". We only stayed there for seven weeks but I've never forgotten it.

I did survive our house in Stretford getting bombed with a direct hit, and going to live with an aunt and uncle in Southport for three years before being reunited with my parents, but I've never eaten sago pudding or set foot in that village again to this day.'

HARD TO FIT IN

'I remember two children coming to Alpraham from Liverpool as evacuees. They ate their food on the back doorstep as they were not used to eating at a table.'

'Norley Bank was converted to a Red Cross hospital and officially opened in October 1940, but the wounded soldiers were not admitted until January 1941. Before that the building was used to house evacuees from London. I was the head nurse and the children, aged between five and ten, were a very destructive lot from poorer homes. There was hardly a visit from parents during the couple of years they were in Norley.'

'Wybunbury received 33 evacuees from Liverpool, aged between four and ten. They attended the village school, and many had never seen a cow or fields before. One called Danny is particularly remembered. Two ladies had cooked a quantity of stew in a tin bath. They had lifted it off the stove on to the floor and Danny put his foot in it (with shoe). It was still served up. The children were all Roman Catholics, and as there was no Catholic church in the village, services were held in the school for them.'

TOO HAPPY

'My father put his head around the bedroom door and called to us "Get up. The war's over! We're going out." My sister, aged twelve, and I, aged ten, got dressed and walked down past the park with Mum and Dad.

We had experienced some of the sadnesses of war. As evacuees we spent an unhappy six weeks away from our parents and with strangers who did not want us. Even now, so many years later, it upsets us to think about that episode in our young lives. Back at home, we hid in the cupboard under the stairs or spent the night in the Anderson shelter during the bombing raids on the docks. Our school, St Albans, received a direct hit. We had lessons in the church hall and played around the crater in the schoolyard.

On that night of celebration in 1945 it seemed to me that the whole population of New Brighton was on the promenade. For the first time in five years the lights of Liverpool blazed across the water. The sight of grown-ups strolling about wearing coats over their night clothes struck me as somewhat improper.

The following Saturday our friend Gladys, aged 13, accompanied us to the pictures. We saw Susan Hayward playing the part of a poor girl in love with a rich man. At a low point in her story she folded her arms across her bosom "That's a sign of insecurity," Gladys informed us in a loud whisper. Gladys would go on to become a teacher. She knew everything and there were times when I longed to tell her to shut up. After the film we went out into the post-war sunshine and Gladys gave us another piece of her wisdom, "There will be a lot of suicides," she said. I stared at her, goggle-eyed. "Now that the war is over people will be too happy. They will not be able to cope," declared Gladys. I walked on down the street, my arms folded over my flat chest muttering to myself, "I must not be too happy. I must not be too happy." '

WE DID OUR BIT

Women who were called up for service had a choice of working in munitions, in the services such as the ATS, or in the Women's Land Army, and many chose the latter. It was hard and essential work, producing food for a besieged nation.

MY LIFE AS A LAND GIRL

'During 1940 I was teaching at my old school in Wallasey. My ambition at that time was to become qualified to teach History and English Classics. The war, however, played havoc with ambition and the school eventually closed, owing to most of the pupils having been bombed out or evacuated. This, of course, meant I was out of a job and on the first Friday after the termination of my work I joined the dole queue. Three weeks of this was quite enough, during which time I did a lot of thinking and came up with the idea I would like to join the WRNS, but decided my mathematical prowess was not good enough so finally I decided on the Land Army. At least, I could count cattle, sheep and pigs etc on my fingers!

The war years subjected us to some of the severest winters I have ever experienced and 1941 was no exception. I then lived in Marine Terrace, Wallasey which was halfway between Egremont and New Brighton; we were thus provided with a ringside seat for the nightly enemy aerial bombardment. From this setting I woke on the morning of 24th January, my 21st birthday, to see ice floes floating along the shoreline of the Mersey. After breakfasting, I took myself off to the Town Hall and was recruited for the Land Army.

On 17th February, just three weeks after recruitment, I was off to Reaseheath College of Agriculture for a month's training. As the men's college was officially closed at that time, it was opened for the training of land girls. I arrived at Nantwich station on a wintery afternoon – here I met another girl called Iris who was also going to the college and we were offered a lift by a local farmer which we took with gratitude as motor transport was very scarce owing to petrol rationing. On arrival we were given our uniform, instructions, and our number, thus I became WLA 37606. We were then shown our bedrooms. I shared with three other girls a large freezing room with four single beds, a rug by each bed on a linoleum covered floor and provision for our private possessions. After this we went down to our first meal which consisted of boiled fish (it being Friday), boiled potatoes, boiled parsnips, never my favourite vegetable since, and slabs of dry bread. After this repast, we were allowed to settle in and sort out our uniforms: corded breeches, cream aertex shirts, lovely warm V-necked green pullovers, greatcoat, hat, badge, tie, woollen socks and stout shoes. For work we had stone-coloured dungarees and wellingtons. Your one aim was to organise a change of jumper and a best pair of breeches as most of the time you smelt very strongly of cows!

Our first morning we reported for duty at 6 am. There was frost an inch thick on the yard gate. We then went into the shippons where we very quickly learned how to hand milk. An accomplishment I was intensely proud of as I was a "town girl" and for some years after my marriage I still continued to hand milk as we had no electric on our small farm and in the beginning, no generator, only our hands. After evening milking we would comb our hair over a piece of white paper to rid ourselves of unwelcome visitors collected from our proximity with the cows' flanks; hair washing was therefore a very necessary, if somewhat basic exercise. Baths were hardly a bundle of fun either, perhaps they were deemed to be part of the toughening up process. The atmosphere was freezing. They had to be taken at set times obviously because of the heating of the water.

During that month we went through every possible facet of farm work that could be done. It really was a very intensive month of training and we did feel the better equipped to cope with most eventualities. Sadly, I lost touch with the girls who were with me, we all got on wonderfully well together.

I went home for the weekend after finishing at Reaseheath and on 17th March 1941 I started at Morris Done's farm – Larkton House,

Proving that land girls could be as glamorous as the next woman was Pat Grainger-Smith, who was posted to Malpas in 1941.

Malpas. Another girl joined me there called Daphne; we shared a room and were very comfortable and lived with the family.

My duties began at 6 am when I started the fire in the boiler house, which was a little hampered at times as we had a searchlight battery billeted on our farm, and for some reason a driver and the cook from this outfit slept in the boiler house. After this I went straight to the dairy and brought the milk up from the shippon which was put through the cooler. At this time we were bottling milk; Dones were one of the big names for tuberculin-tested milk in the area. After breakfast back to the dairy to wash and sterilise all the vessels used for milking and dairy equipment plus bottles. At intervals the rubbers and liners of the milking machines had also to be scrubbed out and sterilised. We had to use quite a lot of soda so it was a bit hard on the hands and I certainly wore out wellingtons on the dairy floor. In the afternoons we did field work. Summer of course brought hay and corn harvests with their long working hours and overtime at one shilling and sixpence per hour for us. We girls did unloading and stacking – the latter both at the hay-bay and down the field on the trailers, knowlege of which came in very useful after my marriage as our place was small and the work on it very much a family affair. We girls also did a 60 hour basic week for which we were paid, if my memory serves me right, £1 7s 6d after deduction of board and lodging. Winter work included muck spreading, threshing and a multiplicity of other jobs in between.

One of my early leaves was in May 1941 and I arrived home to experience the horrendous fire blitz on Liverpool. After another leave I returned to find a Heinkel bomber had been shot down on John Done's land – father to my boss. The flight path of these bombers was always a worry to me, as regularly we saw them over Liverpool and Wallasey. We could hear the dull thuds and see the flashes. One night at the Manor House there was a disastrous stack fire and everyone was working desperately to get it under control because it made a perfect target. There was no sleep for any of us that night.

We had lots of fun in our free time. Daphne and I organised Land Army dances with other land girls from neighbouring farms. We had no lack of support because at Cholmondeley Park there was no shortage of soldiers, sailors and airmen of various nationalities throughout the war, including Americans. A local lady started a club which operated once a week for local land girls. This we enjoyed very much as it gave us a chance to meet and discuss all sorts of things, as with a big workload girls on individual farms tended to become a little isolated. In summer we played tennis. She was very good to us and had the welfare of the girls at heart. There were drama and operatic groups we could join and these being the days before universal television, we played to full houses for a week at a time. Sometimes, after all this, 6 am came rather quickly and was somewhat unwelcome on a cold winter's morning.'

HORSES AND MOLES

'I was 17 when I joined the Women's Land Army. My first job was on a farm at Sydney near Crewe, called Pump House Farm and owned by a Mr J. Green. The farm has long since gone and a new housing estate is there now. I did a milk round in the morning and general farm work in the afternoon. I drove a horse and float with milk tankards on and as it was wartime there were very few milk bottles so the milk was served from a two gallon can with a pint or half pint measure into the customer's jug.

One of the first jobs I was given to do was take Bonny, one of the carthorses, to the blacksmith's. I was supposed to walk from the farm at Sydney to the blacksmith's in Rainbow Street off Earle Street in Crewe, about two and a half miles. I set off walking down the road and about 100 yards away I thought, "This is daft, why am I walking when I could ride?" I stopped at the nearest gate, climbed up and got on the horse, no saddle or stirrups, legs wide apart because of her size. When I arrived at the smithy I didn't know how to get off so I fell off, landing under the horse's tummy and she never moved a muscle. The blacksmith could not stop laughing.

Later on I was sent to a farm at Macclesfield Forest roughly three miles from the Cat and Fiddle Inn. It was a coincidence because my mother was brought up at Wildboarclough, where my great-grandfather was headmaster of the village school and was quite well known round there.

It was very hard work, as the farmer and I worked the 80 acre farm between us. We milked 40 cows twice a day by hand, and did the rest of the farm work during the day. We used to get snowed in every winter and all the farmers used to get together and dig the roads out so the milk waggon could get through to collect the tankards of milk.

The farmers' wives got in stocks of flour, vegetables, dried peas etc ready for the winter. Then they could make their own bread and cakes. We cured our own bacon and ham. What a job it was rubbing salt and turning the sides of bacon every day – did your hands a power of good!

After two and a half years there I hurt the muscles in my tummy with all the hard work and lifting. I was given a job with the "War-Ag" (the Ministry of Agriculture, Fisheries and Food) as a mole catcher. I trained and was sent to Cholmondeley in "digs". I covered 1,600 acres on a bike provided by the Ministry, loaded up with traps, a little spade and knee pads, plus sandwiches. The farmers had a contract with the Ministry and paid one shilling an acre for two visits a year by the mole catcher. When I first started I used to skin them and pin them on a board to dry and then send them off to a firm who made moleskin fur coats. They paid four pence each but each time I sent a batch they rejected some of them so in the end I gave up because it was a lot of work for very little return. Incidentally, it takes 800 skins to make a full length fur coat.'

CAT IN THE MILK

'I spent four years in the Women's Land Army. One morning at Preston Brook, Warrington, I arranged the milking units in the steriliser. For a few minutes there was quite a clatter and I assumed something had overbalanced. Unknown to me, sensing the heat, the farm cat had slipped inside. Later as I switched off and opened the door, out fell the stiff, wet body of the cat. The lorry driver who called to collect the milk remarked, "I knew this was a clean farm but I didn't know they even sterilised the b . . . cats!" '

IN THE ATS

'I joined the ATS in May 1939 and from a holiday in Brighton I was called up to Chester Castle on 3rd September 1939. I had volunteered as a cook and was put into the officers' mess, where my first job was to "cut peeled potatoes into even sizes" for roast potatoes. In those days the men did all the roasts and main courses and the girls were responsible for the sweets. I received my first stripe for making a Charlotte Russe for Princess Mary. At this time I was "local service", which meant that I couldn't be posted away from Chester and I went home every night when my duties were finished.

I was attached to the Cheshire Regiment and a new barracks was being prepared for them at The Dale near Chester. I was sent (by this time I had achieved my full corporal's stripe) in 1940 in the advance party to open up the officers' mess, and as the kitchen in the lovely big house was not yet ready, we cooked in the row of married quarters houses not far from the mess. These houses were of course equipped with small domestic cookers and we pulled down the fences between each house and cooked meat in one house, roast potatoes and vegetables and sweets in another. It was a good job that the weather was fine – it was the summer of Dunkirk and so many of us will remember how beautiful it was.

I changed to general service and was posted to Saighton Camp, Chester as mess steward with the two Royal Artillery regiments who were stationed there. The camp was still only a stone's throw from my home. During my time there, the camp housed the Army School of Physical Training and also for a time an American hospital. High jinks between the officers and the American nurses! I left Chester in 1942, leaving with the regiments who were posted to Park Hall Camp, Oswestry which was a training camp taking the boys from "civvy street" and giving them their initial training. Many sports stars passed through including footballers Joe Mercer, Tommy Lawton and Frank Swift, actors Leo Genn and John Witty and artist David Wright who used to do "Ladies out of uniform" in the *Tatler*.

I was demobbed with my age group in 1945 – going to Manchester on a Saturday where I received my issue of clothing coupons and I returned to Park Hall Camp on the Monday doing the same job as a civilian – the only difference was the pay!'

AT CREWE WORKS

'During the war, with a "control of engagement order" in operation, when my age group "came up", I went to register at the then Local Labour Exchange. Despite my own personal choice, I was informed that I would have to go into "industry" which was, at that time, the main priority and I had a choice of Rolls Royce or Crewe Works. As a number of girls from Bunbury were working at Crewe Works, I chose this and with fear and trepidation presented myself at the allotted time, complete with boiler suit or dungarees, as they are now called. (I had previously been informed that I could not work in the offices, despite my training, but would have to go into the workshops.) I reported at the Brass Finishing Shop, arriving by train and journeying out to the West Street area. I had not long left a girls only school in Chester and the sight that met my eyes was unbelievable, to say the least!

The "shop" was designed with benches down the centre and lathes operated by shafting (belt systems) from the ceiling along both sides. The noise was deafening (no wonder, someone told me, you became deaf or daft, when you'd worked there for some time). I was taken along to a large machine, operated by an equally large lady, turning out brass tail pipes, with a coolant pouring on to the metal. This liquid smelled abominably, the smell seemed to cling to your clothing, and needed strong disinfectant to get rid of it. The machine was never idle, as it was operated in two shifts, a day and night shift. All the machines were huge, with mainly female operatives, and each section had its own male "setter" who set up each job to specification.

There were quite a number of men in the shop, each section being divided up under the supervision of a "leading hand" who dished out the work and a great deal of criticism each day. Girls were only allowed a few minutes' break, when an ancient wooden tea-trolley was pushed in selling tea, which I can visualise now, like thick black coffee, and rock buns, which lived up to their name. We were only allowed to visit the "ladies" once, and we had to go in twos, never alone. This place was most primitive, with loos in a line and the washing facilities in a trough down the middle, with water coming from a pipe with perforations all along. You turned it on with a wheel at the end and hoped the water wasn't scalding hot, as there was *no* way of cooling it down. A lady supervisor timed you, to see how long you'd been away and woe betide you if she had to come and look for you. I didn't smoke but many girls were glad of a quick "ciggy" and the dash to conceal the tell-tale evidence when Ma Green (as she was called) appeared, was to say the least, extremely comical.

The work here was chiefly repairing the railway engines, and making new components, and the girl fitters did everything required, from stripping down, cylinder release valves, pressure gauges, water pipes and numerous other requirements. On the lathes, the work was continuous and monotonous with a stipulated number to be turned out each shift.

Travelling from Bunbury, we had to cycle down to Beeston station to catch the early train to Crewe and get to the works in time to clock on. This was hard on the ones who had to work on the night shifts, as the Crewe residents were home and in bed long before we'd reached home.

One very strong impression became quickly evident, there was no class distinction here, everyone worked hard for the war effort, and alongside each other were ex-shop girls, clerical people, models, teachers, etc – no one seemed to worry about servile jobs or the rough and ready and the primitive facilities. We dashed out at lunchtime to a British restaurant, bought our tickets for a soup, meat and sweet (if money allowed) and took our place in the queue for the meagre helpings. Then we dashed into town and joined the first queue we saw and didn't find out until we reached the head if it was for buns, or maybe silk stockings.

I shall never forget my time at Crewe Works, with latterly my promotion to the office region, with its high stools, ancient phones and horrific work load, and the constant dust which infiltrated into every nook and cranny. It was an experience which, in this day and age of technology, now seems so incredible that I often think of it as perhaps merely a "figment of my imagination".'

HIGHDAYS & HOLIDAYS

MAKING OUR OWN ENTERTAINMENT

Even the smallest village seemed to have a wealth of home-grown talent in the past, and enough enthusiasm to ensure that whist drives and dances were hugely popular and well supported. Those were the days before television, of course, and when even radio was in its infancy. Then there were the royal occasions, such as coronations, when we organised celebrations that included young and old alike.

ENJOYING LIFE TO THE FULL

'Today it's hard for people who have never known any difference to imagine a world without television, films and all the other entertainments available in the late 20th century. Our grandparents had none of these, but enjoyed life to the full regardless.

Sport was always popular. Some of the local Great Sutton men who worked at the factories in Ellesmere Port played football or cricket for their firm's teams. The cement works even boasted a ladies' soccer side in the 1920s.

However, in the village itself more sedate sports such as bowls and tennis were favourites. The Owen family, patrons of St John's church, provided the community with a fine bowling green in 1913, this being situated behind the building called the reading room.

At the request of Mrs Stanley Owen, the green stood unused for the duration of the First World War. It was felt inappropriate to indulge in leisure pursuits while others were fighting and dying for their country. This was also observed during the Second World War. In fact between 1939 and 1945, sheep were grazed on the bowling green, and it needed considerable work to restore it when hostilities ended.

There was also once a bowling green belonging to the Bull's Head Hotel in the village. However, a modern building now stands in the place of the old Bull, and the green is now a car park.

Founded in 1946 and still going strong is Great Sutton Women's Institute. The men had their organisations too. The Oddfellows Society walked from Little Sutton to Great Sutton each year. One year they would stop for a drink at The Bull's Head, the next, at the other hostelry in the village, The White Swan.

In September 1951 the foundation stone of the village hall was laid. Villagers purchased bricks at two shillings and sixpence a time to finance the building work. The hall was opened in Coronation Year (1953), in time for the celebrations, and a grand concert marked the completion.

For several years a carnival associated with the hall was held each September. The high spot of this was the crowning of the Queen. She and her attendants toured the local area on a coal lorry converted for the occasion into a royal coach. It was decorated with hundreds of paper rosettes lovingly made by villagers. It was part of the Queen's official duties during her year of office to raise funds for charity. The carnivals ended after a few years, and an attempt to revive them in the 1980s proved unsuccessful.

There were in addition, sports days held on the field at the rear of the village hall. The hall also boasted tennis courts in its early days, but these no longer exist.

A summer pastime enjoyed for generations by local children prior to the last war was swimming in the local ponds, affectionately known as the "pits". These included the pools in William's Meadow and Dane's Meadow. However, only the most reckless ventured into the deepest of all, "Kelly's Pit".

The village boasted two local inns before its post-war development. These were The Bull's Head and The White Swan. They stood then on the main road to Chester, before the construction of the A41, attracting much passing trade.

The White Swan or "Mucky Duck" as it's affectionately known is still more or less the 18th century inn visited by generations of Great Sutton residents. Its nickname is thought to come from the days when it was called The Black Swan for a short time.

My father remembered a former landlord who kept a small three-legged dog. The little creature had been born with this handicap, but was a happy, friendly dog who managed to get about quite easily. The landlord boosted trade by advertising his unusual dog. Posters invited people to "come and see the wonder dog of Great Sutton", and it seems many responded. They came on foot, by bicycle and in horse-drawn transport.

While he must have earned quite a bit for his master, as he sat on the bar loving the attention, the star attraction did also help others. A cup was placed in front of him, and the proceeds went to charity.'

THE LIGHTER SIDE OF LIFE

'Most of the lighter side of Pickmere life was centred around the various clubs (licensed) in the village, ie the Jubilee, the Happy House, Lake House and the Country Club.

Until about 1914 dances were held weekly in the upper room of the stables adjacent to The Red Lion. When this was demolished for a car park, Lake House took over. Mrs Doris Robinson is still remembered for her many hours of nonstop piano playing, completely by ear, only needing a song title or the humming of a bar or two for her to play and improvise so entertainingly and so very willingly, all on a glass of lemonade!

The funfair at the lake was established in 1925, along with rowing and fishing boats,whilst the *Princess Irene* took all the family on a tour of the lake.

Every weekend from Easter until late September people came on foot, by cycle and by charabanc to picnic, fish, row and swim in Pickmere Lake. The "chara" dropped them at The Red Lion where they returned later for their homeward journey to Manchester and Liverpool. Mrs Thow and Edie Blain satisfied the "inner man" with fish and chips and strong sweet tea at the lakeside café and the tearoom in Mere Lane. Cyclists and walkers thronged both venues and laughter and happiness were the order of the day.

Evening mystery trips from a very wide area ended up in our village too. These were usually on a Sunday evening throughout the summer and drew people from almost every area of the North West.

Many visitors only came at first to sample Mr Hassell's scrumptious home-made ice cream and Mrs Hassell is still remembered touring Tabley, Arley, Wincham and Pickmere with her pony and trap carrying the large tub of ice cream for sale.

During the winter, both children and adults played ice hockey on the lake, skated and sledged on the banks and fishing was also a very popular sport. Mainly because of the latter pastime, the men of Pickmere and district claimed the lake for Pickmerians by staying in every craft imaginable on the water for seven days and seven nights. It became known as the "Battle of Pickmere" and had been planned in The Red Lion. No doubt wives, girlfriends and other Pickmerians made sure that they were suitably fed during their vigil. But it is also said that Tabley Estates who owned most of the land around and about Pickmere gave the mere to the people of the district for their use and pleasure.

The football team was known as the Pickmere Water Lilies and many an exciting game was played against the Wincham Warblers.

The Pickmere Boating Company was brought into being by Mr Davis and carried on by his son Joseph until it was finally taken over by Cheethams, the owners of the fairground on the banks of the lake.'

WHIST DRIVES AND SPORTS

'For three years (in April 1935, 1936 and 1937) a point to point was held in Crowton with the public viewing from the highest field. There was a tote and people came from the surrounding villages to watch the fun.

There were regular dances in the village with a live band, and a thriving tennis club met at the vicarage garden tennis courts. During the summer months the river Weaver was a very popular venue for camping, boating and swimming. Visitors would come up by boat from Frodsham and Runcorn.'

'When I lived in Pensby in the 1930s, the local residents decided they wanted to start a bowls club, so to raise money they held fairs on a field at the Orchards, kindly loaned by the owner, Mrs Ball. They sold flowers and vegetables, and had various stalls including a fortune teller. The land where the green was laid was left to the people of Pensby for recreation, and the bowls club was started in about 1934. A sandpit was made so that the children could amuse themselves while their parents played bowls.'

'We had whist drives and dances in the school at Antrobus and we cycled to other villages for similar events. It was quite lethal really, because in those days long dresses were worn and we had to tuck

Most villages could field a cricket or football team, starting them young like these lads from Over Peover in the 1920s.

229

them up round our waists to be able to ride our bikes, hoping it would not be wet or windy. If we wanted to go to the cinema or variety theatre we had to cycle five or more miles to the nearest towns. Oh, the relief when buses started to run.'

SO MUCH MUSIC

'We used to have three dance halls and a cinema at Heswall, all gone now. I remember as a child being allowed to stay up late when my parents had a "musical evening". Friends who could play the piano, violin etc or could sing used to come along and join together to provide entertainment. We also had a very good village brass band which provided music for all sorts of occasions. We children were always told not to shout to our relatives who were in the band, but the temptation was usually too great when we saw them marching along and we were so proud of them.'

'During the 1920s and 1930s many homes had a piano and ours was no exception. It gave us a lot of pleasure when the family gathered round the piano: Auntie played, my father sang rousing songs in a deep bass voice and my mother sang old favourites in a soft soprano. My elder sister played beginner's pieces on the piano and my younger sister and I recited poems – under protest! Other relations also sang or played the piano, so there was no shortage of family gatherings.'

'When I was a young girl, a great Barn Ball was held in the autumn at Baguley Fold Farm, Ollerton. People came from miles around on their cycles. The barn was lit by "stone" lamps and after the dancing they had a parish tea. The music was provided by a piano and a violin, the pianist being one "Wiggy" Johnson, a teacher at the local school so nicknamed by the children for obvious reasons!'

'In the 1920s dances were held at the local school, which had a large screen which folded back against the wall to give plenty of room for dancing. Before these took place, however, a chalk line was drawn across the floor indicating that the young, boisterous boys and girls of the village should dance on one side, and the more genteel on the other. One can imagine this caused many arguments, and I wonder how many girls would have preferred the boisterous side of the line!'

'Coming more up to date, though still over 30 years ago, Barnston WI had its own hall which it let out to a local jazz group to hold events in the early 1960s. It was there that the Beatles performed on several occasions in 1962, and where they are remembered to have carried their new collarless suits up the path in polythene bags, and to have sported their distinctive new hairstyles for the first time.'

THE PIG ON THE WALL

'Higher Bebington boasted a band, which by all accounts was a very lively and important feature of village life from the late 1800s to the outbreak of war in 1939.

When the band paraded, its members, often in fancy dress, marched down to the farm at the bottom of the hill. There a pig was put on the stone wall to watch the parade.

The pig was again present each time the band, duly dressed up in all manner of strange attire, met outside The George prior to setting off for a day out in a well stocked and provisioned charabanc. As children we watched these goings-on by our fathers, uncles and big cousins, and, like the pig, we wondered.'

THE FIRST RADIOS

'In 1926 I was seven. My father was going to sing on the wireless that evening. He was a well known professional singer in the Manchester area. He had made a crystal set so that Mother and I could listen to him. My grandmother, a very severe Victorian lady, was visiting us. We all sat in the big kitchen, tuned the cat's whisker, Grandmother put the headphones on and said "Shush!" – and we had to sit for 20 minutes in dead silence while she listened to my daddy. My father took me with him the next time he sang on the wireless!'

'In the early days of the wireless, I went to Granny's house to listen to Children's Hour. We used headphones then, and if I didn't approve of what I heard I took off the headphones and shouted down them, thinking the people the other end would hear me.'

'Entertainments consisted mostly of visits to the cinema – practically everyone went to "the pictures" once a week (and the cinema would be full of smoke from so many cigarettes). During the 1930s and 1940s we all listened to the wireless as well. Children's Hour with "Toytown" and "Romany" were special favourites for the children. On Saturday night the family would gather round the wireless set (usually one that contained several valves and ran from a battery or accumulator that had to be recharged weekly for threepence or fourpence) to hear "In Town Tonight" at 7.30 and "Music Hall" at

8 pm. Sunday programmes were rather dreary so sometimes at Sunday teatime families tuned in to Radio Luxembourg to hear The Ovaltinies and The Hughie Green Show.'

SATURDAY MORNING PICTURES

'The cinema was very popular when I was a child and Ellesmere Port had two cinemas: the Hippodrome, later converted into a car showroom and the Queens, now a bingo hall.

The Hippodrome had a children's cinema show on Saturday morning and the Queens on Saturday afternoon. We saw lots of cowboy films – Roy Rogers and the Lone Ranger were our favourites and Laurel and Hardy gave us the comedy. In the interval a man used to play the organ and there were talent competitions. You didn't need much talent, just the nerve to go up on the stage and sing or dance. The prizes were an orange, an apple or an ice cream, all highly appreciated. I sang Al Jolson's song, *April Showers*, and won a choc-ice. I was delighted and thought I would take it home to my mum to prove I had sung on the stage and that she would enjoy the choc-ice. By the time I arrived home it had melted and there was hardly any left!'

ROYAL DAYS

'The Coronation of George V in 1911 was celebrated at Adlington by holding races for the children and dancing. My brother won a race, and won a writing desk. My cousin Fred won a leather coal box. It was a first class day and a morning-till-night do, paid for by the Leghs.'

'For the Coronation celebrations of George VI in 1937, Chester held its own illuminations. The suspension bridge looked like something from fairyland with lights all along it. There were so many people standing on it that it swayed. All the trees in the park were full of coloured lights and many of the buildings in the city were floodlit, including the cathedral and the castle.'

'One of the big events in my early life was the Coronation of our present queen in 1953. We didn't have a television set and were allowed to watch some of the ceremony at my uncle's house. There was a fancy dress competition in the field opposite our house at Dunham Hill and, as sweets had just come off ration, I was dressed up as a big box of chocolates and was thrilled to win. Then there was a party at the church hall. Our house, like everyone else's, was all dressed up in patriotic colours and my father had also had all the garden done in flowers of red, white and blue.'

A visit by the Queen to Wallasey in 1957 brought the Wrens out to march down Brighton Street to the town hall.

'At Acton Bridge in 1953 there was a full programme of entertainment from 2.15 pm to a firework display at midnight. Every child received a souvenir mug. There was a communal television at both chapels, very few homes then having sets of their own.'

ROYAL VISITS

'When the first tunnel (Queensway) under the Mersey for road traffic was opened in 1934, we were allowed to walk through before the cars started. It was quite the dullest and most tiring walk I can remember and the slope from the middle seemed very steep.

King George and Queen Mary came to Merseyside for the big event and after driving through the tunnel their open carriage came to the new library in Borough Road, Birkenhead. We were sitting in a shop window right opposite the library and had a splendid view. The Queen sat with a very straight back and looked neither right nor left, while the King got out of the car, walked up the steps and turned the gold key of the library door.'

'Queen Elizabeth II and the Duke of Edinburgh were due to pay a visit to Wallasey during their tour of Cheshire on 11th July, 1957.

I was a member of the Women's Royal Naval Volunteer Reserve attending HMS *Eaglet*, Liverpool each Wednesday evening. Volunteers were required to line part of the route for the Royal visit to the borough, so I happily joined the contingent of Wrens. Permission had first to be obtained for half a day's leave from my employers, Lloyds Bank.

The Naval party assembled a short distance from the town hall and we were given instructions and marched down Brighton Street to take up positions along the route. The weather was fine at first but rain descended before the Royals' arrival. As the official party passed by in the cars I had a splendid view of the very handsome Duke of Edinburgh, who gave us a cheery wave and smile, and also of the Queen, dressed in blue and wearing a most attractive petal-shaped hat, who was much prettier and more dainty than in her photographs. The day was an occasion to remember.

On being dismissed, I discovered the white blanco from my hat had dripped down over my suit. I received a very small remuneration for expenses, but it cost about twice as much to have my uniform cleaned!'

ALL THROUGH THE YEAR

Shrove Tuesday, May Day, fairs, wakes and revels – the calendar was full of days of celebration that came around with seasonal regularity, most of them bringing the whole community together.

SHROVE TUESDAY

'Until I reached my nineties a few years ago, I always rang the Pancake Bell at twelve noon on Shrove Tuesdays to remind people to mix their pancakes. The little bell on the top of the church at Prestbury has been there since the Reformation so it is very old. You can hear it all over the village.'

'At our house in Daresbury, the mistletoe from Christmas was always kept and put on the range to be burned under the pancakes on Shrove Tuesday.'

234

SPRINGTIME TREATS

'The Good Friday Ball was a custom which seems to have been confined to the Winsford area. Every child expected to receive a ball on Good Friday and Woolworths and other shops were fully stocked with various colours and sizes of balls the week before Easter.'

'Easter at Siddington church was marked by a special afternoon service for the children. At this service they brought decorated eggs, these were judged and the prize winners received a large Easter egg provided by the vicar. No one went away unrewarded for all the entrants received a small Easter egg. After the service they would go Egg Rolling down a hill on a local field. (It was said the two youngsters whose eggs rolled furthest would marry first.)

An Animal Service was held in early June. All ages brought their pets to be blessed. At first the area near the church door was sufficient, but over the years it extended into the churchyard and finally into the farmer's field next to the church.

On Ascension Day, to mark the ancient custom of beating the bounds, the vicar would take some of the boys and girls to various prominent places on the boundary of the parish.

Since 1930 our village Water Lily Queen has been rowed across the Redesmere Lake in a sword-shaped boat to meet her King. This colourful ceremony precedes the opening of the village fete each year.

Roping the drive was a custom after a wedding at Siddington church. The choir boys and girls would not allow the bridal couple to pass until they had been suitably rewarded with a handful of pennies thrown by the bridegroom.'

'Most of the charming customs practiced in Cheshire such as souling and May birching have not been seen in the memory of today's Great Sutton residents. However, a verse does survive in Ellesmere Port concerning Oak Apple Day. This, once a popular holiday, was held to celebrate Charles II's escape from capture by hiding in an oak tree, during England's Civil War. The rhyme goes as follow –

Oak Apple Day, the 29th May,
If we don't get a holiday,
We'll all run away,
Where shall we run to?
Down Stanney Lane,
Here comes teacher with a big fat cane.

Maypole dancing at Over Peover in the 1920s, always a popular part of May Day celebrations.

The verse is probably known countrywide with local variations. I remember a similiar version as a child in Lancashire in the 1950s applied to Shrove Tuesday.

Despite the custom known as May Birching, the decoration of homes on the first of the month, having long declined, the coming of summer was celebrated, the local girls vying to be chosen as May Queen. There was a parade through the village, and also maypole dancing. Fun for the girls but not quite so popular with the boys.

Something the boys did enjoy was the seasonal battle each Good Friday in nearby Little Sutton. The boys from that village would have a mock fight with the Ellesmere Port "town lads". The victors of the affray would then have unofficial ownership of the area called "Sutton Valley" for the next twelve months. Sadly, road construction destroyed the valley, and the late author L.G. Lynch records the last battle as having taken place in 1933.'

MAY DAY

'We used to hold May Day celebrations in Over Peover, but later they changed it to a Rose Day in June because it always seemed to rain in May. All the farmers would dress their flat carts up and decorate the horses' manes, and my aunt would sit for hours making róses out of crepe paper. The entries were judged and the May Queen would ride on the winning cart. She only had an ordinary

236

kitchen chair to sit on and it was very frightening up there! We went on to the field for the crowning, there was maypole dancing, and then we had a sit-down tea in the village hall – sandwiches and cakes and jelly. The May Queen was presented with a watch.'

'We lived for Shavington May Day. My friend, now aged 93, was crowned the Queen one year by Mrs Hunter and she was given a gold brooch. The Queen's transport was a donkey, on which she sat and was led round the village. Her headdress and train were made from lace curtains we had begged. I was in one of the dancing troupes in a white frock, with paper roses in my hair and carrying a half hoop decorated with more roses. Afterwards we had a little tea consisting of penny jellies, blancmanges and small cakes, in a field in Rope Lane.'

'The school at Ellesmere Port always celebrated Empire Day on 24th May, Queen Victoria's birthday. We marched into the schoolyard and we sang patriotic songs and carried flags. The girls wore red, white and blue ribbons in their hair.

May Day was another very exciting day when I was a child. There was great rivalry as to which street could produce the best procession. The May Queen was chosen by the simple method of whose mother could provide a suitable dress for the Queen to wear. We also had to beg and borrow ribbons to decorate the maypole and we had to learn the songs to sing as we walked along the streets and danced around the maypole, such as –

Hurrah for the May day
Hurrah for the May day, Hurrah! Hurrah!
Each with his bonny lass
A-dancing on the grass
With a fa-la-la
With a fa-la-la-la-la.

The girls walked in the procession and the boys knocked on the doors and collected pennies in the street. We discussed where these pennies should go. Sometimes we walked to the local hospital and gave the money to the matron and we felt very self-righteous; sometimes we shared it among ourselves. There was never much money collected, but it seemed a fortune then when we were so hard up.

One year when I was small I collected a bunch of May blossoms, with great difficulty, and took it as a gift to my mother as I thought it was really pretty. My mother was horrified when I gave it to her at home and she shouted, "Take it outside quickly, don't bring it in here!" I was really upset that my mother wouldn't accept these lovely flowers but she said that someone in the family would die if May blossom was brought into the house. Isn't that a strange, sad superstition?'

FAIRS AND WAKES

'The Dahlia Queen festival was a highlight of the year at Burtonwood in the 1920s. The queen was chosen by lottery between all girls of suitable age, and the choice alternated between the Roman Catholic school and the Protestant school. The queen's dress and her attendants' dresses were given by the Forshaw family, who owned the brewery. There were two maids of honour.

There was maypole dancing, morris dancing and folk dancing, then a procession with a tableau. All the schoolchildren walking were given a tea and a shilling. Boys practised for months to become "soldiers" to escort the queen.'

'The Moulton Crows have been renowned for many years and over a large area – in fact, they were banned from some fetes as they won all the awards. I can remember as a little girl standing in Winsford High Street on fete day after the Second World War. As I looked down the street towards the river bridge I could see these tall black figures swooping and diving and flapping their wings. No faces showed, they were completely black with big yellow beaks This was very frightening and with shotguns going off as well, it was all too much for me. I had to resort to peeping from behind my father's legs to see the Moulton Crows go past.'

'The Park Fete was held annually at Crewe, starting with a procession through the town and ending up at the Queen's Park. It took about an hour for the procession to pass, and there was always a fair on the field behind the park. The Scouts, Girl Guides and other local organisations took part and collections were made for the local cottage hospital, which stood alongside the park.'

'On the first Sunday after the 2nd March, which is St Chad's day, Wybunbury Wakes were held. This was when fig and apple pies were rolled down the church bank. Visitors used to walk here from Nantwich, Crewe and the surrounding area to come to the Wakes and the pubs would have pieces of fig pie on the counters to give to their customers.'

'I remember entering the fancy dress competition at the Wallasey village festival in 1938. My mother had a crinoline dress made of

crepe paper, and a poke bonnet and umbrella, in the fashion of the Quality Street lady. The dress was a wonderful pink and lavender colour, tinged with very pale gold.

The parade started with a service at St Hilary's church and then we paraded to the playing fields in Leasowe Road where we were judged. I was lucky enough to win the overall prize for the best fancy dress.

The festival was never held again, as war came in 1939, and so died a wonderful old tradition. What happy times we children of the 1930s had on festival day.'

'Every year at Tattenhall, we had a wakes week. They held a gymkhana and sports on a field along the Burwardsley Road, and the fair came. The children made wands with wild flowers and were judged and awarded prizes. It was a time young and old alike looked forward to.'

'I heard an old song on the radio the other day which reminded me of the Hollins Green village carnival. The carnival was quite an event in the area. There were numerous jazz bands, troupes of morris dancers, decorated floats and of course a May queen.

The song was *When the moon comes over the mountains* and I recalled one year one of the bands had cardboard scenes which they set up on the field and a small boy with a "moon" on a stick moved the "moon" over the various scenes as the band played. We thought it was marvellous. I was about ten years old at the time.

For three years my friend and I were chosen as attendants to the queen. We were so excited on the day and later we were presented from the stage of the local cinema and received a present and also had our pictures in the paper.

Situated at the other end of the village was a pig farm. The pigs were sent to market by rail and had to be driven by the men along the roads. We could hear them coming, mothers shouting to the children to come inside the gate. We would all stand in the gardens laughing at the pigs, grunting and squealing. One would always get away and a man would have to chase it through the gardens, causing much laughter when he fell down.

At the village sports day one of the events we had much fun watching was a man trying to catch a "greased pig". Of course it slipped out of his hands many times before he finally managed to hold its back leg. The prize was the pig for his dinner.'

'One of my most treasured memories is that of the Alderley and Wilmslow Flower Show, advertised as "England's largest one day show".

On entering the ground where it was held, one was aware of great expectancy and excitement with the great marquees and tents set out in rows housing the various exhibits from all the well known seedsmen and growers. I recall the wonderful displays of herbaceous plants by Bees, "The seeds that grow", Allwoods the carnation growers, and Suttons' sweet peas with displays occupying the whole of one end of the marquee. The British Delphinium Society showed spikes of flowers to marvel at and wonder just why the ones you'd grown in your garden were not quite as tall as theirs. The perfume where the exhibits were staged was a real joy. Nearer to home, Cheadle Royal took over the complete end of a marquee with an exhibition of vegetables, many of which were in several varieties, different shapes and colours, some wired into moss-covered conical shapes in perfect order. You name it, it was there.

The children's classes proved the interest in wild grasses and flowers, each neatly labelled with the name of the particular specimen. The table decoration with wild flowers was, for me, a particularly wonderful event. On completing the job and vacating the area for the judging to be done, we peeped under the canvas to find out who had won, and there on my card was the pink label which said I had won first prize!

Apart from the marquees and various tents for the press and officials, there was the beer tent and the refreshment tent; Bass and Worthington displaying their signs and Booths advertising refreshments. Waiters and waitresses were smart in their black and white uniforms.

There was always in attendance a brass band of great repute – Black Dyke Mills, Fodens Motor Works, Grimethorp Colliery to name but a few. Sometimes on display was a model of Crystal Palace, which indicated success in the competition held there.

Stallholders abounded selling celluloid dolls, resplendent in the crepe paper dresses which sparkled with glitter. Also, birds on sticks which made a lovely whirring sound when pulled to and fro in the wind and white balls on elastic, with red and blue striped cotton netting covers, just pleasant to bob up and down.

At six o'clock the nurserymen dismantled the wonderful displays and sold them to the public who would make their way home proudly clutching their purchases. Masses of the exhibits were reserved, to be arranged in Alderley and Wilmslow churches on alternate years when the Gardeners Service was held. I remember the glorious sight to be seen on looking down the main aisle in Alderley St Philip's. In the umbrella stands, filled with water, stood great spikes of delphiniums in a breathtaking haze of blue. The choir members all sported a red flower buttonhole. Then, for me, came the highlight of the service. That wonderful poem, *The glory of the garden* was read; a true account in verse of a gardener's lot in the stately gardens of yesteryear.'

'A village highlight at Acton Bridge was the annual fair, situated opposite the then Railway Hotel, where members of the Order of Oddfellows met, my father among them. They would walk in procession carrying beautiful banners behind a brass band to Christ church, Crowton, where a service took place and then they would walk back through the village to a dinner at the Railway Hotel. The children were left to enjoy the swingboats, hobby horses and coconut shies. I know memory plays tricks with one, but the sun always seemed to shine on that day.'

'Older villagers at Thelwall recall their parents talking about Thelwall Wakes held on 1st or 2nd November, the patronal festival of All Saints church. The old custom of soul caking took place. Stalls set up near the smithy next door to the pub sold gingerbread, brandy snaps, toffee, ribbons, knives, marbles and frumenty, and as dusk fell naphtha flares were lit. This custom died out just before the end of the last century.'

'Peover Club Day was held the first week in June. It was the "Ancient Order of Foresters".

The day started with a service in the church. All the local men were members. They all wore their sashes and carried banners. My father at one time was the chairman of the Foresters. After the service they went to Plumley station to meet the band and most of the local children would go with them. We called at all the farms on Plumley Moor, then on to Peover Hall, Smithy Green, the Mill, Free Green Farm. The men were given beer and cups of tea, we children

241

Harold Smart and his landau take part in Stretton Walking Day in July 1963.

were given milk and cakes. I would never drink milk, so all I was looking forward to was The Crown where we were each given a small bottle of lemonade. These bottles had glass marbles in the neck – much to our frustration.

We children had tea in the schoolroom – seed cake (which I hated) and currant bread. It was not much of a treat for me. The men had a dinner in a large tent on the Bells field. In the evening the band stayed on and played for a dance in the tent. I can remember seeing my parents whirling round the room like a couple of tops, in fact everybody seemed to be whirling round the tent at a terrific speed.

Peover Sports Day was held later on in the year – it was a big day in Peover. People came from far and near (which in those days meant Sale, Macclesfield, Northwich, etc). We had a grandstand on the sports field (put up by the Goughs). In front of the grandstand was a long table full of prizes – clocks, silver cakestands and teapots, cases of cutlery. These were supplied by Sam Gough who had a jeweller's shop in Middlewich. We still have a clock which my brother won and a silver teapot which my mother always used to water her plants with. Silver teapots were not much in her line as teapots.

242

I was quite a good runner and however much they handicapped me I always came in first or second. This was good for my ego, as I was always much nearer to the bottom of the class than the top at school.'

RUSHBEARING SUNDAY

'The second week in July in Pulford, they had what was called a Wakes or Rushbearing Sunday. The memorial stones in the churchyard were all scrubbed and cleaned. You would see the women there, it was a hive of activity, some you never saw from one year to the next. Then they were decorated with flowers and ferns. On the Sunday, there was a special service in the church.

The following Tuesday, all the members who could attend gathered outside the village hall. These were members of the Lord Belgrave Lodge of the Manchester Unity of Oddfellows. All dressed up with their scarves across the shoulders and chests, with the banner and brass band, and walked in procession round the village, stopping occasionally at farms and larger houses to give them a little extra music and usually they would get a donation. These would go to a fund for widows and orphans in need. They ended up with a service in the church followed by a cold meal in the village hall. The evening was spent dancing on the Grosvenor Hotel lawn. Across the road were amusements, the usual side-shows and hobby horses for the children.'

DUCK APPLE NIGHT

'On Halloween we would fill a large galvanised bath in the basement laundry with water, and duck for apples. You were not allowed to use your hands and had to capture an apple between your teeth and lift it out of the bath. On the clothes ceiling airer we would also tie strings of different lengths and attach an apple to each. You found an apple at the right height for your mouth, and again with no help from your hands, ate it nibble by nibble. This all took place with the cellar lit only by turnip lanterns cut like a face and with a nightlight inside.'

SOUL CAKING

A old Cheshire custom, soul caking is still carried out in certain areas of the county.

A LONG TRADITION

'In one form or another the mummers play is common to many areas of England and there is an intriguing homogeneity discernible in its many variations. At the present time mummers plays in Cheshire are confined to the two neighbouring villages of Comberbach and Antrobus who perform a soul-caking play featuring the same characters with a similar script and costumes. This play is performed for about two weeks commencing with Halloween, 31st October, and All Souls Day, 1st November.

During this period these groups perform their play probably four times per night at various public houses and clubs or at any function which requests them, and great care is taken that each group of mummers or soul cakers do not infringe the other group's territory. History tells us that if this happened a fight would ensue for the horse's head which each gang carries. Legend has it that this is a symbol of fertility – the spirit of corn and grain. The victors of the fight would take their rivals' horse's head and bury it as an augury for a good harvest for their own village. This rivalry which supposedly existed in a bygone age has now disappeared and the two groups mentioned now operate with a friendly attitude to each other. The horse's head is still a prominent feature in both groups but the Antrobus dialogue about theirs mentions "Antrobus Moss", whereas reference to the Comberbach Wild Horse concerns Marbury Hall, which until 1930 was the nearby home of the Smith-Barry family. The Comberbach group actually hand out soul cakes to the audience after each performance.

The outstanding feature of both versions of the play is a fatal sword fight between King George and Black Prince followed by the restoration to life by a quack doctor. The latter was the medicine man of primitive tribes which forcibly reminds us that the mummers play is pagan in origin and was being performed long before the advent of Christianity.

The characters in the Comberbach soul caking play are: the Letter-In, King George, Black Prince, Old Woman, Quack Doctor, Dairy Dout, Beelzebub, Lord Nelson, Driver with "Horse", and Man under Horse's Head.'

244

THE SOUL CAKE

'I remember a night in 1950 when the mummers came to my father's (now my) farm at Whitley. My mother baked the soul cake – a delicious parkin made of home-ground wheat which was traditionally served to the audience.'

SOULING SONGS

'Soul a soul a soul cake
Please good missus, a soul cake
Apple, a pear, a plum or a cherry
Any good thing that'll make us a merry.
One for Peter, one for Paul,
One for Him who made us all,
Through the kitchen out the hall,
The road is very stoney, my shoes is getting thin,
But I have a little pocket to put a ha'penny in.
If ye hav'na got a ha'penny a farthing will do...,
If you hav'na got a farthing then God Bless You.

This was sung to a dirge tune, parties of four to six carrying lanterns of hollowed-out swede turnips with faces cut into them and a tallow fat candle set inside for light. Parties were kept low in number because the collection was distributed between members and so went further!

Local soul-caking songs includes –

Old Guy Fawkes, set him up on high
Hang him from a lamp post there to die
An ha'penny bun to feed the post and
A red hot fire to roast him.

Sung to the tune of Old King Cole! Followed by three loud knocks on the door (usually successful, not always). Certain houses would throw a bowl of water from the upstairs window down onto you. At these, you stood into the door porch, or well back, after the three knocks.

According to a local soul caker who performed the plays around Manley and Frodsham, a lot of the words were spoken in a broad Cheshire dialect. Soul caking, as he knew it, was a spin-off from the old mummer plays of the late 1800s and early 1900s that consisted of a number of players, twelve to 15, which had characters such as the King, the Fairy, the Evil Lord, the Horse's Head, etc.'

'The words to my version of the souling song are slightly different to some, although I am sure the tune is the same as the metre is identical:

A soul, a soul, a soul cake
Please, good misses a soul cake,
An apple, a pear, a plum or a cherry,
Any good thing to make us all merry.
One for Peter, two for Paul,
Three for Him who made us all.
Christmas is coming, the geese are getting fat
Please to put a penny in the old man's hat,
If you haven't got a penny, a ha'penny will do
If you haven't got a ha'penny
God Bless You.

This was sung by children, the door would then be opened and a present given to the group. In my day this was usually money, which was promptly used to buy fireworks! The words have altered little over the years as an aunt of mine sang this song 75 years ago – probably with a good deal more religious fervour than I did.'

CHRISTMAS JOYS

Christmas past evokes such nostalgia – for happy family occasions, mouthwatering food and simple but wonderful presents.

BEFORE THE ICE AGE

'It is, perhaps, difficult now to remember a time when chicken, indeed poultry generally, was a luxury reserved for "high days and holidays". But this was the case in the pre-war and immediate post-war years when the age of the oven-ready chicken lay some years ahead. Most poultry in those days was fresh and prepared for market as near as possible to the feast day.

We kept, at best, a free-range laying flock of about 300 birds and, ready for Christmas, about 35 cockerels, all of them spoken for, either by family or long-standing customers.

The approach of Christmas was, therefore, a time of unremitting toil. We hoped for cold weather in the absence of refrigeration and the timing of the killing, plucking and dressing was critical. Ideally, we looked to preparing all 35 birds on 23rd December which meant that they could be collected by the customers on Christmas Eve. So we would start – and all the family were involved – at 6 am and toil throughout the day in a snowstorm of feathers.

Our home then was of sandstone, with 18 inch walls, and the pantry was the coldest room imaginable with temperatures very close to those achieved by the modern refrigerator.

By 6 pm on the big day all the birds lay, in serried ranks, on the stone slabs in the pantry. It was customary to put a small peeled onion inside each bird to keep them fresh. This was an old country method. Plucking was manual and non-mechanical with no use of hot water to loosen feathers. The "drawing" technique would have graced a Fellow of the Royal College of Surgeons! Skewering was with wooden skewers whittled specially for the purpose and no metal skewers were used.

We were glad to see Christmas Eve and the pantry, freezing still, but empty except for the one large chicken which would grace our table.

One memory stands out over the years. One year, after completing the work, my father suggested that we (my husband and I, recently married) should accompany him to the village Fur and Feather whist drive. We were not, as I remember it, over-keen for fairly obvious reasons but we went and, guess what, my husband won first prize, a cockerel, very much alive. They offered to kill it but we declined the offer and I remember carrying the reprieved bird home where he enjoyed a few extra months of life.

As to Christmas dinner – after all that, I would have settled for beans on toast!'

GIFTS FROM THE ESTATE

'Most of the people at Aldford were employed by His Grace the Duke of Westminster. At that time Pulford had not been sold to the tenants so Pulford, Eccleston, Saighton and Aldford all more or less worked for the estate. Every worker had a gift of a joint of meat according to the size of their family and, as far as I remember, widows received a gift of a blanket and the children were given a present off the Christmas tree at Eaton Hall.'

WONDERFUL CHRISTMASES

'I look back in admiration of my parents for the wonderful Christmases of my childhood. I was first-born of seven children, the sixth being born when I was ten and the seventh when I was 17. As

Dad was a wood-cutting machinist operating a large automatic saw, his pay was not good. He came from a family of twelve and Mum from six. Money had always been short.

Christmas was the highlight of the year for us. The wonderful feeling of anticipation was fostered by my parents for weeks, commencing with the mixing of the puddings at the beginning of December. These were boiled in the copper boiler and I can still smell the wonderful damp, steamy, spicy smell which would greet us at lunchtime. Thursday was pay-day and Friday evenings Dad was always a little later home. He would go straight to their bedroom to hide the goodies he had bought in the wonderful Birkenhead market.

School nativity plays and parties with jelly and custard continued the excitement. We hoped we wouldn't fall ill and miss out on anything. Christmas Eve dawned. The turkey was bought and the cupboards bulged with food. A trip to town with Mum had bought new socks, a dress and cardigan. These were part of our present and would be set out with them.

Evening brought baths all round. Scrubbed and clean we attached name tags to one of Dad's washed socks and hung them over the end of the bed. Sleep eluded us and we awaited the thump of a newly filled stocking on our bed. Then the intriguing rustles as parcels were fetched in. I always fell asleep and was woken by one of the younger children opening their stocking. The true surprise and delight of these stockings is hard to imagine now. The contents never varied but were eagerly awaited; an apple, tangerine, banana, Mars bar, few nuts and sweets and a sixpence! Presents were handkerchiefs, paint boxes and board games. I remember the moment I was given my first watch. I was so excited I dropped it. The watch was a present to mark the magical age of eleven when I went to the big school.

On Christmas morning we would rush into the living room and "ooh" and "ahh" at the sight we beheld. The Christmas tree lit up in the corner, the garlands, balloons and bells hung from the ceiling. Our old sideboard groaning with food. In the centre the Christmas cake surrounded by bowls of shiny apples, tangerines and pears. Nuts in their shells, a packet of dates and a packet of orange and lemon slices, all surrounded by Christmas cards and on the large mirror the words "Merry Christmas" stuck on with cotton wool. We never failed to be thrilled with it all. We older girls retained our feelings and perpetuated the myth of Father Christmas, we wouldn't dream of spoiling it for the younger ones.

With hindsight I can see that the magic of childhood was engendered and sustained by the wonderful love and attention of both my parents. They allowed us to be children and protected us from the bad and evil of the world.'

A BUSY, HAPPY TIME

'When I was a child Christmas was a busy, happy time. The preceding week was exceptionally hectic. Poultry had to be dressed and prepared for numerous Christmas dinners. Then, when all had been weighed and despatched, there were feathers peeping out of every corner! No matter how careful were the pluckers, the wind still had its bit of fun and it was quite a job to get rid of them all. However, turkey wing-feathers were saved for oiling, and goose's for cleaning the machinery. The thresher usually came that week – must have plenty of corn to grind and straw for the cattle over Christmas – and (folk being just the same in those days) assistants for the thresher were more likely to turn up before than after!

At last, all extra work finished, Dad went off to the wood nearby to collect a Christmas tree and holly. The holly always seemed to have lots of red berries in those days. We placed a sprig on every picture. The tree was always fastened to the strong double cheese press (painted deep blue) in our kitchen. A trip to the apple room next to get rosy, golden ones to thread with cotton and hang on the tree to add to the decorations. When we had hung the paper chains, the kitchen looked quite festive. In the pantry was the plum pudding which, weeks ago, everyone had stirred as they gave a wish.

We had written our letters to Father Christmas and thrown them into the fire. If they wafted up the chimney, all was well, and we were not very big before we knew that to bang the door at the right moment helped! Next, to Dad's drawer for an inspection of his stockings – must measure and get the longest! We wrote our names, Lucy, Olive, Joseph or Ethel, on a piece of paper and then firmly sewed it onto the stocking – a pin might fall off. On Christmas Eve to bed early because we must be asleep when Santa visited, or at least eyes firmly closed because it was very unlucky to catch a glimpse of a red robe. We hung our stockings on the bed-rail in readiness. In those days we had four-poster beds with curtains. Just fancy what they would be worth today if we still had them. I was the eldest in our family and Mother would tell of the first time my stocking was filled. All the house, including the baby, was wakened up by a loud cry that Father Christmas had been! The first Christmas I remember was the year when I announced that, as my doll was broken I was going to ask Father Christmas for a new one, and Mother replied that there was a war on and he might not come. Never having heard of war, it was explained that people disagreed and then fought to get what they wanted. I wondered why they had never thought of asking Father Christmas! War must be terrible, I thought. However, each Christmas morning found our stockings filled and a parcel or two around. Such a thrill in the dark to feel the stocking and guess. An orange? Or was it a ball?

Grown-ups had to milk and feed as usual but after that they had time to see our gifts and join in the fun. No TV or even radio, but our day was full. Friends called and often it seemed to snow (nice, dry stuff, not wet and cold)!

In the evening, all the family (indeed practically all the village, for Plumley was not very big) wended their way to the chapel schoolroom. What a crowd! By 6.30 pm when the door opened, we saw the huge Christmas tree, often touching the ceiling, laden with numbered gifts. On a side table were books – large, small, fat and thin. And it was there that I looked – would my prize be a fat book? I hated large thin books! The most cherished one I ever received was red and about three inches thick, and I kept it for years. Prompt at 6.30 the minister took the chair and, to the wheezy harmonium, we sang *O come all ye faithful*. Always that carol first. After a prayer, another carol. Next, a number of girls recited – I never recall a boy taking part. Each reciter climbed on to the platform, bowed, fixed her eyes on a spot near the ceiling, clasped hands behind her back, and began. Without exception, somebody recited "Hang up the baby's stocking, be sure you don't forget. For the dear little dimpled darling, has never seen Christmas yet." After the recitations, a member of the school would render a Lancashire reading in dialect and as we children did not understand what he was saying, we were glad when it was finished. It was lucky, too, if the oil lamps had not smoked and had to be turned down before then! Next, the lovely part – we each received our book for regular attendance, after which a teacher came round with the offertory box – no, not to collect, but for each child to take out a number and to receive the correspondingly numbered gift from the tree. One year, we three girls each got a gun and our brother a doll! He was so disgusted that he carried it by its toe. Still, we could always swop.

So ended Christmas Day. Boxing Day we always had guests we loved coming. Finally, on the day after, we took the apples and small gifts off our own tree but, before that was done, we tried to copy the Christmas evening entertainment. All the family had to perform. One year we taught the younger member a recitation – "Behold the spider on the wall, spinning its web and that's all." But she burst into tears and said she did not like spiders!'

MY FATHER WAS THE BUTLER

'We always went to Dane Bank for tea on Christmas day. My father was the butler there and as this was his busiest time of year – early mornings, late nights, lunch and dinner parties, we saw very little of him. The only time he had Christmas at home was the year he had pleurisy and he was allowed, by the doctor, to come down in his dressing-gown for tea.

At a certain hour on Christmas Day we would all go into the drawing room, where the family was assembled. This was a long room with a large window at one end and in a corner of this was a huge Christmas tree, beautifully decorated and lit with coloured candles – someone standing by with a long-handled snuffer, in case of fire. At the base were presents for everyone, family, outdoor staff and their families; this was always a happy time for us because we received lovely books and toys. Later we had a jolly tea in the servants' hall: we were really spoiled by the indoor staff, who were missing their own families. There was lots to eat as well as large boxes of chocolates and fruit, given by the family, and we also had crackers. We stayed until late in the evening. Mother helped Dad in his pantry, washing the silver and glass, while we curled up in front of a roaring fire.

Before the gong sounded for dinner for the family, Dad let us creep down to the dining room to look at the table. What a sight – beautifully polished, laid with sparkling glass, silver candelabra, cutlery, flowers, crackers too pretty to tear apart, and all in candlelight. Often a choir or Scout handbell team called, then we peeped through the banisters of the front stairs or in a group by the back stairs. Mother took her sleepy children home, but Dad would not leave till the early hours and then have to be back before seven o'clock, to start another day.'

WELCOMING THE NEW YEAR

'On New Year's Eve all the boats on the river Mersey would sound their horns to welcome in the New Year.'

Index